Adelaide: a literary city

This book is available as a free fully-searchable PDF from
www.adelaide.edu.au/press

Adelaide: a literary city

edited by

Philip Butterss

Discipline of English and Creative Writing
School of Humanities
The University of Adelaide

UNIVERSITY OF
ADELAIDE PRESS

Published in Adelaide by

University of Adelaide Press
The University of Adelaide
Level 1, 254 North Terrace
South Australia 5005
press@adelaide.edu.au
www.adelaide.edu.au/press

The University of Adelaide Press publishes externally refereed scholarly books by staff of the University of Adelaide. It aims to maximise access to the University's best research by publishing works through the internet as free downloads and for sale as high quality printed volumes.

© 2013 The Authors

This work, with the exception of the poem, *New York Nowhere: Meditations and Celebrations, Neurology Ward, The New York Hospital* by Geoffrey Dutton, is licenced under the Creative Commons Attribution-NonCommercial-NoDerivatives 4.0 International (CC BY-NC-ND 4.0) License. To view a copy of this licence, visit http://creativecommons.org/licenses/by-nc-nd/4.0 or send a letter to Creative Commons, 444 Castro Street, Suite 900, Mountain View, California, 94041, USA. This licence allows for the copying, distribution, display and performance of this work for non-commercial purposes providing the work is clearly attributed to the copyright holder. Address all inquiries to the Director at the above address.

New York Nowhere: Meditations and Celebrations, Neurology Ward, The New York Hospital by Geoffrey Dutton is reproduced by arrangement with the Licensor, The Geoffrey Dutton Estate, c/- Curtis Brown (Aust) Pty Ltd. Apart from any fair dealing for the purposes of private study, research, criticism or review as permitted under the *Copyright Act 1968*, no part may be reproduced, stored in a retrieval system, or transmitted, in any form or by any means, electronic, mechanical, photocopying, recording or otherwise without prior written permission.

For the full Cataloguing-in-Publication data please contact the National Library of Australia: cip@nla.gov.au

ISBN (paperback) 978-1-922064-63-9
ISBN (ebook) 978-1-922064-64-6

Project editor: Patrick Allington
Book design: Zoë Stokes
Cover design: Emma Spoehr
Cover image: Mark Grivell

Contents

Acknowledgements		vii
List of Contributors		ix
Adelaide as Literary City: Introduction		1
Philip Butterss		
1	Acts of Writing	19
	Kerryn Goldsworthy	
2	A Colonial Wordsmith: George Isaacs in Adelaide, 1860-1870	39
	Anne Black	
3	Scots and Scottish Literature in Literary Adelaide	57
	Graham Tulloch	
4	'An entertaining young genius': C.J. Dennis and Adelaide	77
	Philip Butterss	
5	Adelaide Around 1935: Stories of Herself When Young	95
	Susan Sheridan	
6	Adelaide and the Country: the Literary Dimension	111
	Jill Roe	

7	'Fearful Affinity': Jindyworobak Primitivism *Peter Kirkpatrick*	125
8	The Athens of the South *Alison Broinowski*	147
9	Max Harris: a Phenomenal Adelaide Literary Figure *Betty Snowden*	163
10	Geoffrey Dutton: Little Adelaide and *New York Nowhere* *Nicholas Jose*	183
	New York Nowhere: Meditations and Celebrations, Neurology Ward, The New York Hospital *Geoffrey Dutton*	199
11	A Coffee With Ken: Ken Bolton's Adelaide *Jill Jones*	239
12	'A Dozy City': Adelaide in J.M. Coetzee's *Slow Man* and Amy T. Matthews's *End of the Night Girl* *Gillian Dooley*	253

Acknowledgements

I would like to express my special gratitude to a number of people who have helped with this book. Firstly, thanks to all the team at University of Adelaide Press, in particular, to Patrick Allington, for his enthusiasm about the project, for his rigorous editing, and for his excellent advice, but also thanks for the invaluable input from John Emerson, Zoë Stokes and Julia Keller.

I'd like to thank Sarah Tooth and Malcolm Walker from the SA Writers' Centre for their suggestions. I'm very grateful to History SA, and, particularly, Margaret Anderson, for generously supporting my research on literary Adelaide.

I am delighted to be able to include Geoffrey Dutton's long poem 'New York Nowhere', and would like to thank Robin Lucas, the Geoffrey Dutton Estate (c/- Curtis Brown (Aust) Pty Ltd) for generously providing permission for this republication.

Finally, I'd like to acknowledge, with much gratitude, the considerable hard work and good grace on the part of all the contributors to this volume.

List of Contributors

Anne Black is a postgraduate student in the Discipline of English and Creative Writing at the University of Adelaide, where she is writing a thesis on the life and work of George Isaacs. She hopes that the result will find a publisher and that Isaacs will be accorded greater recognition for his contribution to South Australian literature.

Alison Broinowski was an Australian diplomat until 1996. Her last overseas assignment was at the Australian Mission to the UN in New York. Her PhD is in Asian Studies at ANU. She has written or edited 11 books on Australia's interface with Asia and with the United Nations, three of the latest being *About Face: Asian Accounts of Australia* (2003), *Howard's War* (2003) and *Allied and Addicted* (2007). She is a Visiting Fellow at ANU and is a research associate at Macquarie University. In 2013 she stood for the Senate in NSW for the WikiLeaks Party.

Philip Butterss teaches Australian literature and film at the University of Adelaide. Over the past 25 years he has written widely on Australian cultural history. His recently completed biography of C.J. Dennis will be published by Wakefield Press. He is currently working on a history of literary Adelaide.

Gillian Dooley is Special Collections Librarian and Honorary Senior Research Fellow in Humanities at Flinders University. Her publications include *V.S. Naipaul, Man and Writer* and *J.M. Coetzee and the Power of Narrative*, and essays on writers ranging from Jane Austen to Iris Murdoch.

She is a regular book reviewer for *Australian Book Review* and founding editor of two journals, *Transnational Literature* and *Writers in Conversation*.

Kerryn Goldsworthy was born and educated in South Australia and then lectured in literature at the University of Melbourne for 17 years before moving home to Adelaide, where she has lived and worked as a freelance writer and critic since 1998. She is the author of three books: a collection of short stories, a book of literary criticism, and, most recently, *Adelaide* (2011) in the NewSouth Books 'Cities' series. She was a member of the editorial team that produced *The Macquarie PEN Anthology of Australian Literature* (2009), and won the 2013 Pascall Prize for Critical Writing, earning the title Australian Critic of the Year.

Jill Jones has published seven full-length books, most recently *Ash is Here, So are Stars* (Walleah Press 2012). A new book, *The Beautiful Anxiety*, is due from Puncher and Wattmann in 2014. She won the Kenneth Slessor Poetry Prize 2003 for *Screens Jets Heaven: New & Selected Poems* and the Mary Gilmore Award 1993 for *The Mask and the Jagged Star*. Her work has featured in a number of recent anthologies including the *Macquarie PEN Anthology of Australian Literature* and *The Penguin Anthology of Australian Poetry*. She is a member of the J.M. Coetzee Centre for Creative Practice, the University of Adelaide, and teaches there in the Discipline of English and Creative Writing.

Nicholas Jose is a novelist, essayist and playwright, whose thirteen books include the novels *Paper Nautilus*, *Avenue of Eternal Peace* (shortlisted for the Miles Franklin Literary Award), *The Custodians* (shortlisted for the Commonwealth Prize) and *Original Face*; two short story collections; a volume of essays, *Chinese Whispers*; and the memoir *Black Sheep*. He is general editor of the *Macquarie PEN Anthology of Australian Literature* (also published as *The Literature of Australia*). He was Visiting Chair of Australian Studies at Harvard University 2009-2010 and taught there again in 2011. He is Professor of English and Creative Writing in the School of Humanities at the University of Adelaide, Adjunct Professor with the Writing and Society Research Centre at the University of Western Sydney, and Professor of Creative Writing at Bath Spa University.

Peter Kirkpatrick is a senior lecturer in Australian Literature in the Department of English at the University of Sydney, and is the author of *The Sea Coast of Bohemia: Literary Life in Sydney's Roaring Twenties* (2nd edn API Network, 2007). He has co-edited, with Fran De Groen, *Serious Frolic: Essays on Australian Humour* (University of Queensland Press, 2009) and, with Robert Dixon, *Republics of Letters: Literary Communities in Australia* (Sydney University Press, 2012).

Jill Roe AO is Professor Emerita in Modern History at Macquarie University, Sydney, where she was recently awarded a D. Litt as a higher research degree for her work on Australian writer Miles Franklin. Her publications in Australian social and cultural history include numerous entries in the *Australian Dictionary of Biography*. She has also been a contributor to the *Wakefield Companion to South Australian History*. She is currently working on aspects of the history of Eyre Peninsula, where she was born and spent her first fourteen years.

Susan Sheridan is Professor Emerita in Humanities at Flinders University and a member of the Australian Academy of the Humanities. She has published widely on women's writing, feminist cultural studies and Australian cultural history. Her latest book is *Nine Lives: Postwar women writers making their mark* (University of Queensland Press, 2011).

Betty Snowden has a PhD in art history and has lectured in art history and theory in South Australian universities and art institutions. She has regularly presented conference papers and published in the field of art history. For nine years she was an art curator at the Australian War Memorial, and prior to that at the Flinders University Art Museum. In 2006 she worked in Federal Government arts policy and program, in particular Collections Development and in Private Sector Support, at the Department for Communications, Information Technology and the Arts (DCITA). She has qualifications in music from the University of Adelaide and teaches piano privately. She is also completing a major biography on Adelaide-born poet, writer, journalist, critic, publisher and bookseller, Max Harris.

Graham Tulloch is Professor of English at Flinders University and has written extensively on Scottish literature and language. He has edited Scottish and Australian literary texts, including *Scott's Ivanhoe* (1998), Clarke's *His Natural Life* (1997), Martin's *An Australian Girl* (1999) and, with Judy King, Hogg's *The Three Perils of Man* (2012) and Scott's *Shorter Fiction* (2009). He is the author of *The Language of Walter Scott* (1980) and *A History of the Scots Bible with Selected Texts* (1989) and has a long-standing interest in Scottish language and literature in Australia, particularly South Australia, and has published a number of articles in this field.

Adelaide as Literary City: Introduction

Philip Butterss

THE ORIGINS OF LITERARY ADELAIDE

All cities are literary cities: places where people read, places where people write, places people write about. Perhaps, though, not all cities can claim to have their very origins in the domain of the literary. The theory of 'systematic colonisation', on which the European settlement of South Australia was based, received its first book-length airing in 1829 in Edward Gibbon Wakefield's *A Letter from Sydney*, but the volume was hardly the straightforward, first-hand account of life in New South Wales implied by its title. In her essay in *Adelaide: A Literary City*, Kerryn Goldsworthy describes Wakefield's volume as 'a factual document using fiction-writing techniques' (23). A recent PhD thesis calls it 'largely a work of imaginative speculation' (Radzevicius 8).

Even if *A Letter from Sydney* counts in some senses as 'literary', much more relevant to Adelaide's future life as a literary city is its central argument. Wakefield's book sets out a utopian vision of a new colony in which literature might have an integral place. Its narrator criticises Sydney, finding that 'intellectual society' is notably absent and observing that writers, scientists and philosophers are unlikely to emigrate to locations where their skills will not be valued and rewarded (40). By contrast, he asserts that a colony based on his principles will attract a long list of British citizens, including all the components of a literary culture: 'printers, schoolmasters and schoolmistresses, booksellers, authors, publishers, and even reviewers' (187).

Unlike New South Wales as he imagined it, Wakefield's ideal colony was intended to replicate the institutions of the old country. It was crucial that there should be no convicts, that land should be priced so labourers might buy it only after an appropriate period of employment, and that the settlement should be concentrated. In other words, Wakefield wanted a respectable society, with a middle-class whose members were guaranteed a supply of employees, and where people lived in proximity to each other. More than all the other Australian colonies, then, South Australia was envisioned as having an ordered provincial English city at its heart, one with all the preconditions for a literary culture.

However, although literature might have been part of Wakefield's overall conception, it was hardly a priority, either for him or for his followers. Among the proponents of systematic colonisation were those keen to solve the problems of overcrowding, unemployment and poverty in Britain. At the other end of the spectrum were those who wanted to make a fortune for themselves. For both groups and everyone in between, economic success was at the heart of the enterprise.

The South Australian Literary Association was founded in London on 29 August 1834, just two weeks after the South Australian Act received royal assent. In spite of the name, though, its focus was resolutely pragmatic and material. One of the organisation's original aims was to establish 'a library of reference and circulation' for the use of people in the new colony, but the literature which members wished to share was 'useful knowledge' rather than creative or artistic writing (Minute Book). To better reflect this emphasis, within a few months it was calling itself the South Australian Literary and Scientific Association. Members were wealthy and educated, and included a number of men who were to be prominent in Adelaide, such as Osmond Gilles, Robert Gouger, Thomas Gilbert and George Kingston. Wakefield, himself, was not a member, but his brother Daniel was. They met regularly in Adelphi Terrace, London, for what were known as *conversaziones*—lectures and discussions on topics of relevance to the colony, such as natural history, geology, horticulture, astronomy, Aborigines, policing, and a monetary system. It was not until the fifteenth *conversazione*, a year after the association had been formed, that Robert Owen, the controversial Welsh social reformer, gave the first explicitly literary paper: 'on the influence of Literature on the institution of nations, and habits of the people'. His audience consisted of thirty-six ladies and gentlemen. Captain John Hindmarsh, soon to be governor, had been elected President and was in the chair.

To further the association's initial aim of establishing a library, Robert Gouger made a donation of more than fifty books and four volumes of collected pamphlets. One of the authors whose works were included was Barron Field, represented by a dry account of the colony of New South Wales rather than by his *First Fruits of Australian Poetry*, the first book of verse published in Australia. Similarly, the library included William Charles Wentworth's *A Statistical, Historical, and Political Account of the Colony of New South Wales* rather than his long poem, *Australasia*, runner up for the chancellor's gold medal at Cambridge in 1822 (Minute Book). The rest of the material, too, consisted of factual accounts of existing colonies and information of practical use. Wakefield's *A Letter to Sydney* was probably the most literary of all the books in the library, though it was valued not as imaginative writing but as analysis and theory. By the time that the colonists began to sail to South Australia during 1836, Gouger's donation had been supplemented with a range of accessible and informative volumes published by the Society for the Diffusion of Useful Knowledge and with religious tracts provided by George Fife Angas. The library was packed into a large iron chest and shipped on the *Tam O'Shanter* (Hailes 3-4). It might not have been full of poetry or novels, but it was a collection of reading material that could later be developed in different directions.

An indication that, unlike the penal colonies of New South Wales and Van Diemen's Land, the cultural institutions of Britain were to be replicated from the outset was the foundation of the *South Australian Gazette and Colonial Register*. More than thirty years earlier, Robert Thomas had established a printing, bookselling, and law stationery business in Fleet Street. Now, attracted by Wakefield's ideas, he decided to join the new colony as publisher of a newspaper, to be edited by his friend, George Stevenson, who was also the governor's secretary. So keen was Thomas to get his venture off to a good start that he issued its first number in London on 18 June 1836, before setting sail. Among a handful of advertisements on the front page was one for Black and Armstrong, a London publishing and bookselling company which offered to fill any orders for books, paper or other stationery that might be required in South Australia.

As the nine ships set out during 1836 for the new colony, there were mixed signs as to the likelihood of a successful literary culture. In the first place, five hundred and fifty people was a tiny group to support any kind of artistic pursuits. Nor did some of the most influential among them show an interest in such matters. Governor Hindmarsh's presidency of the South Australian Literary and Scientific Association had derived from his office rather than his commitment to its original aims, and, on the *Buffalo*, he clashed with his secretary over the establishment of a public library. According to Stephenson, the governor asked scornfully 'What good will books do our Colony?' (Stevenson, 13 September 1836).

Nevertheless, among the new colonists were those had worked in the British book industry, like Robert Thomas, or who had moved in literary circles, or tried their hand at writing, and literature was not an interest they left behind. Mary Thomas, his wife, had published *Serious Poems* in London in 1831. In the preface, she claimed modestly that it had been written 'with a sole view to the instruction and amusement' of her family (v), though in fact, as its title might indicate, the book included several long and ambitious pieces. It ran to 276 pages. She continued to write during the passage to South Australia, recording in her journal a riddle in verse about the death of her cat on board ship and composing a couple of more sombre poems—'A Farewell to England' and, on the same theme, 'Adieu' (Evan Thomas xiii-xiv; 112-13). Many of the colonists had packed their favourite books or their hand-copied albums of much-loved poems. In addition, Robert and Mary Thomas brought with them on the *Africaine* some essential infrastructure: the colony's first printing press, a large quantity of type and paper, and even an apprentice printer.

On the *Buffalo*, commanded by Governor Hindmarsh, was Fidelia Hill, whose luggage included a body of poetry in manuscript that she had been encouraged to publish in England prior to departure. While in the harbour at Rio de Janeiro, she composed a poem remembering her brother, Thornton, who had earlier died in Jamaica (33-4). Others on board also used writing to pass the time, and enough contributions were received for at least two issues of an amateur literary magazine, handwritten on sheets of foolscap under the title of the 'Buffalo Telegraph'. As in the Adelaide of the future, critics could be harsh, with passengers describing the second number as 'a dead failure' containing 'scarcely a redeeming point of intelligence or wit' (Stephenson, 4 August 1836).

Among the passengers on the *Buffalo* with connections to literary life in Britain were George and Margaret Stevenson, who had married in London just before the ship sailed. George had written articles for the London *Globe*, edited by Margaret's father, who was an accomplished writer and translator. Margaret was a friend of Kate Hogarth, who would later marry Charles Dickens. One of the guests at the Stevensons' wedding was Henry Lytton Bulwer, a poet, among other things, and brother of the famous novelist, Edward Lytton Bulwer. Margaret's elegant prose can be seen in the diary she wrote with her husband in 1836 and 1837; she also composed a ballad about what she saw as Hindmarsh's stupidity and incompetence on the voyage.

Not surprisingly, it was a tough environment for the pursuit of literature in the early days of the colony, as is clear from the fate of the Literary and Scientific Association's library at the end of its long journey. On the 18 December 1836, the *Tam O'Shanter* ran aground on a sandbar in the Port River and began taking on water. Colonel William Light, who was nearby on board the *Rapid*, records that it was only after four days work by the crews of both vessels 'lightening her and pumping' that the *Tam O'Shanter* was freed (Elder 90). During the process, the books were damaged, and water stains can still be seen on some of them in the State Library of South Australia (Bridge 7). In explaining why the trunk had still not been unpacked, over a year later, Thomas Horton James offered evidence to support the views attributed to Hindmarsh:

> Young Colonies are not very anxious about books, and reading is but little indulged in generally, the amusements during day light at least, being entirely out of doors, in these fine climates, and of a much more attractive and stirring interest than any thing within. (James 172)

At the same time, though, there were those for whom reading and writing was an essential part of the educated, cultivated life that they saw themselves leading, or to which they aspired. In seeking to make the colony, in Wakefield's words, an 'Extension of Britain', they used literature as a pastime, as a means of reflecting quietly, or as a way to help cope with personal difficulties, just as they had in the northern hemisphere.

Sixteen years had elapsed between the establishment of a penal colony in New South Wales and the appearance of the first piece of original poetry in *The Sydney Gazette*; sixteen months after Governor Hindmarsh's arrival in Adelaide, the *Southern Australian* published Nathaniel Hailes's 'South Australian Melodies. No. I.' (8 May 1839, 3). Robert Gouger, the Colonial Secretary, was one who wrote verse privately. As they had in Britain and on the passage to the southern hemisphere, Mary Thomas, Margaret Stevenson and Fidelia Hill also continued to produce poems. When the last of these imagined what the settlement might become, the result was a piece called 'Adelaide', in which the future city was described as a version 'of London and of home' (Hill 42). In 1840, Hill became the first woman and the first South Australian to publish a book of poems in Australia with *Poems and Recollections of the Past*. From the start, then, although it was small and fragile, the city had a literary life and it was making its own contribution to what would become the nation's literary history.

ADELAIDE: A LITERARY CITY

Earlier versions of almost all the essays in this book were delivered as papers at a symposium on 'Literary Adelaide' in February 2012. *Adelaide: A Literary City* is not, therefore, an attempt to provide any systematic or exhaustive treatment of the history or present state of Adelaide's literary output or literary culture. Instead it brings together a number of separate contributions addressing, in often quite different ways, a range of connected topics: in particular, the representation of Adelaide in literature, literary culture in Adelaide, and the place of Adelaide writers and writing within Australian literary history.

Writing from Adelaide is acknowledged but, not surprisingly, under-examined in the major literary histories of Australia: Oxford, Penguin, and Cambridge. Partial, but for different reasons, is Paul Depasquale's *A Critical History of South Australian Literature: 1836-1930*, which contains much useful information for the period it covers but could fairly be described as idiosyncratic. Australian literary journals include a selection of valuable articles on Adelaide writers, and *Southwords: Essays on South Australian Writing*, which I edited in 1995, also brings together a range of essays by scholars in the field. In addition, there are fine biographies of individual South Australian writers, such as Catherine Helen Spence by Susan Magarey, Matilda Evans by Barbara Wall, and Barbara Hanrahan by Annette Stewart, to name three. Carl Bridge's *A Trunk Full of Books* and Michael Heyward's *The Ern Malley Affair* are both examples of the excellent research on specific aspects of Adelaide's literary history. Nevertheless, countless gaps in the scholarship remain, and the work in *Adelaide: A Literary City* helps to fill some of them.

Many of the essays address questions about Adelaide as it is represented in writing about the city. Kerryn Goldsworthy suggests that, with the notable exception of Barbara Hanrahan, there is relatively little literature evoking the texture of Adelaide life in comparison to David Malouf's Brisbane, Helen Garner's Melbourne, or Patrick White's Sydney. Alison Broinowski agrees with this assessment, proposing Patrick Allington as one of the few fiction writers who today succeed in capturing 'the look and feel' of the city. Goldsworthy suggests that Adelaide originated in a series of acts of writing, and goes on to present a fascinating case that the relative absence of evocative writing about place is the result of a long tradition of representing it as a planned city, a utopia, or a paradise.

Other essays turn their attention to the kind of Adelaide that *does* emerge from the literature written about the city. Peter Kirkpatrick opens his account of the Jindyworobak movement with an analysis of a striking Rex Ingamell poem in which Adelaide is viewed perhaps from Mount Lofty, and is depicted as having a 'spiritually abiding Aboriginal presence' (126), and he continues, among other things, with a larger exploration of the Jindyworobaks' treatment of place. In discussing a series of autobiographical novels by women who grew up in the city during the 1920s and 1930s, Susan Sheridan acknowledges the dominance of Barbara Hanrahan's impressions of Adelaide during second half of the century, and wonders whether her authors were in some ways responding to Hanrahan's vision. She finds that Nancy Cato, Geraldine Halls and Nene Gare 'write the Adelaide of this period into existence—its city shops, dance halls and cinemas, its suburban homes and schools' (95). Fragments of a more recent Adelaide consistently emerge in the poetry of Ken Bolton, as discussed by Jill Jones: glimpses of the slightly edgy Hindley Street and its surrounds, occasionally of the eastern side of the city or of the inner southern suburbs.

Among the contemporary representations of place examined in *Adelaide: A Literary City* is the work of Amy T. Matthews and J.M. Coetzee. In *End of the Night Girl* (2011), Matthews, who grew up in Adelaide, vividly depicts the city as experienced by a waitress in her twenties, struggling on a range of fronts. Coetzee's *Slow Man* was published in 2005, three years after his relocation to South Australia, and two years after he received the Nobel Prize for literature. As Gillian Dooley points out in her essay, he takes from the real city a set of briefly sketched places and uses them not to depict an accurate Adelaide but an Adelaide that serves the novel's purposes. He explores a different phase of life to that of Matthews's protagonist, but one similarly difficult. Dooley concludes that, in contrast to its reputation as a city with a dark side, these two novelists both present it as 'a relatively benign, safe place' (254). This version of the city is, in fact, not unlike the nurturing and sedate Adelaides found by Sheridan in the autobiographical novels of Cato, Halls and Gare.

Though in Wakefield's initial conception, the ideal colony might have had at its heart a city where the literary could flourish, often the relationship between Adelaide's literary culture and the society of which it forms a part has not been easy. The early tension between the economic and the literary has given way to other more complex relations, sometimes fraught in different ways.

In the middle of the nineteenth century, George Isaacs relished taking the fight to conservative Adelaide society, as Anne Black shows in her essay on this now virtually unknown writer. Black's research brings to light not only important information about the author of the first novel published in South Australia, but also invaluable detail about the difficulties in surviving as a writer in the Adelaide of the 1860s. Early in the twentieth century, it was C.J. Dennis and a group of like-minded bohemians who were trying to prick and sting the politically and socially conservative members of Adelaide society with their satirical weekly, the *Gadfly*, as my own essay on Dennis outlines. Betty Snowden's chapter offers readers some of her biographical research on Max Harris, who, by the mid-twentieth century was pricking pretensions almost as a vocation. In all three cases the forces of conservatism responded in kind, with Isaacs's reputation severely damaged by an obituary in one of the newspapers he had attacked, with Dennis's *Gadfly* forced to close because it relied for advertising on those whom it mocked, and with Harris under siege, particularly in the Ern Malley hoax and subsequent *Angry Penguins* obscenity trial.

Not surprisingly, *Adelaide: A Literary City* gives a good deal of attention to particular periods when literary life was at its most creative and energetic. Kirkpatrick's research on the Jindyworobaks is a significant re-examination of that important Adelaide-based poetic movement from the late 1930s, giving, among other things, an acute reading of the racial politics of the poems.

Several essays examine specific aspects of the 1950s and 1960s, while Alison Broinowski takes a broader view of that exciting period when the creative energies of people such as Geoffrey Dutton, Rosemary Wighton, Max Harris, Mary Martin, John Bray and Ninette Dutton meant that Adelaide could be known as 'the Athens of the South', though possibly with just a trace of irony. As well as giving a personal perspective on this period, Broinowski takes account of other crucial fundamentals for a flourishing literary culture, for instance the bookshops like the WEA, the Argonaut, and Mary Martin's, and the publishing houses like Griffin, Wakefield, and Rigby. Jill Roe's essay, too, mentions the vibrant literary life of mid-twentieth century Adelaide, similarly giving attention to the infrastructure on which that culture depended. Also playing a surprisingly significant role in supporting Adelaide's literary life at this time—perhaps because of the city's size—is the University of Adelaide. Several essays point, for instance, to professors J.I.M. Stewart and Charles Jury's role in encouraging young writers, and Geoffrey Dutton's input is also stressed.

At the same time, however, Broinowski's is a justifiably ambivalent account of the city, drawing attention to the dangers of smugness, of looking inwards, of complacency, and of resenting those who choose to leave. Jill Jones's essay on Bolton is similarly aware of the advantages and potential disadvantages of a city the size of Adelaide. As she points out, when Bolton arrived from Sydney over thirty years ago, he was attracted by the anonymity that Adelaide offered. But she goes on to delineate gently the provincial nature of the city, mainly tracing the positives in its relative distance from larger metropolises, but also hinting at the drawbacks. The dangers of a small town mentality might well be evident, too, in the nervousness that Sheridan discerns in Nancy Cato about the reception of *Marigold*, in which she had criticised the strait-laced Adelaide of many decades earlier.

Another related and important question is how Adelaide may have shaped the writing that took place within it. Sheridan asks whether the experiences of growing up female depicted in the novels of Cato, Halls and Gare could have been located in any other Australian city. Nicholas Jose hints at a connection between the 'flat grids' of Adelaide and the 'honest discipline' of Geoffrey Dutton (197). Peter Kirkpatrick argues that the 'modern urban life' of the Adelaide-based Jindyworobak movement was 'the precondition' for the primitivism at the heart of their poetic project (126). And Jill Jones considers whether there might be a difference in Bolton's mood in his Adelaide poems in comparison with his earlier Sydney poems—a shift that perhaps corresponds with his move from 'Sydney's multitudinous curves to Adelaide's flatter, less frenetic ways' (243). She finds a greater calmness in his Adelaide work, perhaps connected to its slower pace of life.

Sometimes *Adelaide: A Literary City* reveals surprising contributions that Adelaide has made to the nation's literary history. For example, William Storrie's *Letters frae Saunders McTavish to his Guid-brither in the Kintra*, as Graham Tulloch points out, stands alone in 'South Australian (and Australian) literature ... as a full-blooded expression of Scottish identity in an entirely Australian setting through the use of the Scots language' (71). Better known is C.J. Dennis's *The Songs of a Sentimental Bloke*, which today retains its position as having sold more copies than any other Australian book of verse. Although written near Melbourne and published in Sydney, my essay argues that the style and ideas that flourished in that volume had largely been developed before its author left Adelaide, where he received his first encouragement to write, and where he cut his teeth as a poet and journalist.

This collection of essays also adds an Adelaide dimension to literary criticism—and, sometimes, historical research—that has been carried out in relation to other parts of Australia. Since the institutional rise of Australian literary studies, the question of the relationship between Sydney and the bush and Melbourne and the bush has received much study, for example, in Wilde, Hooton and Andrews's *Oxford Companion to Australian Literature* and the work of Chris Wallace-Crabbe. Here, Jill Roe begins the process of examining the literary dimension of a similar relationship in South Australia, taking her cue from John Hirst's influential history, *Adelaide and the Country*, which addressed the social and political connections between metropolitan and rural South Australia. In looking at the literary impact of the city on the country and vice-versa, she finds that the divide was seldom as marked in South Australia as it was in those eastern states. Similarly broadening existing scholarship is Sheridan's work, which augments Joy Hooton's classic account of Australian women's autobiography, *Stories of Myself When Young*, by examining Cato and Halls, whose material was published after Hooton's book.

Peter Kirkpatrick notes, in passing, that Adelaide falls outside 'the dominant literary axis of the eastern states', and that this might have played some part in the reception of the Jindyworobaks' poetry. His revision of the usual readings of the movement argues that their primitivism should be seen as 'a distinct mode of Australian modernism' (128).

In their essays, Betty Snowden and Nicholas Jose provide new information about Max Harris and Geoffrey Dutton, both probably better known in Adelaide than nationally. Snowden stresses the contribution of the larger-than-life Harris to the literary and cultural world of Adelaide, as a precocious young student, as poet and novelist, as editor of literary magazines, and as energetic participant in the book trade. As she points out, Harris had a close partnership with Dutton, whose reputation is examined in Jose's perceptive analysis of *New York Nowhere*, Dutton's last substantial poem. Using this autobiographical piece as 'a lost key', Jose moves between a detailed knowledge of the poet's personal history and a subtle interpretation of the poem to throw much light on both.

I'm very pleased that this volume is able to include the text of Dutton's *New York Nowhere*. It was originally published in 1998 in a lavishly produced and expensive limited edition of just 175 copies, which included etchings by John Olsen, photographs by Robert Littlewood, and a recording of Dutton reading the work. *New York Nowhere*'s release was overshadowed by its author's death, a few weeks earlier. It is here made widely available for the first time.

Adelaide has inevitably played its part in the lives of writers from other regions of Australia, and one example of this is its role in Patrick White's career as a playwright. Several of the essays in *Adelaide: A Literary City* refer to the opposition to White from conservative elements in the city, and the efforts of people like Harris, Dutton and Harry Medlin in ensuring that *The Ham Funeral*, *The Season at Sarsparilla* and *Night on Bald Mountain* received their premieres in productions from the University of Adelaide Theatre Guild. In addition, Jose uses his examination of *New York Nowhere* to counter the unfair assessments by Patrick White of Geoffrey Dutton, through which, he suggests, many today have gained their opinions of the latter.

And finally, at a time when literary criticism is stressing 'the transnational', it is worth noting that, of course, writing in Adelaide has always been strongly connected with literature throughout the rest of the world, and this is something that emerges in many of the essays in this volume. Graeme Tulloch's chapter on the surprising prominence of Scots and those of Scottish descent in Adelaide and its literary life examines the complex and multiple identities negotiated in and through

Scottish literature during the seventy-five years after the proclamation of the colony. He details the popularity of Robert Burns and Walter Scott, delineates the ambiguous position of Scottish writing within English literature, and discusses writing in Adelaide, including the importance of Scottish identity as a strand in the work of Catherine Helen Spence. While it is Tulloch who examines the transnational in the most focused way, the interconnectedness of literary Adelaide with international literature is everywhere through this volume: in C.J. Dennis's reading of Rider Haggard and Charles Dickens and in the importance of Rudyard Kipling to his work; in the reading material consumed by country readers surveyed by Jill Roe; in the traces of Christina Stead and Henry James in the writers examined by Susan Sheridan; in the Jindyworobaks' connection with international modernism; in Max Harris's voracious reading; in the breadth of Geoffrey Dutton's literary references, as evidenced by *New York Nowhere*; and in Ken Bolton's connections with Manhattan, to name only some examples.

ADELAIDE AS A LITERARY CITY

Like all cities, Adelaide has, in its own smallish way, always been literary — as producer and consumer of literature and as subject of literature. It was never going to have a large literary culture in relation to its counterparts elsewhere in Australia, and therefore it was never likely to have a creative output to rival those places.

However, the literary has always had a significant place in Adelaide's identity — arguably for much of its life a more significant place than in other Australian capitals. When the colony was founded, the centrepiece in many South Australians' sense of their difference was the idea that their new home was untainted by the transportation of convicts. Adelaide's belief that it was more respectable, more cultured, and less brash than its colonial neighbours, was augmented through the nineteenth century by a series of factors. These included the enduring legacy of Wakefield's rhetoric, the prominence of dissenters, the number of churches, and the absence of a large-scale South Australian goldrush. But its interest in literature, and in high culture, more broadly, has figured prominently in the city's self-definition from early in its life, becoming increasingly important after the cessation of transportation to the other colonies.

By the mid-1890s, before William Mitchell left London to take up the chair of English Language and Literature at the University of Adelaide, he was informed that 'Adelaide, in proportion to its population, might claim to be the most literary city in Australia'. On his arrival, he was struck by 'the widespread interest in literature' in the city, as demonstrated by attendances at public lectures on literary topics, and by the memberships of literary societies (*Advertiser*, 19 December 1895, 7). Perhaps interest in the literary was actually no greater than in any Australian capital city, but it may well be that Adelaide's sense of itself as a cultured and civilised place was more significant to its inhabitants than was the case elsewhere. Throughout the twentieth century, the city has continued to value the literary, and to take pride in some of its formidable achievements in this area, such as Writers' Week, Australia's oldest literary festival; the Friendly Street Poets, Australia's oldest public reading community; the South Australian Writers' Centre, the first such body to be established and a model for others throughout the country; and the establishment of the first chair in creative writing in any Australian university, and the highly successful program which that has allowed. During that period the connection between the literary and respectability has probably largely disappeared, but a focus on creativity and culture remains prominent.

Today, literary Adelaide is thriving. The 'printers, schoolmasters and schoolmistresses, booksellers, authors, publishers, and even reviewers' that Wakefield imagined more than 180 years ago have been supplemented by the infrastructure just mentioned, by ArtsSA and its support mechanisms, by an online literary culture that connects the city to the rest of the world, and by countless reading groups and public readings. Adelaide is home to a vast array of interesting writers, such as

Peter Goldsworthy, Anna Goldsworthy, Sean Williams, Dylan Coleman, Vikki Wakefield, Jan Owen, Mem Fox, Stephen Orr, Brian Castro, Hannah Kent and many others, including some contributors to this collection of essays. Its flourishing literary life continues to be an important component of one of Adelaide's most significant identities. *Adelaide: A Literary City* hopes to broaden and deepen our understanding of that long strand in the city's life.

WORKS CITED

Bridge, Carl. *A Trunk Full of Books: History of the State Library of South Australia and Its Forerunners*. Netley, SA: Wakefield Press, 1986.

Butterss, Philip. Ed. *Southwords: Essays on South Australian Writing*. Kent Town, SA: Wakefield Press, 1995.

Depasquale, Paul. *A Critical History of South Australian Literature: 1836-1930*. Warradale, SA: Pioneer, 1978.

Elder, David. Ed. *William Light's Brief Journal and Australian Diaries*. Adelaide: Wakefield Press, 1984.

Hailes, Nathaniel. 'Institutional Dawnings in South Australia'. *Educational Journal of South Australia* 1.1 (15 August 1857), 3-4.

Hill, Fidelia S.T. *Poems and Recollections of the Past*. Sydney: Trood, 1840.

Hirst, John. *Adelaide and the Country, 1870-1917: Their Social and Political Relationship*. Carlton, Vic.: Melbourne University Press, 1973.

Hooton, Joy. *Stories of Herself When Young: Autobiographies of Childhood by Australian Women*. Melbourne: Oxford University Press, 1990.

Horton, James T. *Six Months in South Australia*. London: Cross, 1838.

Magarey, Susan. *Unbridling the Tongues of Women: A Biography of Catherine Helen Spence*. 1985. Adelaide: University of Adelaide Press, 2010.

Marr, David. 'So much of our life is in it'. *Australian Book Review* (May 2012): 12-17.

Minute Book of the South Australian Literary and Scientific Association, GRG 44/83, South Australian Archives.

Radzevicius, Michael. 'England Elsewhere: Edward Gibbon Wakefield and an Imperial Utopian Dream'. PhD thesis, The University of Adelaide, 2011.

Stewart, Annette. *Barbara Hanrahan: A Biography*. Kent Town, SA: Wakefield Press, 2010.

Stevenson, George and Margaret. 'Extracts from the Journal of a Voyage in His Majesty's Ship Buffalo, from England to South Australia'. Angas Papers, State Library of South Australia, PRG 174/1 Quarto Series.

Thomas, Evan Kyffin. Ed. *The Diary and Letters of Mary Thomas (1836-1866)*. Adelaide: Thomas, 1925.

Thomas, Mary. *Serious Poems*. London: Whittaker, Treacher, 1831.

Wakefield, Edward Gibbon. *A Letter from Sydney*. Ed. Robert Gouger. London: Cross, 1829.

Wall, Barbara. *Our Own Matilda: Matilda Evans 1827-1886, Pioneer Woman and Novelist*. Kent Town, SA: Wakefield Press, 1994.

Wallace-Crabbe, Christopher. *Melbourne or the Bush: Essays on Australian Literature and Society*. Sydney: Angus & Robertson, 1974.

Wilde, William H., Joy Hooton and Barry Andrews. Ed. *Oxford Companion to Australian Literature*. 1985. Melbourne: Oxford University Press, 1994.

1 Acts of Writing

Kerryn Goldsworthy

The city of Adelaide existed extensively in writing before one house had been built, before one street had been surveyed, before the place had been named or its site determined. It was built on acts of writing, and it had existed in writing, a city built of paper and parchment, for years before it became a physical fact. The city itself, with its geometric streets and quarried stone, seemed to be somehow absent from all the documents surrounding its establishment, as though it were the hole in the middle of a large discursive doughnut.

That might be understandable, given that the focus was on establishing the laws and limits of the colony, rather than on the city itself. But throughout the history of South Australian writing there seems to be surprisingly little emphasis on, or representation of, the city of Adelaide itself. South Australia has writers associated with Mt Gambier, Auburn, Penola and Eudunda; it has writers who write about China and Russia; it even has writers who write space operas. But by comparison with Brisbane or Perth or Hobart, much less with Melbourne and Sydney, there is relatively little writing grounded in the city of Adelaide, at least not in a way that brings it to life after the fashion of

Patrick White's Sydney or Helen Garner's Melbourne or David Malouf's Brisbane.

In the many historical accounts, certain key documents are repeatedly mentioned as crucial points in the establishment of the colony of South Australia and the city of Adelaide. The earliest of these was published in 1829: Edward Gibbon Wakefield's *A Letter From Sydney*, in which he outlined his scheme for 'systematic colonisation', on whose principles the colony of South Australia was subsequently founded. The next is *Two Expeditions Into the Interior of Southern Australia*, published in 1833 by Captain Charles Sturt, whose description of the country around the lower reaches of the Murray and whose recommendation of it as a good place for settlement was influential both in the decision to establish a colony and in the choice of where the earliest arrivals would land. A third is the *South Australia Act of 1834* (or 'Foundation Act'), which wrote the future establishment of the colony into British law, and a fourth is the Letters Patent of February 1836, which brought the colony into being as a geopolitical reality. A fifth, and the one that has had the most lasting resonance for South Australians, was the Proclamation that was read to the assembled colonists under the Old Gum Tree—or possibly under some other gum tree; the point is still disputed and the truth may be permanently lost—at Holdfast Bay on 28 December 1836.

These are the five key documents on the basis of which the Province of South Australia and its capital or 'principal town' were established. But the word 'Adelaide' does not appear anywhere in any of them, and on the day that the Proclamation was read, the city's site was not yet decided on.

Writing about place is almost always an act of mimesis. The writing is a response to and a representation of something that already exists. But although these early documents are all about the colony of South Australia, and by extension the city of Adelaide, this process is reversed in them: the city of Adelaide did not yet exist except as an imaginary place, and did not begin to exist until a fortnight after the Proclamation was read, when Colonel William Light began his survey near the corner of what became North and West Terraces. The city of Adelaide was brought into being by a succession of acts of writing: acts not of mimesis, but of projection.

On the voyage out, the three earliest boatloads of settlers likewise kept shipboard diaries of a voyage whose destination was as yet non-existent. It was an imaginary basket into which they had put every egg of their lives and futures. In describing their fellow emigrants and anticipating their lives in the new country as they wrote their shipboard letters and journals, they were writing the community into existence, as were the settlers who followed in their wake.

This chapter considers the genesis of Adelaide in acts of writing, tracing its beginnings as a planned city not only in terms of its physical layout, but also in terms of its social, political and economic workings. It looks at some of the literary aspects of the documents that brought the city into being, and at a tradition of literary references to Adelaide either as Paradise or as Utopia. And it gives some examples of the ways in which the idea of Adelaide as an abstraction, an ideal or an absence—and sometimes as more than one of those things at a time—has persisted as an influence and as a motif in writing about the city. It's a given that the establishment of the city of Adelaide was an act of Aboriginal dispossession; in spite of the surprisingly detailed and contemporary-sounding paragraphs concerning the rights and treatment of the Kaurna people of the Adelaide Plains in some of these early documents, Aboriginal culture here as elsewhere was literally overwritten by the process of white settlement. The condition of written-ness was one that automatically excluded, if not erased, the Aboriginal culture of the time and place.

* * *

On 14 May 1827, Edward Gibbon Wakefield, then 31 years old, was sentenced to three years' imprisonment in Newgate for the abduction of a teenage heiress, something he had already done once before and so much more successfully that when the first one died in childbirth, her fortune had set him up financially for life, which did not stop him from trying it again. While in prison, he became interested in the fates and life stories of his fellow-prisoners, including men who had been or were about to be transported as convicts, and many of whom as victims of the Industrial Revolution had found themselves with no legal means of support.

During this period Wakefield became a strong and inspiring advocate of emigration as a cure for the overcrowding and underemployment of the times. The study that he made of colonisation resulted in the writing and publication, in 1829, of his highly influential book *A Letter From Sydney, The Principal Town of Australasia*. It was, in fact, a letter from Newgate — in the event, Wakefield never set foot in Australia, much less in South Australia — but it used the reported weaknesses and failures of other Australian colonies as a basis for the scheme that he called 'systematic colonisation', as summarised here in Graeme Pretty's entry for Wakefield in the *Australian Dictionary of Biography*:

> Wakefield claimed that Australian colonies were suffering from chaotic granting of free land, shortage of labour and consequent dependence on convicts. He argued that if settlement were concentrated, waste lands of the crown could be readily sold and the proceeds applied to the emigration of labourers, preferably young married couples, thereby giving maximum population relief in Britain and ensuring a balanced, fruitful colonial society. But if the price for crown land were made high enough to discourage labourers from immediately acquiring land they could not use, such tribulations as those of the Swan River settlement would be avoided. Sufficiency of labour and a congenial society would attract capital, encourage emigration, assure prosperity, and justify the rights of a colony to elect representatives to its own legislature.

Ideally the plan was self-perpetuating, like an executive toy. And it was a version of this scheme, though tinkered with here and watered down there, that was eventually put in place to establish the province of South Australia. Although reality intervened fairly quickly, the essence both of the plan and of the ideals behind it were enshrined in British law and in the history of South Australia.

A Letter From Sydney is what we'd probably now call creative nonfiction. It's a factual document using fiction-writing techniques, most notably the invention of a first-person narrator purporting to be a colonist in Sydney who has observed what works and what doesn't in the Australian colonies, and is offering his scheme for colonisation from the point of view of imaginary personal experience. Wakefield makes his argument persuasive by the use of literary techniques: turning it into a dramatic monologue and a narrative, not to mention the exotic setting. It also, on its title page, contains in large letters the words 'Edited by Robert Gouger.'

In one of the neater ironies of the only convict-free colony in the country, South Australia's two earliest founders and enthusiasts, Gouger and Wakefield, had both seen the inside of a jail. In a further irony, Gouger's imprisonment was for a debt to a printer, incurred by the costs of printing and distributing Wakefield's first outline of his theories. It was during Gouger's brief imprisonment in 1829 that he first learned of the explorations of Flinders and Baudin, and late in 1830 he heard of Charles Sturt's epic journey down the Murray through southern Australia and turned his attention there, thinking it sounded like an ideal place for an experiment in systematic colonisation.

The eventual success of Gouger's tireless efforts over the next few years to establish one of Wakefield's ideal colonies in southern Australia was due largely to Captain Charles Sturt's account of the countryside on the Fleurieu Peninsula, in his book *Two Expeditions Into the Interior of Southern Australia*. After this influential account appeared in 1833, the hitherto hostile Colonial Office in London appears to have changed its collective mind in the face of widespread public interest.

At this point, however, it is instructive to look at what Sturt actually said. Having reached the Murray mouth at the end of his epic journey to map the river, and having realised that not only had the promised support ship failed to arrive but that it was going to be impossible to sail safely out of Encounter Bay and back around the coast to Sydney, Sturt's already exhausted crew turned around and began the 1500-kilometre row upstream, back to their depot on the Murrumbidgee. Sturt never explored the land to their west, between the river and St Vincent's Gulf, at all; the closest he came was a quick glimpse across to the western side of the Mt Lofty Ranges as they set off back upstream:

> reduced as [we] were from previous exertion, beset as our homeward path was by difficulty and danger, and involved as our eventual safety was in obscurity and doubt, I could not but deplore the necessity that obliged me to re-cross the Lake Alexandrina ... and to relinquish the examination of its western shores. We were borne over its ruffled and agitated surface with such rapidity, that I had scarcely time to view it as we passed; but, cursory as my glance was, I could not but think I was leaving behind me the fullest reward of our toil, in a country that would ultimately render our discoveries valuable, and benefit the colony for whose interests we were engaged. (Chapter 8)

Closer inspection was left to the doomed Captain Collet Barker, sent by Governor Darling the following year, on the basis of Sturt's report, to explore the area. Barker and his party had made and recorded a fairly detailed exploration of the Adelaide Hills and the land on either side of them by the time of his death; he was killed by a group of Ngarrindjeri men after having swum across the Murray mouth, with his compass tied to the top of his head to keep it dry, in order to take bearings from the other side. In writing up his own journals for publication in book form, Sturt included the report from a member of Barker's party, which was a fairly detailed description of the coast, the Adelaide Hills and the Adelaide Plain—although, with the landscape's geographical features described but as yet unnamed, even readers familiar with the landscape might struggle today to recognise some of its features. At the beginning of *The Road to Botany Bay*, Paul Carter writes 'If we believe the name, the place is still recognisable. Or is it? Before the name: what was the place like before it was named?' (xiii)

Under the heading 'Adaption of this part of the country for colonisation', Sturt wrote

> From [Barker's] account it would appear that a spot has, at length, been found upon the south coast of New Holland, to which the colonist might venture with every prospect of success, and in whose valleys the exile might hope to build for himself and for his family a peaceful and prosperous home. All who have ever landed upon the eastern shore of St. Vincent's Gulf, agree as to the richness of its soil, and the abundance of its pasture. (Chapter 8)

Sturt's diction and cadences there are poetic and almost biblical, with exiles and valleys and pastures, and alliterative v's and p's. The rhetorical power of this passage no doubt played its part in engaging the British public and persuading the Colonial Office to change its mind, in spite of the fact that Sturt had never laid eyes on the place himself. His biographer J.H.L. Cumpston, writing in 1951, claims for Sturt's book that

> It had one immediate and most important result. ... The movement towards the foundation of a 'Wakefield' colony had languished, but the publication of Sturt's story of a large river, and his almost lyrical praise of the fertile river valley, brought the whole movement again into vigorous activity. He was invited by the Under-Secretary Hay at the Colonial Office to give his views as to the geographical prospects of a settlement in South Australia in the region of the Murray River. He gave these views in a long memorandum dated 17th February, 1834, in which, having the benefit of Barker's survey ... he recommended the vicinity of Port Adelaide River as the site for

the first town, 'because [wrote Sturt] it appears to me that when the distant interior shall be occupied, and communication established with the lake and the valley of the Murray, the banks of this creek will be the proper and natural site for the capital'. (Chapter 5)

This is the first mention that I know of in any document of plans for a capital city. Only six months later, in August 1834, the South Australia Act was passed through the British Parliament. Written in impenetrable nineteenth century legalese, this document enshrines in law the basic premises of Wakefield's scheme to achieve a balance of labour, land and capital and to establish an Emigration Fund through the sale of South Australian land, as well as showing the kind of social engineering that Wakefield argued would 'ensure a balanced, fruitful colonial society' (Pretty) but that also looks, to the contemporary reader, ominously like a plan to breed a labouring class:

> [the] 'Emigration Fund' ... shall without any deduction whatsoever ... be employed in conveying poor emigrants from Great Britain or Ireland And to the said province provided also that the poor persons who shall by means of the said 'Emigration Fund' be conveyed to the said province shall, as far as possible, be adult persons of the two sexes in equal proportions, And not exceeding the age of thirty years.

This document contains no mention anywhere of a capital or 'principal town'. Nor do the Letters Patent of February 1836 in which King William IV, who had been empowered by the Act of 1834 to establish the Province of South Australia, duly and officially did so. Again, there is no mention of a capital or principal town in this short document, and nor is there in the Proclamation that was read to a crowd of over 200 colonists in the shade of a gum tree outside Robert Gouger's tent—Gouger having by this time been appointed Colonial Secretary—at Holdfast Bay, a little way inland in what is now North Glenelg. Clearly showing the hand of Gouger, whose concern for the Kaurna people is expressed again and again in his own diary, the Proclamation consists of three short paragraphs, two of which consist entirely of calls upon the colonists to cooperate in securing Aboriginal rights, freedoms and safety.

Since the Province of South Australia had come into being as a geopolitical reality in February 1836 with the issuing of the Letters Patent, it's not clear exactly what was being proclaimed on Proclamation Day. The opening sentence begins 'In announcing to the Colonists ... the establishment of government', which suggests to me that the proclamation was simply Governor Hindmarsh's announcement of his own arrival. Robert Gouger had woken up on that hot morning, had gone out of his tent to feed his precious cashmere goats, and had seen the Governor's ship, the *Buffalo*, in the distance, sailing up the gulf; the proclamation ceremony was held that afternoon, in 39°C heat. Geoffrey Dutton and David Elder, in their unashamedly partisan biography of Colonel William Light, refer to the proclamation ceremony as 'Hindmarsh's little circus' (Dutton and Elder 134).

But although there's no mention in the Proclamation of a capital or a city, there is an exhortation in the first paragraph to behave as an orderly society, and perhaps this is the moment at which the colonists' sense of themselves as a community began to cohere. The Proclamation calls upon the colonists 'to conduct themselves on all occasions with order and quietness, duly to respect the laws, and by a course of industry and sobriety, by the practice of sound morality, and a strict observance of the Ordinances of Religion, to prove themselves worthy to be the founders of a great and free Colony'. Order, quietness, industry, sobriety, morality, religion: perhaps this document was the genesis of Adelaide's largely undeserved reputation as a city of wowsers, goody-goodies and 'churchianity'.

In another kind of early document, the shipboard letters and journals written by the colonists on the voyage out, their destination is likewise strangely absent from their writing. Although the place to which they're going is the end and aim of their journey and the whole point of being at sea, their letters and journals concentrate almost exclusively on shipboard conditions, companions and tribulations; on the seasickness, the boredom, the food and the weather. In 2011 History SA established a website called *Bound for South Australia: Journey of a Lifetime*, structured like a blog with weekly entries, in which the voyages of the first nine ships out to South Australia were recreated through weekly updates over 45 weeks. The entries included written summaries of events that week, as well as numerous extracts from the shipboard diaries of the colonists, including Governor Hindmarsh's waspish private secretary George Stevenson and the practical, cheerful and energetic Robert Gouger.

But like the recently discovered shipboard diary of the young Scottish Presbyterian emigrant James Bell, these documents concentrate almost exclusively on shipboard happenings from week to week; their destination is barely mentioned. The capital city has been well established by the time James Bell takes ship late in 1838, but almost the only time he mentions the place where he has been bound all along, and which must have been a great deal in his thoughts, is in the final entry: 'Tomorrow I hope to step ashore at Adelaide' (174).

* * *

The representation of Adelaide as some form of absence is not confined to these early documents. Our most thorough, evocative, detailed and beautiful representation of the city in literature is Barbara Hanrahan's first book *The Scent of Eucalyptus*. But Hanrahan wrote this book in London; as with one of her literary heroes, Katherine Mansfield, she wrote one of literature's most memorable accounts of an antipodean childhood home from a self-imposed exile in the northern hemisphere. Both of them needed to be absent from the place, or for the place to be absent from them, in order to see and write about it in so powerful and evocative a way. In her own account of writing *The Scent of Eucalyptus*, Hanrahan is very clear about the psychological mechanics of it: she needs to be separate from her remembered childhood before she can write about it, and that involves both her own absence from Adelaide and the death of her grandmother, the most powerful figure of her childhood. After her grandmother's death, Hanrahan recalled,

> I started keeping a diary again ... The old world was gone from me physically, yet it was inside my body, hurting so much it had to get out ... for the next six months I sat down every day and wrote about my childhood in Adelaide ... Dead, my grandmother had set me free to write. ('Beginnings', 84)

Even one of the most recently published books about Adelaide figures the city as something distantly seen from unfamiliar angles, and sometimes as a looming absence. Michael Ladd's beautiful book about the River Torrens is called *Karrawirra Parri: Walking the Torrens From Source to Sea*. It combines poetry, prose and photographs in its account of our river. It is at once a book about Adelaide and not about Adelaide at all: in its emphasis on Aboriginal sites and stories, on indigenous vegetation and on native wildlife, there's a sense in which it's almost an anti-Adelaide, an evocation of what the landscape and life of the river was like before the city was built on its banks.

* * *

When it comes to theorising about the relationship between writing and place, the three names that come first to mind are those of the philosopher Gaston Bachelard, the Marxist theorist and filmmaker Guy Debord and the great American regionalist fiction writer Eudora Welty. But the ideas of all three are predicated on the assumption that the place pre-exists the writing: that there already exists, to be written about, a place with the dense material reality of an established location with a name and a history. In her luminous essay 'Place in Fiction', Welty is writing for other writers, talking about the importance of writing about place as a creative act of mimesis, a response to and representation of the locations of stories. Bachelard's ideas in *The Poetics of Space* and Debord's theory of psychogeography both presuppose the material density and complexity of a build environment: psychogeography is to do with the effect of urban space, which is often crowded and chaotic, on the human subject, while Bachelard's ideas depend on the contents, structures and functions of intimate space: the house, the attic, the wardrobe, the chest of drawers.

Given the psychological importance that both Bachelard and Debord ascribe to a built environment, in fact, it's interesting to consider the degree to which the colonists might have felt that as a lack. The culture of Victorian England was one that privileged *stuff*, in all its forms: bags, boxes, objects, gadgets, cupboards, drawers and general paraphernalia. The colonists had only such of their stuff as they had managed to bring with them, and were living in makeshift tents and huts while they waited for a city to be created. And many of these people were from cities: an understanding of daily interaction with urban space was a central part of their ontology.

A more useful set of ideas with which to approach the earliest, which is to say pre-Adelaide, white history of South Australia is that to be found in Paul Carter's groundbreaking book from 1987, *The Road to Botany Bay*, which seems to look more valuable and original the older it gets. Some of the uses to which it might be put in a study of this time and place in South Australia's history are suggested by his observation that

> The 'facts' of ... spatial history are not houses and clearings, but phenomena as they appear to the traveller, as his intentional gaze conjures them up. They are the directions and distances in which houses and clearings *may* be found or founded. (xxiv, emphasis in original)

Consider, for example, the case of Colonel William Light: asthmatic, tubercular, already 51 years old, unsupplied with any form of transport apart from boats and his own feet and sent out to the colony much later than he should have been, Light spent the second half of 1836 trudging across the terrain of the Adelaide Plain, Encounter Bay and the Eyre and

Fleurieu Peninsulas during the early months before the arrival of the Governor, struggling to make sense of earlier accounts of the regions and to work out what might be the best place to situate the city and begin his survey.

Another useful theorist in this context is Benedict Anderson, with his notion of 'imagined communities'; while he is specifically talking about nationalism, the idea could apply equally well to a group of colonists trying to bring a new group identity into being in a new place. As well as being a real, if as yet embryonic, community, the colony of South Australia also constituted an imagined community in the Anderson sense: something in which the members of a national community don't all know, and never can all know, each other, yet perceive themselves as related through common nationhood. Many of the colonists regarded the Province of South Australia as a kind of mini-nation, and what Anderson calls 'the Utopian element' in nationalism was certainly present in the establishment of South Australia.

There's a long history of referring to South Australia as Utopia or as Paradise, something that would make many of the early colonists, many generations of bored teenagers, and many contemporary eastern-staters snort with disbelief. But the fact that it's such a very planned city, both in its physical layout and in the ideal structure of its earliest white society, probably has something to do with these recurrent tropes of perfection. Certainly Wakefield's ideas and ideals were Utopian.

References both implicit and explicit to Utopia and Paradise begin to appear early on in writing about South Australia. Catherine Helen Spence wrote an overtly Utopian novel called *Handfasted*, which remained unpublished until 1984, but her better-known novel *Clara Morison* uses mid-Victorian Adelaide as the setting of another feminist Utopia of sorts, disguised as standard nineteenth century realism and frankly imitative in many respects of *Jane Eyre*, which had been published a few years earlier. *Clara Morison* describes in detail and with relish the conditions of life in Adelaide during the gold rushes in Victoria and NSW, when so many Adelaide men rushed off across the border burning up with gold fever and left the women at home to hew wood, draw water, learn to fend for themselves, and keep the city going in a sensible, practical and non-febrile way based on mutual cooperation and sturdy female common sense of the kind Spence personified for all of her long life.

Anthony Trollope, in his 1873 book *Australia and New Zealand*, called Adelaide 'a happy Utopia' in spite of his well-founded disgust at the state of the river at the time: 'Anything in the guise of a river more ugly than the Torrens would be impossible to either see or describe' (181). Mark Twain, writing 25 years later, recalled his attendance at a Proclamation Day ceremony in Glenelg and his bemusement at what he calls Adelaide's 'most un-English mania for holidays. Mainly they are workingmen's holidays,' he wrote,

> for in South Australia the working-man is sovereign ... The working-man is a great power everywhere in Australia, but South Australia is his paradise. He has had a hard time in this world, and has earned a paradise. I am glad he has found it. (94)

Douglas Pike titled his magisterial and still definitive early history of the colony *Paradise of Dissent*, a clever, multi-layered, and only slightly ironic title that makes reference, among other things, to the principle of religious freedom that was part of South Australia's attraction for many immigrants. And Peter Goldsworthy's novel *Three Dog Night* begins with a hymn of praise:

> There might be higher mountains on the planet than the Adelaide Hills, but they are no closer to heaven. Each valley is a little deeper and greener than the last, and each ridge, a little higher and bluer, seems another step in some sort of ascension. Even the names of the steps have a heavenly sound. (3)

Even J.M. Coetzee is uncharacteristically hyperbolic in his account of his first visit to Adelaide: 'It was March, it was hot, but there were shaded walks to be had along the Torrens River where black swans glided serenely. "What kind of place is this?" I asked myself. "Is this paradise on earth?"' ('Coetzee shares his wisdom').

The representation of Adelaide as a paradise is the reverse of the more usual nineteenth and twentieth century representations in both English and Australian literature of Australia as a dumping ground for convicts: merely to be sent to this country was a punishment, and the country was therefore, implicitly, Hell. Even Adelaide was only briefly convict-free; many of the transported made their way here from other colonies. The difference was that they had wanted to come here because it was by comparison a desirable place, rather than having been sent here as a form of punishment. Adelaide was the one Australian colony not officially constituted by the British legal system as a hell on earth.

Paradise and Utopia are two different things. 'Paradise' is a word from the discourse of the sacred, with its connotations of innocence and of reward. 'Utopia' is a profoundly secular idea, and suggests a place where the ideal social organisation is the result of some hard thinking and regulated conduct by human beings, not created by any god or gods. What the two things do have in common is their status as ideals and the fact that neither of them actually exists except as an abstraction.

For Wakefield's perfect society did not perpetuate itself in practice, any more than Colonel Light's beautiful design for the city guaranteed, at least in the early days of settlement, that a citizen might be comfortable and happy in it. The lived experience of making one's way through the perfectly planned city was very different from the way it looked on paper, and Governor Gray's account of Adelaide society in 1845 stands in vivid contrast to the Noah's Ark prescriptions of the South Australia Act. One early colonist, James Hawker, later recalled his arrival in the Colony in 1838:

> Owing to the buildings in Adelaide being very much scattered, the streets were scarcely defined. Hindley to Morphett Street—Rundle to Stephens Place and Currie Street to Light Square were the only

ones that could be designated as such, as some tenements were erected on each side. Few and far between, however, they were. The greater part of King William Street was scrub, and so was the southern part of the town (M. Carter 195-6).

Another colonist, William Mann, wrote of his experiences earlier the same year:

> ... I lost my way one day going from one house to another, and perceiving a fowler at some distance, I walked up to him to enquire the way to Adelaide, particularly to Hindley Street. He said 'Why Sir, you are now in the very centre of the city! The place you are in is Victoria Square', and pointing to a wooden hut about half a mile distant, he told me to follow the path through the forest that led to it, and the inmates could show me the way to Hindley Street. (M. Carter 196)

The population, by 1845, was very far from being the orderly society of strong young British and Irish couples that Wakefield had envisaged. Governor Grey, who like so many British gentlemen of his era had a remarkable gift for words, described it in a letter to his uncle in London in January 1845:

> The European population are collected from almost all parts of the world. They were wholly unacquainted with one another previously to their arrival here. You meet Scotchmen in kilts and plaids, Irish women without bonnets and their cloaks thrown over their heads, Germans in their national costumes and very picturesque they are (we have about 1,000 Germans here who have abandoned their country upon account of religious persecution), Chinese with their wide trousers, Indians in different costumes, natives with kangaroo skin cloaks, Frenchmen, runaway convicts who have come overland, with large beards & bush appearance, Catholic priests, English country bumpkins with smock frocks, Irishmen with frieze coats, London dandies, all mixed in our streets—all accustomed to different laws and usages, all ignorant of one another, of the country into which they have come, of its seasons, of its soils and their

different degrees of productiveness, of the crops which are most remunerative (indeed until lately of those that would grow here), never accustomed to act in unison, having no common interest, ignorant of the nature of the Government under which they were to live, of the personal character and capacity of their Governor who had arrived from the other extremity of the earth to govern them, they did not know how—such was the nature of the Society into which I was thrown. (M. Carter 247)

Perhaps the city's origins in idealism are one reason for Adelaide's comparative lack of representation in literature. Adelaide is a difficult place to write about: the extremes of heaven and hell in its history make the city hard to see clearly. We have a handful of novelists and poets who did and do engage directly with the streets, mean or otherwise, of the city. But we have no robust body of such work: no equivalent of Sydney according to Ruth Park, Christina Stead, Kenneth Slessor or Patrick White; of Melbourne according to Henry Handel Richardson, Frank Hardy, Ray Lawler or Helen Garner; of Brisbane according to David Malouf, Andrew McGahan, Venero Armanno or the young Gwen Harwood.

Why in the twenty-first century is there still so little writing about the lanes and gutters and cafes and factories of Adelaide, about the body of the city? About its heart, its gut, its muscles and its little capillaries; about its circulation, its digestion, its breath; about its beauties and its bruises? I think South Australia is still haunted, even now, by the oppressions of perfection, even if only, ever, in theory: by the myths of a planned city and an ideal society. If the map is already perfect, then it doesn't leave you anywhere new to go. And if the society is already perfect, then it doesn't leave you anything new to say.

Works cited

Anderson, Benedict. *Imagined Communities: Reflections on the Origin and Spread of Nationalism*. Revised edition. London and New York:

Verso, 2006.

Bachelard, Gaston. *The Poetics of Space*. 1958. Trans. Maria Jolas. Boston: Beacon, 1969.

Bell, James. *Private Journal of a Voyage to Australia 1838-39*. Ed. Richard Walsh. Sydney: Allen & Unwin, 2011.

Carter, Max. *No Convicts There: Thomas Harding's Colonial South Australia*. Adelaide: Trevaunance Pty Ltd, 1997.

Carter, Paul. *The Road to Botany Bay*. 1987. Minneapolis: University of Minnesota Press, 2010.

Cumpston, J.H.L. *Charles Sturt—His Life and Journeys of Exploration*. 1951. Project Gutenberg Australia. <http://gutenberg.net.au/ebooks07/0700391.txt>. Accessed 1 July 2012.

Debord, Guy-Ernest. 'Introduction to a Critique of Urban Geography.' 1955. <http://library.nothingness.org/articles/SI/en/display/2>. Accessed 2 July 2012.

Dutton, Geoffrey and David Elder. *Colonel William Light — Founder of a City*. Melbourne: Melbourne University Press, 1991.

Goldsworthy, Peter. *Three Dog Night*. Camberwell: Penguin Books Australia, 2003.

Gouger, Robert. 'Proclamation'. *The South Australian Gazette and Colonial Register*. 3 June 1837. 10.

Hodder, Edwin. Ed. *The Founding of South Australia: as recorded in the journals of Mr Robert Gouger, first Colonial Secretary, edited with additional material by Edwin Hodder*. London: Sampson Low, Marston and Company, 1898.

Hanrahan, Barbara. 'Beginnings.' 1982. *Eight Voices of the Eighties*. Ed. Gillian Whitlock. St Lucia: University of Queensland Press, 1989. 81-7.

___. *The Scent of Eucalyptus*. London: Chatto & Windus, 1973.

Ladd, Michael. *Karrawirra Parri: Walking the Torrens From Source to Sea*. Kent Town, SA: Wakefield Press, 2012.

Pike, Douglas. *Paradise of Dissent: South Australia 1829-1857*. London: Longmans, Green & Co., 1957.

Pretty, Graeme L. 'Wakefield, Edward Gibbon (1796-1862)'. *Australian Dictionary of Biography*. National Centre of Biography, Australian National University. <http://adb.anu.edu.au/biography/wakefield-edward-gibbon-2763/text3921>. Accessed 1 July 2012.

Rushdie, Salman. 'At the Adelaide Festival.' 1984. *Imaginary Homelands: Essays and Criticism, 1981-1991*. London: Granta Books in association with Penguin Books, 1991.

Spence, Catherine Helen. *Clara Morison*. 1854. Kent Town, SA: Wakefield Press, 1994.

___. *Handfasted*. Ed. Helen Thomson. Ringwood: Penguin Books Australia, 1984.

Sturt, Captain Charles. *Two Expeditions into the Interior of Southern Australia During the Years 1828, 1829, 1830, 1831*. <http://ebooks.adelaide.edu.au/s/sturt/charles/s93t/v2ch8.html>. Accessed 1 July 2012.

Trollope, Anthony. *Australia and New Zealand*. Vol. II. London: Chapman and Hall, 1873.

Twain, Mark. *Following The Equator*. 1897. <http://www.gutenberg.org/catalog/world/readfile?fk_files=2408411&pageno=94>. Accessed 2 July 2012.

Wakefield, Edward Gibbon. *A Letter From Sydney, the Principal Town of Australasia*. Ed. Robert Gouger. London: Joseph Cross, 1829.

Welty, Eudora. 'Place in Fiction'. 1956. In *The Eye of the Story: Selected Essays and Reviews*. London: Virago, 1987.

ONLINE WORKS WITHOUT AUTHORS

South Australia Act: *Transcript of the South Australia Act, 1834*. National Archives of Australia. <http://foundingdocs.gov.au/item-sdid-37.html>. Accessed 1 July 2012.

Letters Patent. 'Documenting a Democracy'. Museum of Australian Democracy. <http://foundingdocs.gov.au/item-did-2.html>. Accessed 3 July 2012.

History SA. *Bound for South Australia: Journey of a Lifetime*. <boundforsouthaustralia.net.au>. Accessed 2 July 2012.

'Coetzee Shares His Wisdom'. *The 7.30 Report*. Transcript. ABC TV, Adelaide. 3 March 2004. <http://www.abc.net.au/7.30/content/2004/s1058394.htm>. Accessed 1 July 2012.

2 A Colonial Wordsmith: George Isaacs in Adelaide, 1860-1870

Anne Black

One hundred and fifty years ago, a popular author with the mythological pseudonym 'A. Pendragon' walked the streets of central Adelaide, but his significance and his story—a complex drama of one man's efforts to establish himself as a colonial writer—have been long forgotten. In 1858, George Isaacs made his mark on Australian literature as the author of the first novel published in South Australia, *The Queen of the South*. Yet in terms of literary output, his most prolific years were in Adelaide during the 1860s, when newspapers, poems, stories and plays flowed from his pen. At the start of that decade he had modestly declared: 'I believe there is a vacant place in our colonial literature. It is my aim to fill it' (Pendragon, *Number One*, 3). This chapter examines Isaacs's efforts to achieve that goal in an unsupportive environment, and the huge personal cost that it entailed.

Born in London in 1825, Isaacs was the eldest son in a prosperous Jewish family. During his youth he dabbled in literature, hobnobbed with the titled, was a *flâneur* in Paris, collected medieval antiques and, despite his tender years, became a precocious antiquarian. This pleasant existence ended suddenly with the pregnancy of Marion, his non-Jewish partner, who was probably only 15 years old. Isaacs sold off his treasures, farewelled his friends, indicated he was leaving for a healthier climate and boarded the former convict ship, the *Mountstuart Elphinstone*. The couple and their baby arrived in Port Adelaide in March 1851.

Isaacs now faced the novel prospect of employment. Armed with recommendations from prominent English authors plus examples of his own poetry, he approached the editor of the *South Australian Register*, John Taylor. No doubt Taylor had met many newly-arrived amateur scribes hoping for a career in journalism, so it is not surprising that his polite but tardy reply did not include the offer of a job. Forced to earn a living, Isaacs opened a stationery business next to the Royal Exchange Hotel in Hindley Street with Samuel Copland Allday, a fellow immigrant from the *Mountstuart Elphinstone*.[1] Shortly afterwards, Isaacs became the sole operator of the business, but either it did not prosper or he was restless. By 1852 he had settled in Gawler, north of Adelaide, where he again ran a stationery shop, this time on behalf of Burnet Nathan, an Adelaide-based merchant and importer.

Following the discovery of gold in late 1851, a large proportion of South Australia's adult male population was lured to the Victorian goldfields. Isaacs joined the throng. Nothing is known of his success there, but when he returned to Gawler in early 1856 he had only two pounds. His experiences in Victoria, however, did provide the basis for his novel, a tale of the goldfields. Back in Gawler, an abortive attempt to found a reading room led Isaacs to insolvency and the Adelaide Gaol. Eventually, with other clever young men, he became a prominent citizen of the 'Colonial Athens' of Gawler, a vigorous promoter of its Institute and a founder (and the 'Surprising Sham') of its once-famed anti-humbug fraternity, the Humbug Society. His first 10 years in the colony

---

[1] No cargo on the *Mountstuart Elphinstone* was listed under Isaacs's name, so it appears that he did not bring stock with him from England. This suggests that the stationery business venture was opportunistic rather than planned.

established his reputation as an independent, colourful character who did not fit comfortably into conservative Adelaide society. The appearance of his novel *The Queen of the South* and a few published poems marked his first decade as a colonial writer.

By 1860, the now 35-year-old Isaacs was determined to advance his literary career. While toiling as a clerk, he wrote a letter to the *South Australian Advertiser* that expressed his latent editorial ambitions:

> But if circumstances have placed us in a sphere uncongenial to us, we are not to be restrained from our endeavor to emancipate ourselves. Why should I, for instance, always be as I am? May I not, like others, have my small ambition and desire to write myself M.P. or Editor? (31 July 1860, 3)

Isaacs's 'small ambition' was a conceit. He yearned for influence and for recognition from his fellow citizens. From his diverse literary output over the following decade, it is clear that he ached for publication, irrespective of literary genre. He happily jumped from one literary form to another, apparently on a whim or as circumstances prevailed.

By nature, Isaacs was suited to the role of editor. He liked to collect, arrange, inform—and to correct his fellows. In April 1861 he boldly launched a monthly journal of prose and poetry, named *Number One*, in Adelaide. This was his first attempt in Australia to publish his prose and poetry, although ostensibly he was doing it not only for himself but for the greater good of other aspiring writers. *Number One*'s introduction stated that its editor, A. Pendragon, hoped to 'provide a vehicle for imaginative writing' (3), but, probably by necessity, Isaacs himself supplied most of the contents. He also received minor support from his Gawler friend Doctor George Nott, who contributed material under the pseudonyms "G. N." and "Ignotus" (Latin for unknown). 'A. Pendragon' outlined the journal's scope: 'Politics and News as generally understood, would have no place in it, Wit, Humour, Agreeable narrative, History, Travel, Poesy, the Arts and Sciences, the movements of the Philosophical, and other literary associations—would.' (3) The booklet was a geographical hybrid, compiled in Gawler, printed at the *Northern Star* office in Kapunda and published by the bookseller W. C. Rigby at 53 Hindley Street in Adelaide.

Number One was a hybrid in a different way too. It juxtaposed European recollections with impressions of Australian colonial life. Most of Isaacs's poems are permeated by nostalgia for his European past, a universal concern of South Australian immigrants of the time. Thus, in *Number One* he recalls European birds in the anthropomorphic 'The Owl and the Lark' (22) and English plants in his poem (and later published song) 'The Myrtle' (31). This probably provided a comforting and familiar context for his readers. However, the *Register*'s reviewer was more impressed by the journal's inclusion of Australian themes:

> One of the best things about this new production is that it is 'racy of the soil'. In matter, tone, and spirit it is generally Australian. The writers deal chiefly with subjects familiar to the reader, and this of itself is so great an advantage that it will be readily excused if a thought is sometimes crude, or if an idea here and there wants 'fencing in'. (16 May 1861, 2)

The *Advertiser* also joined its daily rival in adding a mildly sanctimonious rebuke to its review: 'We suggest, however, that certain expletives which Police Court reporters usually indicate by an initial letter and a long dash, might with advantage be omitted from a magazine which we presume is intended for all circles' (18 May 1861, 2). *Number One* garnered supportive reviews—'The number before us is really a good colonial shilling's-worth' (*Advertiser*, 18 May 1861, 2)—but despite an extensive nine-month advertising campaign in the Adelaide press, *Number One* did not progress to *Number Two*. In his introduction, A. Pendragon had stated that the journal's fate 'rests with the public of South Australia'; their response was apathy, as it was to most of the city's new magazines of that era.

Isaacs's editorial ambitions were inflamed rather than dampened by the demise of *Number One*. He could not resist the freedom and the discipline of the editorial role for long. If overseeing the birth of *Number One* had been satisfying for him, the prospect of becoming the editor of a weekly newspaper was irresistible. With supreme confidence he moved again to the city and probably invested all his money in the new project. Adelaide's inhabitants awoke on 4 October 1862 to find a new sixpenny Saturday weekly, the *Critic*, edited by A. Pendragon. From his upstairs office in Waterhouse's Buildings in King William Street, Isaacs provided readers with an independent view of life in the colony. On the opening page he stated that the *Critic* aimed:

> not to advance the opinions of any political party, but to comment, in a candid and impartial spirit, on the Events of the Week, and on the various sentiments initiated by the Daily Journals. SATIRE— generally recognized as one of the most effective correctives of folly and abuses, will be by 'THE CRITIC' somewhat freely employed. (4 October 1862, 1)

An inveterate critic, Isaacs was hardly impartial where political parties were concerned. His paper promised 'Fun without coarseness/ Humour, free from vulgarity/ Wit devoid of bitterness, and/ Ridicule, clear of personalities'. Its launch was noted by the *Register*: 'Its editor, long known under the nom de plume of 'A. Pendragon,' is a man of undoubted ability, and the first number of the new journal fully sustains his reputation' (7 October 1862, 2). The same article also graciously added that 'there is ample room in the colony for such a publication', even though the first issue had chastised the established paper for suppressing negative correspondence. Isaacs did not attempt to align himself with Adelaide's literary establishment. Brave (or perhaps foolhardy), and politically astute (but with few social inhibitions), he preferred an independent path.

Isaacs ensured that his paper lived up to its name. The *Critic* held local politicians to account and offered topical opinions on world affairs. It reviewed new publications (such as John Gould's *The Birds of Australia*) and was not afraid to address current scientific controversy (with a spirited defence of Darwinism). For light relief it also included puzzles, gave news from the local racetrack and theatre, and entertained its readers with gossip, poems and stories. Isaacs's still-strong attachment to European literary culture showed in his inclusion of extracts from the recent works of European writers. Thus, a translated excerpt from Victor Hugo's latest sensation *Les Misérables*, courtesy of Mr Rigby, appeared in the *Critic* not long after the novel's debut in France. From a technical perspective the *Critic* expected other papers to match its own high standards, and it gleefully exposed examples of grammatical imperfection, typographical errors and careless prose in the Adelaide press. Isaacs, at least as an editor, was a perfectionist.

He was also responsible for most of the *Critic*'s content. It was a huge task, but it did allow him to indulge himself extravagantly. He printed an image of his own rebus (two eyes over an axe, eyes-axe = Isaacs), recalled his early days in 'Twainbridge' (a thinly-disguised reference to Gawler) and described an adventure he had experienced with his friend, the Adelaide photographer 'Professor' Robert Hall. He also included, in two parts, the full text of his own rather strange lecture, 'Ancient Superstitions'. On cool evenings in August and September 1862, just prior to the *Critic*'s launch, Isaacs had delivered this hour-long speech to appreciative audiences in several towns scattered around Adelaide. The dense subject matter must have demanded the full attention of the colonists who sat in those draughty local halls, and it illustrates the general thirst for novelty. A reviewer captured the complexity of the talk, and also the depth of Isaacs's knowledge in this rarefied field, writing that the speaker:

> commenced his subject by referring to the Jewish caballists as the earliest teachers of magic science,—the science and mysteries of numbers, judicial astrology, invocation of Saints, and the labours of the alchymists, in their endeavours to transmute base metals into gold, and the search after the philosopher's stone, were severally touched upon. The lecturer then proceeded to give an account of love phyltres, amulets, and charms, and of the universal belief in, and horrors of, witchcraft in England up to the last century. The celebrated Dr. Dee, and the pranks he played on Queen Elizabeth, were referred to, and the lecture concluded with a brief notice of

theomania of fairies, gnomes, and sprites. (*Advertiser*, 25 August 1862, 3)

The lecture and its publication are indicative of the driving force behind most of Isaacs's writing—he wished to entertain and inform his fellow citizens. Yet despite his enthusiasm, erudition and effort, the paper was soon in financial trouble. Debtors did not pay their bills, illness intervened and there was a legal dispute with the printer, the Adelaide publisher George Dehane. Isaacs's grand vision of founding and editing his own paper collapsed within six months, after only twenty-one issues. Undaunted, he co-founded and contributed his wit to the Humbug Society's new satirical paper, the *Bunyip*.

It would be six years before Isaacs was again the editor of an Adelaide paper. This venture was the threepenny weekly, the *Licensed Victualler*. Printed at the City Steam Press in Gawler Place, its purpose was to advocate on behalf of the colony's publicans, who were then facing onerous proposed legislation. Isaacs frequented hotels and hated injustice, so he took up their cause with glee. The first issue appeared on 27 November 1869, and it opened appropriately with a two-page article on defamation law. Then in a familiar Pendragon tone, but rather violent language, the editor announced his aims:

> to ridicule, pretension—to hold up to scorn, cant and humbug—to denounce abuse and jobbery, and to seize with an unflinching hand the public thief and oppressor, however he may deem himself protected by the bristles of the law, and to gibbet him as an example to evil doers in all times to come. (27 November 1869, 4)

The *Licensed Victualler*'s masthead was adorned with a typical Isaacs's device—a grandiose motto. This particular example came from the works of Francis Bacon, 'Magnanimity consisteth in contempt of peril, in contempt of profit, and in meriting of the times wherein one liveth.' It sounds an appropriate motto for Isaacs, but its relevance to publicans is a bit vague. Isaacs used the paper to promote his own causes, as well as those of the licensed victuallers. Not only were there articles on liquor regulations, diatribes against the unjust treatment of the inebriated and a footnote on the derivation of the word 'grog', but readers could also enjoy a humorous article on the rival colony of Victoria or a comment on South Australia's neglect of intellectual worth. Once again, Isaacs used his paper as a platform from which to attack the relevance of the major Adelaide newspapers. His audacity is apparent in this example from the seventh issue:

> THE 'Register' and 'Advertiser' have had a grand controversy regarding the respective right of each to claim to be at the head of the Press. The question may not be considered by an indifferent reader to be of any great moment to the public, but it is certainly as instructive as most of the subjects presented in those journals, and, without dispute, as amusing as the majority of reports given by them of tea meeting[s], bazaars, good young men's associations, lectures, and the various other sources of bewilderment and beguilement presented by sanctimonious scavengers to their silly supporters. (8 January 1870, 3)

The *Licensed Victualler* ran for thirteen issues and then disappeared, a victim of Isaacs's poor health[2] and financial difficulties.

Elizabeth Webby, writing on literature in colonial Australia, has noted that 'Few authors were able to make a living from writing and these few depended heavily on journalism, supplemented in some cases by the writing of serialised fiction or plays and pantomimes' (46). Isaacs was typical in this regard: his first novel had initially been released in parts, he dabbled in journalism and throughout the 1860s he wrote plays. Life was difficult for a playwright, not only in Adelaide, but nationally. In the absence of local copyright laws and royalties, many Australian theatre managers chose to stage pirated (and therefore free) versions of English

---

[2] Throughout his life Isaacs suffered from chronic asthma, and there are many references to his illnesses (including typhoid in 1866) in letters to him, and in the press. His ill-health certainly had a negative impact on the production of his newspapers, which were temporarily or permanently suspended during such bouts.

plays, in preference to paying local writers for new works. Isaacs railed against this practice in print, especially when he was unable to stage his burlesque of *Frankenstein* (an unperformed but printed play, now of interest to science fiction buffs) during his time in Melbourne in 1864-65.[3]

One of the two venues that hosted performances of Isaacs's plays in Adelaide still exists. The Victoria Theatre (now known as the Queen's Theatre building) remains on its original site in Gilles Arcade in the CBD. The other theatre, White's Assembly Rooms in King William Street, has not survived to the present. Following several reincarnations (from White's, to the Majestic Theatre, then the Majestic Hotel) it was demolished in 1981.

A thorough review of Adelaide theatre advertisements in the 1860s reveals that Isaacs's first play was *That's Smith*. According to the *Register* it promised 'a great amount of amusing business and many laughable situations such as generally secure the success of compositions of that character' (22 July 1862, 2). The two act farce, which had been expressly written for the Victoria Theatre, opened on the stormy evening of 22 July 1862:

> It was very successful with the audience, who imperatively demanded the appearance of the author. He was, after some delay, led to the front by Mr. Greville, the living picture of sweet bashfulness and unsophisticated confusion. He bowed his acknowledgments, and retired amid a storm of applause. (*Register*, 23 July 1862, 2)

Despite this pleasing reception it seems that there were only two performances of *That's Smith*. By June 1863 Isaacs had completed his next play, *Major Blaze*, but he was unable to secure a backer or find a

---

[3] Isaacs's description of the difficulties he faced in staging the burlesque, plus the text of the play, can be found in his book, *Rhyme and Prose, and, a Burlesque and its History*, published in Melbourne in 1865. The play was new, but much of the other material in the book had already been published in Adelaide in the *South Australian Advertiser*, *Number One*, the *Critic* and in Isaacs's occasional leaflet, *Colonial Lyrics*.

venue for its production. The *Advertiser*, which was generally supportive of his literary efforts, provided the following titbit to its readers:

> We understand that Mr. George Isaacs not having succeeded in arranging for the production of his new comedy, 'Major Blaze,' in Adelaide, and there being no local copyright law in South Australia to protect his work, he has decided to enter it at Stationers' Hall, according to the provisions of the Imperial Act. Before doing so, however, he intends to give a private reading of the comedy to a few literary friends. (20 June 1863, 2)

A check of the records of Stationers' Hall,[4] the London-based registry of literary works, has found no evidence that *Major Blaze* was ever lodged there, under Isaacs's name or under that of his pseudonym. Possibly procrastination, frequent ill-health or his chronic poverty had prevented its deposition. Perhaps the manuscript's details did not survive the long sea voyage 'home'. *Major Blaze* disappeared without a trace.

Isaacs's ephemeral entertaining comedies, performed competently by well-known actors, were always well-received by Adelaide's audiences and critics. In terms of longevity, his most successful play was *Our Trip to the Rhine*. He wrote it and several other sketches at the request of the visiting English entertainers Grace Egerton and her concertina-playing husband and sidekick, George Case. Egerton was wildly popular in Australia (amongst other things, a gold reef, a mining company and a racehorse were named after her) and she was famous for her quick change routines, her astonishing impersonations and her sweet singing voice. Isaacs employed all her skills when he wrote *Our Trip to the Rhine* for her in late 1864 during his stay in Melbourne. The play premiered there, but by March 1865 it had opened in Adelaide at White's Assembly Rooms. Its plot was a silly confection of improbable characters and situations

---

[4] 'Stationers' Hall', now the Worshipful Company of Stationers and Newspaper Makers, is a London organisation that was founded in 1403, originally as a Guild of Stationers. In Isaacs's time, authors could enter their name and work in a Register, thereby establishing an early form of copyright.

interspersed with popular songs and concertina solos, all staged against a painted alpine backdrop. The critics were thrilled by Egerton's skills. Isaacs received named credit for the play in advertisements during its Melbourne run, but by the time it was staged in Adelaide, and from then on, all trace of his authorship was erased. Over the next fifteen years *Our Trip* was performed throughout Australia and around the world, from Cooktown to Perth and from India to Nova Scotia. Although the sketch probably evolved over time, its title was retained. Isaacs was almost certainly unaware of his play's reincarnation overseas, and he received neither much-needed money nor the recognition he craved from the popular production.

During the couple's next Australian tour, Egerton performed Isaacs's latest play *The Lost Party or the House Warming: Too Warm to be Pleasant*[5] at White's Assembly Rooms. It had first appeared in Sydney in September 1866 and reached Adelaide in April of the following year. The *Advertiser* clarified its origins for its readers and once again offered subtle support for its creator:

> We understand 'The Lost Party,' now being presented to the public at White's Rooms, and the well-remembered 'Trip to the Rhine,' and several minor pieces with which Mr. and Mrs. Case have delighted Adelaide audiences, are from the pen of the popular writer 'Pendragon' properly known as Mr. George Isaacs. (25 April 1867, 2)

Isaacs's final known play, a brief farce called *Our Uncle*, appears to have had only one performance, at the Victoria Theatre on 7 June 1867. It was included in the benefit night for the popular actor William Hoskins, whom Isaacs had met a few years earlier in Melbourne. The

---

[5] The Mitchell Library holds a 'book of words' of *The Housewarming: Too Warm to be Pleasant*. It is undated and printed by Charles Troedel in Melbourne. A later version of this play was advertised as having been revised by Edmund Yates, a friend of Dickens, so it is possible that this is the version published. However, there are clear similarities in content between newspaper reviews of the initial performances of the play, and the extant copy.

audience and the local papers gave the play an enthusiastic reception, with one reviewer noting that 'its chief merit lay in the dialogue, which was racy, and abounded in local allusions' (*Register*, 8 June 1867, 2). This play was not published, but contemporary reviews provide a summary of the implausible plot in which, thanks to a series of coincidences, the impoverished lawyer Fluke eventually marries the heroine, Miss Honeydew.

As the 1860s advanced, Isaacs's own life became a drama. Following the demise of the *Critic* he moved to Melbourne with his wife Marion and seven children. He was optimistic that the city offered more scope for his literary talents and for the production of his plays, but by early 1865 he was dangerously impoverished. Demanding creditors, family illness, little literary success and insufficient employment as a 'theatrical agent' led to his second imprisonment for insolvency—this time in the Melbourne Gaol.

Following his release (and the birth of his eighth child) Isaacs published a new compilation of his work, *Rhyme and Prose, and, a Burlesque and its History*. Its timing and contents suggest that it may have been prepared during his incarceration. Many of the poems and short stories had already appeared in Adelaide, but Melbourne offered a new audience. Then Isaacs fled the city, to reappear in Adelaide alone. Perhaps his wife, worn down by years of strife and poverty, banished him from the colony and her life, although how an unsupported woman survived in that circumstance is difficult to imagine. Perhaps Isaacs was avoiding creditors and intended to return once he was financially stable. Maybe, exhausted and disillusioned, he simply deserted his family. Whatever the catalyst for the separation, he never reunited with his wife and family.

The ability to write was now Isaacs's only remaining asset, so he offered his services to the Adelaide public. During August 1866 he promoted his abilities in the *South Australian Advertiser*: 'TRADESMAN'S BOOKS MADE UP. Letters for the press revised, lectures written, advertisements and circulars drawn up, petitions prepared, &c.' (4 August

1866, 1). A journalist added wryly: 'Amongst his other offers, Mr. Isaacs undertakes to revise letters intended for publication in the press; an office for which there is, as we know by experience, abundant occasion' (*Advertiser*, 31 July 1866, 2). Evidence suggests that Isaacs's advertisements were successful. The State Library of South Australia holds a manuscript in his handwriting, entitled 'The Origin, Rise and Progress of British Song', along with affectionate notes from the celebrated English musician George Loder to Isaacs. Much to the delight of musically inclined citizens, Loder had recently settled in Adelaide. He delivered the lecture to an appreciative audience at the Adelaide Town Hall in December 1866.

Another example of A. Pendragon's writing from that year can be found in the State Library of New South Wales, in the form of a charming 12-page advertising brochure entitled *Twenty-four Hours' Adventures of a New Arrival in South Australia*. Isaacs created this fictional story to promote the local Adelaide traders. In an amazing feat of stamina and retail therapy, its protagonist Augustus Fastman traipses around the city streets on his first day in the colony. Unable to resist the city's bountiful offerings, Augustus purchases everything from cigars to wine, a haircut, a piano, a saddle and a ticket to a performance by Lyster's Opera Company. He even has time for a trip to the beachside suburb of Glenelg and for jewellery repairs. (Isaacs was rather fond of beautiful jewellery.) At the mention of each purchase, Isaacs carefully identifies and praises the vendor. In addition to being a novel way to advertise goods, this little work provided new immigrants, as well as twenty-first century readers, with a comprehensive overview of the products, shops and services available in Adelaide in 1866. Neither the lecture nor the advertising story is a serious literary work, but they illustrate the versatility required by a colonial writer. Unfortunately, these literary pursuits did not save Isaacs from a third insolvency and imprisonment, just as he was struggling to re-establish himself in Adelaide.

Isaacs had an obvious affinity, and a lot of fun, with poetry. He covered the gamut of its varieties—narrative, love ('Enough! That I have loved as few can love' [Pendragon, *Number One*, 19]), satirical, historical, nationalistic and autobiographical ('Evil the deeds that wall my life about—That doom me to this cage' [Isaacs, *Rhyme and Prose*, 55]). These poems reveal much about his nature. They popped up regularly in Adelaide publications including the *South Australian Register*, the *South Australian Advertiser* and *Bell's Life in Adelaide*, as well as in Isaacs's own *Colonial Lyrics* and in his collections *Number One* and *Rhyme and Prose*. They were consistently well-reviewed. In 1869 he launched a new collection of his prose and poetry in the city, *Not for Sale: A Selection of Imaginative Pieces*. Its title advertised his independence and its love poetry reflected his happiness in a new relationship. Isaacs was shortly to marry.[6]

His passionate nature gave rise to brief, sentimental poems filled with memories and regrets. 'The Orange Flower' is an example. Set against the 'tideless sea' of the Mediterranean, it evokes his carefree youth. The harsh realities of his life in Australia did not inspire him to eulogise colonial scenery in a similar way:

> 'Twas by the blue and tideless sea,
> Calm as the Heaven that shone above;
> But what was Heaven or earth to me
> When I saw Dora, fairest dove,
> My only love?
> (Isaacs, *Not for Sale*, 30)

Isaacs responded in rhyme to current events at home and abroad. He had personally experienced revolutionary fervour in France in 1848, and was inspired by the ongoing fight for Italian independence. He rallied the Adelaide citizenry to this international cause with his poems 'Garibaldi: a Rhapsody' (which was first published on 1 September 1860 in the *Register*) and the rousing 'Viva L'Italia: a Voice from Australia', which first appeared in his self-published *Colonial Lyrics No. 2* in 1859:

> Awaken, Italia! The land of the glorious,
>   The Cradle of Art, and the Fountain of Song!

---

[6] Once again, Isaacs chose a much younger partner, 24-year-old Eliza Rice.

> As your aim is impassioned, so be it victorious,
> To Italians may Italy ever belong!

Irrespective of quality, his poems are heartfelt and responsive, none more so than the *Critic*'s poignant 'We all would do Better when we Grow Grey' (11 October 1862, 12) in which he confronts his mortality:

> Grey! Grey! Am I getting grey?
> Yes, it is so, grey I am getting;
> Passions, like ravenous birds of prey,
> Have swooped on my heart, in its blood their beaks whetting:
> And have left on my temples the print of their feet,
> And have left the rush of their wings in my brain,
> And have left my soul sickened amidst my defeat—
> In the past no memorial, the future no gain.
> I used my youth as a thing to endure;
> I used my manhood as not to fade out;
> I played with my love as a thing secure,
> And I looked on all men as a rabble and rout,
> The whom I would bend and mould to my will,
> In the pride of my knowledge and force of my skill.
> But now I am grey; wearied and grey—
> And little I care for the things that were.
> I have squandered my morning, have wasted my day.
> Gave no thought to the night when the world was gay
> We all would do better when we grow grey.

Isaacs's prose during the 1860s, like his poetry, is woven throughout his previously-mentioned newspapers, the *Critic* (1862-63) and the *Licensed Victualler* (1869-70), his journal *Number One* (1861), his books *Rhyme and Prose* (1865) and *Not for Sale* (1869) and other colonial publications. His short imaginative tales, with their oddly-named characters and happy endings, are somewhat contrived, in contrast to the charm and insight evident in his autobiographical stories such as 'Without a Passport' (*Not for Sale*, 31) or 'How We Fared When Hard-up in Paris' (*Number One*, 11). That description of the youthful misadventures of Isaacs and his friend

'Harry R' (the illustrator W. Harry Rogers) in Paris provides a premonition of Isaacs's later financial difficulties—and perhaps a reason for them. He impulsively pursued his ambitions, whether tempted by desirable antiques (as described in 'How we Fared') or, later, by the possibility of literary fame.

Strangely, following the publication of *The Queen of the South* in the previous decade, Isaacs did not attempt another novel. Perhaps during the 1860s he recognised his writing limitations, or more probably he no longer had the freedom, means or stamina to attempt such a lengthy and financially unrewarding exercise. He was also well aware of the colonists' preference for European rather than Australian novels. Instead, he concentrated on shorter prose. Isaacs's gift for writing concisely is best appreciated in his contributions to his own and other colonial newspapers. His rapidly composed editorials, incisive reviews, commentaries on current events and prolific (and frequently aggrieved) 'letters to the editor' enlivened the Adelaide press.

Isaacs made a determined effort to live as an independent writer in Adelaide during the 1860s, but he was unable to support himself or his family on the proceeds of this work.[7] His newspapers, poetry, stories and plays from that time display his versatility, but their irregular appearances failed to produce a steady income. This led to insolvency and imprisonment. Hampered by factors such as ill-health, a conservative public and press, poor remuneration, a lack of copyright and the need for other employment, Isaacs remained optimistic in his quest to entertain and inform. Contemporary reviews make it clear that his status as a littérateur was recognised and that his works were appreciated. But life was clearly tough for a writer in colonial society. Despite these difficulties, George Isaacs made a significant contribution to Adelaide's early literary scene.

---

[7] Of necessity, during this decade Isaacs was also a clerk, a theatrical agent and (most unlikely for a man who had been jailed for insolvency on three occasions) an accountant. None of these occupations appear to have provided him with financial stability.

WORKS CITED

Isaacs, George. *Not for Sale: A Selection of Imaginative Pieces*. Adelaide: Sims & Elliott, 1869.

___. *Rhyme and Prose, and, A Burlesque and its History*. Melbourne: Clarson, Shallard & Co., 1865.

Pendragon, A. [George Isaacs]. *Colonial Lyrics No. 2*. Gawler: W. Barnet. 1859.

___. *Number One*. Adelaide: Rigby, 1861.

___. *The Queen of the South: A Colonial Romance; Being Pictures of Life in Victoria in the Early Days of the Diggings*. Gawler: W. Barnet, 1858.

___. *Twenty-four Hours' Adventures of a New Arrival in South Australia*. Adelaide: George Isaacs, 1866.

Webby, Elizabeth. 'The beginnings of literature in colonial Australia'. *Cambridge History of Australian Literature*. Ed. Peter Pierce. Melbourne: Cambridge University Press, 2009. 34-51.

3 Scots and Scottish Literature in Literary Adelaide

Graham Tulloch

Literature has many roles and serves many purposes. One of the most common uses to which literature has been put, both by its producers and by its consumers, is as an expression of personal, regional or national identity. This chapter is concerned with the reading and writing of literature as an expression of identity, and it concentrates on a particular case: the use of literature as an expression of Scottish identity by Scots living in Adelaide in the first 75 years of European settlement. In doing this, it defines a specifically Scottish 'literary Adelaide' as encompassing both the consumers of Scottish literature (Adelaide readers and performers of works written in Scotland, often themselves of Scottish origin) and the producers of Scottish literature, or Scottish-Australian literature (the Adelaide writers of Scottish birth or descent who produced literary texts with Scottish themes or language). For these two overlapping groups Scottish literature performed a variety of functions but this chapter concentrates on one of these, the use of Scottish literary texts as a marker of Scottish identity.

Before discussing how Scottish literary Adelaide used Scottish literature as an expression of identity, I consider the ambivalent nature of Scottish identity. By the time the colony of South Australia was founded, Scotland had already been part of the United Kingdom for more than a century. Scots could identify themselves as Scots but also as Britons, and even, although much more rarely, as English. Indeed, it was common for Scots to have a sense of dual or multiple national identity. This duality was carried over to the new colonial context where further possibilities offered themselves, including being Australian, South Australian, 'colonial' and members of the British Empire. In South Australia their distinctive speech and their Presbyterian worship set the Scots apart; at the same time, unlike the Irish, they were (mostly) Protestants and fitted into the dominant Protestant (including Anglican) ethos, and were generally well educated in English. The Scots, if not English, were certainly British and, even as a sense of Australian identity began to grow in this country, for many people it was at least as important to be part of the great British Empire. Thus, in 1912 in the introduction to his book *The Australian Citizen*, Walter Murdoch (himself incidentally of Scots birth), without ever addressing his readers as Australians, speaks of 'you and me as members of the British Empire' (13). Nevertheless, their Scottishness was important to Scots in Australia and, being in the minority, they had to work hard to maintain and display a sense of national identity. Scottish literature was one of the tools to do this. It is against this background of a dual national identity, brought from Scotland but continuing in South Australia, that this chapter considers the use of Scottish literature as a expression of identity in Scottish literary Adelaide.

As it happens, Scottish literature was an ideal vehicle for the expression of the dual or multiple identities which were adopted by many Scots: Scottish, British, (South) Australian. The literature of Scotland is, and has long been, in an ambiguous position. It is both part of English literature and not part of English literature. It is both part of British literature and not part of British literature. And, when it is written in

Australia, it is part of Australian literature and not part of Australian literature. Similarly, Scottish dialect shared in this ambiguity. Was it a dialect of English, as is perhaps implied by the title of Robert Burns's collection *Poems, Chiefly in the Scottish Dialect* (1786), or was it a language in its own right, as works such as John Jamieson's *Etymological Dictionary of the Scottish Language* (1808) asserted? This ambiguous position of both the literature and the language can cause real problems of identity for Scottish writers and their readers but, like most ambiguous positions, it can be exploited for their benefit by both reader and writer.

Walter Scott is perhaps the best example of the writer who exploited this ambiguity, both in the content and setting of his novels and in his use of Scots language, and it is worthwhile dwelling on his example for a moment. Even in the Scottish novels and poems, Scott's appeal was not just to Scottish readers but to English readers as well. His books, after all, sold far more copies in the larger English market than in the Scottish market. Waverley is an Englishman with whom English and other non-Scottish readers could identify, but the real interest of the novel which bears his name lies in his encounter with Lowland and Highland Scotland. In this and other novels Scott exploited the two-sided appeal of Scottish language and literature, making sure his Scottish readers had plenty of Scottish meat to chew on but also ensuring that English readers could follow the plot even if some of the dialogue was in Scots. As a result he became the most widely read and loved writer in 'English' literature in the nineteenth century but at the same time he retained a special place in the affections of the Scots. As Ann Rigney has reminded us in *The Afterlives of Walter Scott: Memory on the Move*, the actual reading of Scott came over time to be less important than various kinds of celebration of his work or, to put it another way, his role as a site of cultural memory. As she argues, 'Scott's particular strength as a memory-maker was that his work, as literature, was not tied to any one place or community, but could operate in both national and transnational frameworks' (13-14). In offering this dual attraction he provided a model for Scottish writers who followed him, including major figures like Robert Louis Stevenson, but also minor but extremely popular writers like the now largely forgotten writers of the Kailyard School. Thus the ambiguous position of Scottish writing allows it to be different things to different people: the literature of their nation for the Scots, whether at home or abroad, but also a national literature for the British (including those in the British colonies) and even, for the English, a part of their literary heritage. In the period this chapter considers, all of these functions are present in Adelaide in its literary and cultural circles.

The Scots were always a minority in the population of Australia in general and of Adelaide in particular, although they were often leaders in politics, industry, commerce and the arts. As a minority group they were particularly concerned with the issue of identity and the reading and writing of literature was one of the ways in which they could address this issue. In the 75 years following proclamation of the colony Scots were prominent figures in Adelaide life and many had literary interests, particularly interest in Scottish literature. Important Scottish immigrants who showed such an interest include Allan Campbell (doctor and president of the Caledonian Literary Club), Daniel Fergusson (farmer and orchardist and key figure in the St Andrews Day celebrations), Alexander Hay (first chief of the Caledonian Society in which role he was strongly supported by his second wife Agnes Gosse, who was, however, English), John Hannah Gordon (judge and politician) Robert Barr Smith (South Australia's wealthiest pastoralist), his wife Joanna and her brother Thomas Elder (also a wealthy pastoralist), and Josiah Symon (lawyer, politician and writer on Scottish and English literature). Furthermore, one of South Australia's most important writers in these years, Catherine Helen Spence, was Scots by birth and wrote about Scotland and Scottish people in her novels. Thus Scots were both consumers and producers of Scottish literature.

I first discuss the consumers whose important role in making Adelaide a literary city can easily be forgotten. In Adelaide one of the main ways to celebrate Scottishness was through the annual St Andrews Day celebrations. The earliest I have so far found recorded is from 1847. Scottish literature plays a part from the beginning, with the speeches proposing toasts interspersed with Scottish songs, including Burns's 'My Bonnie Mary', 'John Anderson my Jo' and 'Auld Lang Syne'. In addition, Peter Cumming, president of the Saint Andrew's Society, uses quotations from Burns' 'The Twa Dogs' in his reply to a toast to the Society. However, unlike the lengthy reports on other speeches, the *South Australian* merely reports that the speech on 'The Literature of Scotland' 'referred to its ancient ballad poetry—to its distinguished authors of later days, and the spirited exertions of its publishers' (7 December 1847, 4). Despite its brevity the report thus reveals that the emphasis on ballads which was to remain a staple throughout the century was present from the beginning. The following year's occasion is reported in detail including the toasts 'The Land of Cakes' (which is, of course, Scotland) and 'The Land we live in' (which is, specifically, *South* Australia), so that already there is an attempt to combine a Scottish identity with an Australian one under the umbrella of imperial Britain; such at least was the feeling of the proposer of the toast 'The Land we live in', George Stevenson, who, according to the *South Australian*

> thought no toast could be submitted to a meeting of Scotsmen more welcome than that of 'The Land we live in.' Many could recollect the enthusiasm with which it was drunk at home. ... Our children, happy he trusted here, would never perhaps feel the same towards Scotland, but they doubtless would towards South Australia—the land we live in now. None, who like himself, had seen the grass above the knees, and the rush hut, where now the mansion stands, could refuse the toast. No man who had left his country could find a better end to his peregrinations than South Australia—one of the finest colonies on which the sun shone. (5 December 1848, 2)

There is, however, no mention of literature except for the singing of Scottish songs such as Burns's 'The banks an' braes o' bonnie Doon'.

By the 1852 dinner, however, literature was again playing a substantial part. The traditional toast to 'The Land of Cakes' is full of quotations from Scottish poetry, including a lengthy quotation from Robert Fergusson's 'Hame Content' proudly asserting the superiority of the Scottish rivers Tweed, Forth and Hay to the classic Italian rivers Arno and Tiber.

> The Arno and the Tiber lang
> Hae run full clear in Roman sang;
> But save the reverence o' shools,
> They're baith but lifeless dowie pools.
> Dought they compare wi' bonnie Tweed,
> As clear as ony lammer bead?
> Or are their shores mair sweet and gay
> Than Fortha's haughs or banks o' Tay?
> (*South Australian Register*, 4 December 1852, 3)

There is certainly no diminishing of Scottish identity here, but in the Chairman's speech which followed there is a strong desire to assert again the new and separate identity of South Australia within the British Empire. According to the newspaper's account,

> He did not wish to say anything disparaging of the other colonies, but we had certainly the advantage of them from the nature of our Constitution and the mode adopted here of subdividing the land. There was no doubt we had within ourselves the elements of every success, and that the colony would, in a few years, form one of the brightest gems in the British crown. (3)

By 1873 literature had moved to centre stage and the toast to 'The Land of Cakes' was followed by 'The Literature of Scotland—Burns and Scott'. The speaker, the Rev. James Henderson, suggested that

> though living in a community composed of a variety of national ties, yet there need be no attempt to disguise the object and intention

of such a gathering as this. It is broadly and distinctly intimated that we meet to revive recollections of Scotland. (*South Australian Register*, 4 December 1873, 5)

For him Burns fulfils this purpose perfectly:

> The most cursory reader of Burns is soon made aware that all through his poetry there throbs the pulse of a pure and noble patriotism—a patriotism which binds his countrymen as with a spell, and which no distance from Scotland can weaken ... (5)

With Scott the emphasis is rather different. To be sure, he figures as the chronicler and portrayer of Scotland:

> one who, by the torch of his genius, has lit up every type of Scottish character—every form of the physical landscape[.] From the Cheviots to the furthest shore of the Shetlands the whole land is under the spell of his genius. (5)

But he also transcends geographical and national boundaries:

> In every country, translators, poets, singers, painters, sculptors, dramatists, the whole hierarchy of art, have sought to draw inspiration from the productions of his genius. (5)

Thus Scott served both to reinforce Scottishness and to place Scotland on an international stage.

Finally, at the 1892 St Andrews Dinner it was Josiah Symon who proposed the toast to 'The Literature of Scotland'. Symon was well placed to take this on, as a Scotsman with a passionate interest in Scottish literature, an interest very evident in the catalogue he produced of his personal library and in the collection itself, which he bequeathed to the State Library. At the same time he wrote two books on Shakespeare, one of which was entitled, significantly, *Shakespeare, the Englishman*. Symon managed to bring the two interests together by remarking that 'We know that Shakspeare [sic] was indebted to Scotland for his magnificent tragedy of "Macbeth"'. He also told his listeners that 'There could be no question that Scotchmen should be proud of their grand literature'.

Nevertheless, when he came to speaking of Scott and Burns, it is their universality rather than their Scottishness that he emphasised: so Burns 'was no longer a Scotch possession, but was claimed by the whole world' and 'As novels went; there was nothing so interesting, instructive, and wholesome as the novels of Sir Walter Scott.' Comparing Burns with Tennyson, Symon claimed that 'what struck the reader [of Tennyson] was the art which overlaid his poems, whereas with Burns the reader was carried away by the natural forceful sentiments expressed, overlying art, and putting nature forward' (*Advertiser*, 1 December 1892, 6).

The naturalness of Burns, the 'heaven-taught ploughman', as he was admiringly but condescendingly called in his own time, is a continuing trope of Burns criticism throughout the nineteenth century. A similar idea underlies the address of the Caledonian Society's Chief, Dr Allan Campbell, in 1884 where this quality is considered characteristic of Scottish poetry in general:

> Scottish poetry ... was essentially lyrical in its nature—the embodiment of a musical language of some simple but absorbing emotion ... . She also had her more lofty and ambitious poems, as 'Marmion;' but after all Scottish poetry was essentially of sweet songs of friendship, devotion, valour, and love. (*South Australian Register*, 24 September 1884, 7)

Not very subtly hidden in such comments lies the implication that Scottish people are particularly open and frank in the expression of emotion, something which sets them apart from the stereotypically reserved English.

The other great Scottish day was, and still is, Burns' birthday. In the 1893 celebration once again the speaker, J.H. Gordon, used Burns to argue, as others had before, for a dual identity. On the one hand he noted that

> The splendid audience convinced him that though many leagues of the 'braid sea' divided them from old Scotland, and though many—

perhaps the majority of them—would never see the land of their birth again, the Scottish blood still flowed warm and loyal in their veins. (*Advertiser*, 26 January 1893, 7)

On the other hand he immediately went on to proclaim that

> He had protested before, and would still do so, against the notion prevalent in some quarters that in Australia we should be Australians only and sink all memories of the land from which we came. They were none the worse, but the better colonists, that they remembered the honorable race from which they sprang. (7)

A dual identity, Scottish and Australian, is not just possible but even urged as the only correct course. In this context Burns emerges as an Australian poet by adoption, a role that has been enshrined in the Burns statues throughout the country, far more than for any other literary figure, including one in Canberra unveiled on Australia Day 1935. Thus, speaking of the newly unveiled statue of Burns in Ballarat which he had seen two days before, Gordon envisages him as fully adapted to the Australian climate (both physical and mental), almost breathing Australian air:

> That splendid figure stood in the glorious brightness of the Australian day as if conscious of the busy hum of men around its base and glorying in that free, bright land in which they moved. ... And though silent it still proclaimed with trumpet voice the invocation and the prophecy—
>> Then let us pray that come it may
>> As come it will for a' that,
>> That sense and worth o'er a' the earth
>> May bear the gree and a' that.
>> For a' that and a' that,
>> It's coming yet for a' that,
>> That man to man the world o'er
>> Shall brothers be for a' that! (7)

In expressing such a notion, Gordon was not alone in co-opting Burns as the patron of Australian democracy.

Gordon's enthusiastic praise of the Ballarat statue incited John Darling, Chief of the South Australian Caledonian Society, to start raising funds for a similar statue for Adelaide. The next year, after winning donations from Thomas Elder and Robert Barr Smith, he unveiled a statue of Burns on North Terrace. In Darling's speech on this occasion, Burns once again figures as both a symbol of Scottish and British identity. On the one hand Darling emphasises 'the importance which we as Scotsmen attach to this ceremony of perpetuating in imperishable marble the features and form of one who did so much for his native country' and on the other hand he remarks that 'Wherever the British tongue is spoken—wherever Britons are gathered to express their kindliest, deepest, most genial feelings—it is to the songs of Burns they instinctively turn, and in them find at once an effective expression and a fresh tie of brotherhood' (*South Australian Register*, 7 May 1894, 3). Indeed, despite the fact that it was the Caledonian Society that commissioned the statue and prominent Scotsmen who paid for it, Darling suggests that Burns's appeal is universal:

> with the exception of the birthday of our beloved Queen there is no birthday so universally celebrated over the whole world as that of Coila's sweet singer. Not only in every hamlet, village, town, and city in Scotland is it made the occasion of a Burns' celebration in some form or other, but amid the snows of North-west Canada, on the diamond fields of South Africa, from the banks of the Ganges to the cities and towns of our own land laved 'by the long wash of Australasian seas,' January 25 is celebrated by music, song, and story. (3)

While Darling singles out 'The Cottar's Saturday Night' as the one poem that should never be omitted from any collection of Burns's work (a common attitude at the time but one which moves Burns away from his original radicalism into being primarily the voice of a conservative Scottish peasantry) he also give special attention to Burns' songs which 'interpret the inmost soul of the Scottish peasant in all its modes, and in verse exquisitely and intensely Scottish, without degrading either his sentiments or his language with one touch of vulgarity'. Yet, despite their intense Scottishness, 'It is indeed Burns' songs that will perpetuate his fame, for they appeal to all ranks, they touch all ages, and they cheer toil-worn men under every clime' (3).

As so often happened, a Burns occasion inspired others to emulate him. Consequently, the *Register*'s account of the festivities includes 'Lines on the Unveiling of the Burns Statue' by John Richards. Richards, however, was not himself a Scotsman (as he hastens to tell us in the first lines of the poem) and, not surprisingly, it is Burns's international appeal that he highlights:

> On parched Australian saltbush plains,
>   And 'mid Canadian snow,
> In deadly Indian jungles, and
>   Where icy blizzards blow,
> And Matabele assegais
>   Lay Afrikanders low.
> Where'er the Briton's tongue is heard,
>   As draughts of rich old wine,
> The songs of Burns cheer toilworn men
>   In every land and clime.
> (*South Australian Register*, 5 May 1894, 7)

Burns's songs, here celebrated by Richards, certainly play a key role in expressing Scottish identity but through this period they share that role with those of another Scottish poet, James Hogg, the Ettrick Shepherd. While Hogg is now celebrated as the creator of one of the great novels of the nineteenth century, *The Private Memoirs and Confession of a Justified Sinner*, in that century he was much more renowned for his poetry and songs. Thus, in 1909, right at the end of the period covered by this chapter, we find a report on 'A Nicht wi' the Ettrick Shepherd' where the emphasis is on his poetry. Hogg saw himself as the poet whose gift came from nature not from education, a successor to the ploughman poet, Burns. Hence, in keeping with the attitudes of the time and his own consciously crafted self-image, Hogg is described as 'a man of great natural gifts, of wondrous imagination, and a heart that overflowed with the milk of human kindness'. In the program

> 'The Queen's Wake'—probably the shepherd's best work—received special attention, and the poetic plan of the beautiful fairy story of 'Kilmeny' was outlined. During the social proceedings several of Hogg's songs were sung, including 'Cam ye by Athol,' 'McLean's welcome,' 'Flora Macdonald's lament,' and the evergreen pastoral 'When the kye comes hame'. (*Advertiser*, 4 October 1909, 10)

The newspapers also contain a number of accounts of various lecturers talking about Scottish literature in church halls, the YMCA and other venues, including this from 1885:

> At the monthly meeting of the Port Adelaide Caledonian Society on Monday evening Mr. T. H. Smeaton, of Adelaide, gave a very entertaining lecture on 'Scottish Songs and Ballads'. ... He was also assisted by able exponents in the persons of Miss Mills and Messrs. Eunson and McColl, who sang several of the compositions alluded to in the course of the lecture ... . The historical element contained in numerous ballads was prominently alluded to, as also the rugged grandeur of Scottish scenery in its creative power as the home of the muse. (*South Australian Register*, 13 October 1885, 5)

The emphasis on finding Scottish identity in Scotland's history and scenery is typical, as is the inclusion of performances of songs.

Prominent amongst such lecturers on Scottish literature is William Storrie who, for instance, gave a talk at the YMCA in April 1869. According to the *Advertiser*'s account of this event,

> A very efficient company of amateur singers then gave the glee, 'Now tramp o'er Moss and Fell,' after which Mr. Wm. Storrie, the Vice-President of the Society, read an admirably written paper on 'Scottish Songs.' He confined himself to the love songs—those of Burns principally—and with his well-known ability in a humorous

and deeply interesting manner commented upon the many exquisite gems of this portion of the Scottish literature. (*South Australian Advertiser*, 26 April 1869, 6)

Storrie provides a connection to the other most significant way of using literature to express identity, the writing in Australia of what might be called literature of Scottish identity. He thus provides a bridge between the consumers and the producers of Scottish literature in Scottish literary Adelaide. He was the author of a series of letters in the *Advertiser* supposedly from Saunders McTavish in Adelaide to his brother-in-law in the country. Written in broad Scots and conforming to a model known in Scottish newspapers, Saunders McTavish's letters might be considered as the most extreme expression of Scottishness through writing. The opening letter describes a performance by the Scottish theatrical family the Gourlays and there is certainly plenty of Scottish pride on display:

> to hear Gourlay himsel was a divert. It pit me in mind o' auld times, and gart me think I was in the Gallowgate again. Somehoo maist o' the Scotch that come here seem to be kin' o' shamed o' their ain auld mither tongue, an' when they hae been here twa three years, what wi' their whummlin' the words i' their mooths, an' trying to ca' cannily ower the r's, ye can hardly tell what they're sayin'. But I'm in hopes that wi' the Gourlays' veesit the gude auld tongue 'll come into vogue again, and we'll hae a' the Englishers tryin' to talk Scotch, an' vera richt tae, for its far in advance o' English, baith in soun' an' expression. I've nae doot it was the language Adam and Eve used when they were coortin'. (*South Australian Advertiser*, 8 February 1867, 3)

Pretty obviously there is a satirical purpose here and plenty of stereotypes of Scottish chauvinism are present. In that sense Storrie was not writing in his own voice and this is not an endorsement of such products of a Scottish inferiority complex. Yet, at the same time, the comments about Scots abandoning their speech and making unsuccessful attempts to speak like the English ring true as Storrie's own genuine criticism. We might indeed expect such an attitude of Storrie—several accounts appear of his performing passages of Scots as well as lecturing. For instance, at the Glenelg Literary Association's 'very successful' meeting in 1879, 'The proceedings were commenced by Mr. Storrie reading in his usual happy style the amusing account of "Kirstie Macpherson's trip to London by electric telegraph," which was greatly applauded.' At the end, according to this account, Storrie 'gave two readings, entitled "The Broken Bowl" and "Mansie Wauch at the Play," which created great merriment and pleasure' (*South Australian Advertiser*, 16 August 1879, 5) The comments which follow in the remainder of Saunders McTavish's letter, about the Scots speaking English, also have a ring of conviction about them, although somewhat exaggerated:

> It's aye alloo't that the Scotch speak finer an' purer English than the bodies dae theirsells. We dinna miss oo't oor h's an' pit them in whar they shudna' be; we dinna pit r's to the en' o' sic words as idea, umbrella, an' the like. We dinna pronoonce fellow as if it was written feller nor law lor, an I we ken fine the differ a'tween v an w, and that's mair than thae dae. Besides oor poets an' prose writers can write gude Scots an' the vera best o' English ; an' though I winna deny to the Southern bodies a certain amount o' command o' their ain language, yet I defy ye to produce ony Englisher that ever was cleckit that could either write or speak Scotch. (*South Australian Advertiser*, 8 February 1867, 3)

The use of literature as an argument for Scottish superiority is another familiar trope. Indeed, it is important to realise how literary this is despite being popular writing on a topical subject; the literariness lies precisely in what seems least literary, the representation of the spoken word. This is because Storrie's Scots is in the end a literary language, reproducing the form of Scots traditionally used to represent dialogue in literary texts rather than being the representation of any particular Scottish dialect. Once again it is specifically literature that is evoked to assert identity.

In the event Storrie produced a series of 26 letters, later published as *Letters frae Saunders McTavish to his Guid-brither in the Kintra* in Glasgow in 1874. In South Australian (and Australian) literature they stand alone as a full-blooded expression of Scottish identity in an entirely Australian setting through the use of the Scots language. At the same time they are about Adelaide and proudly so, so that they might also be seen as an expression of South Australian identity: the duality of Scottish identity is once again on show.

There are a number of other Adelaide writers who express their Scottishness through literary texts and the use of Scots language even though their works are not entirely in Scots. The most important of these is undoubtedly Catherine Helen Spence. Spence was intensely proud of her status as an early settler in South Australia and wrote under the name 'An Old Colonist' in the newspapers. But she also never forgot her Scottish heritage even though it was her opinion, as expressed in her *Autobiography*, that 'in the growth and development of South Australia … there have been opportunities for usefulness which might not have offered if I had remained in Melrose, in Sir Walter Scott's country' (37). Her Scottish heritage figures strongly in her autobiography and in her account of her mother's recollections of Scotland which Judy King and I edited as *Tenacious of the Past*. More importantly for the concerns of this chapter, she constantly introduced Scottish characters, settings and language into her novels. Her first novel, *Clara Morison*, published in London in 1854, is set in Adelaide as seen through the eyes of the eponymous heroine, a young Scotswoman who has been forced to emigrate to South Australia after being left penniless on her father's death. Although *Clara Morison* and Spence's next novel, *Tender and True*, were published in London, she contributed more immediately and directly to the literary life of Adelaide by publishing three of her novels in serial form in Adelaide newspapers: in the *Weekly Mail*, *Mr. Hogarth's Will*, under the title *Uphill Work* (1864); and in the *Observer*, *The Author's Daughter*, under the title *Hugh Lindsay's Guest* (1867) and *Gathered In* (1881-82). Spence's novels all have major Scottish characters and several are set in both Scotland and Australia. Although, in accordance with the sociolinguistic realities of her time, her middle-class central characters do not speak Scots, she has a number of Scots-speaking minor characters. In this way all her novels express a strong sense of Scottish identity often within an Australian context.

Finally, I return to the consumers of Scottish literature and consider book and play reviews in the Adelaide newspapers. Book reviews seem to have played a prominent place in the later part of the nineteenth century, with a number of sets of reviews from 'our Special Correspondent' in London. However, when Scottish books are reviewed in this fashion, along with other books, it is unlikely that they will be presented as reading specifically for Scottish-Australian readers and offered for use as symbols of Scottish identity. Rather they will be seen as available to all South Australians with literary interests. By the end of the century the Kailyard School of Scottish writing was in full stream, with its sentimental and nostalgic view of a bygone Scotland, a view particularly attractive to Scots in exile. However, the writers of the Kailyard—J.M. Barrie, S.R. Crockett and Ian Maclaren—had learned the lesson of Scott all too well and their writing was calculated to appeal to an English as well as a Scottish audience. Scottish literature had been absorbed into the English mainstream.

In these circumstances neither the imminent visit to Australia of Robert Louis Stevenson, one of the most popular and famous Scottish writers of the time, nor the appearance of his very Scottish novel *The Master of Ballantrae*, leads to any special address to Scottish readers. The London correspondent makes no mention of Scottishness, merely remarking that

> I hear that Mr. Robert Louis Stevenson is expected in Sydney next month, and that he intends visiting most of your principal cities before returning home. His new book, 'The Master of Ballantrae,' has deservedly scored a great success. It is the best thing he has done since 'Kidnapped,' and should be read by all who enjoy a good book of adventure. (*Advertiser*, 28 October 1889, 5)

In other cases even where Scottish elements or texts are mentioned, the writer takes it for granted that there will be non-Scottish readers. An *unfavourable* review of James Paton's *Castlebraes* in the *Advertiser* seems to assume, while drawing attention to its 'awful dialect', that non-Scots will be able to read it (5 November 1898, 9), as does the *favourable* review in the *Register*, which describes it as 'A book written in the language of the kailyard, with a glossary at the end to help those who are not familiar with the "Scots wha hae" dialect', but also as 'a delightfully readable book' (*South Australian Register*, 24 October 1898, 5). Similarly, even though an article regarding Barrie's play version of his novel *The Little Minister* recognises that 'this attempt to delineate the life and character of a small Scotch town has succeeded admirably', and that it is a useful reminder of 'the delightful humor and the deeply pathetic touch to be found in the books of its author, the acknowledged master of the new school of brilliant young Scots', issues of Scottish identity do not loom large (*Advertiser*, 2 September 1898, 4). The writer is primarily concerned with the problems of adapting novels to the stage and is as much interested in the actress as anything else, remarking that 'It has afforded a chance of welcoming back Miss Pattie Browne, who has achieved, a marked reputation in London, and is therefore doubly welcome' (4).

By the end of the century, then, the wide acceptance of Scottish literature throughout the English-speaking world has robbed the reading and performance of Scottish literature of some of its power to allow Scots in Adelaide (and elsewhere) to express a distinctive Scottish identity. Some of its power, but only some: if Scottish literature now belonged to everyone it still belonged specially to the Scots. at the end of the century, as at the beginning, the ambivalent nature of Scottish literature remained. This ambiguous position is neatly expressed at the end of an article on 'Scottish Story and Drama' where, after referring to a letter deploring the absence of Burns's 'Scots Wha Hae' at the concert in aid of funds for a statue of Thomas Elder, the writer remarks that 'Scottish colonists are entitled to special consideration when the memory of a distinguished countryman is being honoured', but then goes on to add that Scottish literature is not just for the Scots: 'Meanwhile Australian

Scotsmen and Scotswomen and Australian all other men and women will have an enviable opportunity of foregathering on the stage with the delightful personalities of "The Little Minister"' (*South Australian Register*, 26 August 1898, 4).

To summarise, Scottish literature could be a potent means of expressing and displaying Scottish identity in an Adelaide where Scots always remained in the minority and felt a special need to assert their identity. It had a particular potency when used on occasions dedicated to the celebration of Scotland, but Adelaide's group of Scottish-Australian writers could also use literature as a way of expressing their own Scottishness and representing the Scottishness of others. However, as the nineteenth century wore on the ambiguous position of Scottish literature to some extent undermined its role as an expression of Scottish identity and Scottish literature was increasingly absorbed into English literature. There is nothing surprising in this: in fact it is part of a broader trend of critical writing, certainly noticeable in Britain as well as Australia during this period. It has taken until the later twentieth century and the first years of this century for the separate identity of Scottish literature to be once again strongly asserted in critical circles. Nevertheless, as this chapter has aimed to show, for much of the nineteenth century the writing, reading and celebration of Scottish literature served many Scots-born Adelaideans as a powerful way of expressing their sense of themselves as Scottish. In doing so they added another element to the complex notion of literary Adelaide.

Works Cited

Murdoch, Walter. *The Australian Citizen: An Elementary Account of Civic Rights and Duties*. Melbourne: Whitcomb and Tombs, [1912].

Rigney, Ann. *The Afterlives of Walter Scott: Memory on the Move*. Oxford: Oxford University Press, 2012.

Spence, Catherine Helen. 'An Autobiography'. *Ever Yours*, C.H. Spence. Ed. Susan Magarey with Barbara Wall, Mary Lyons, and Maryan Beams. Kent Town, SA: Wakefield Press, 2005.

Spence, Catherine Helen. *Tenacious of the Past: The Recollections of Helen Brodie*. Ed. Judy King and Graham Tulloch. Adelaide: Centre for Research in the New Literatures in English and the Libraries Board of South Australia, 1994.

Symon, Sir Josiah. *My Library at 'Manoah', Upper Sturt, South Australia, Catalogued for Use*. Upper Sturt, SA: J.H. Symon, 1924.

4 'An entertaining young genius': C.J. Dennis and Adelaide

Philip Butterss

In April 1918, a journalist from the Adelaide *Advertiser* might have been slightly starstruck when he described C.J. Dennis as 'an alert, unaffected, and entertaining young genius' (10 April 1918, 7). Dennis had left the city 10 years earlier without fanfare. Now, as the nation's most famous writer, he was returning to negotiate a film version of *The Songs of a Sentimental Bloke*, which had been the literary phenomenon of the war years and which, even a decade into the twenty-first century, has sold more copies than any other book of Australian verse. Today his role as a poet and journalist is commemorated in a plaque on North Terrace, Adelaide's cultural boulevard, while another plaque on the Parade in Norwood celebrates his connection with that suburb.

Dennis's greatest literary successes—the Sentimental Bloke book and its sequel, *The Moods of Ginger Mick*—were written in Victoria, but it was in Adelaide that he received his first encouragement to write, that he cut his teeth as a poet and journalist, and that he established the approach and themes that would prove so fruitful in his writing career. This chapter explores Dennis's life and work during his periods in Adelaide.

Clarence James Dennis began his formal education at the public school in Gladstone, in the mid-north of South Australia, where his father held the licence of the local hotel, but his literary education had its real origins during visits to his grandmother's house in Adelaide a few years later. She and his aunts moved to a comfortable villa at what is now 63 Elizabeth Street, Norwood, when Dennis was eight or nine. On holidays there, he read bound editions of an English illustrated weekly, *The Graphic*, started on the novels of Rider Haggard, and fed his appetite for humour with Metta Victor's *The Bad Boy's Diary* (Innes 1). The contrast between Adelaide's leafy eastern suburbs and the dry plains around Gladstone encouraged his first poem, written on an early trip to his grandmother's house, probably in 1885:

> Oh, I love to live in Norwood
> Where the flowers do sent [sic] the air,
> And take a walk at sunset
> When the evening is cool and fair.
> (Jenkin 17)

In October 1889, at the age of thirteen, Dennis was sent from Gladstone to board at Christian Brothers' College in Adelaide, and during his two years at this school his interest in writing was noticed and fostered. He was encouraged to produce verse and to become involved in the school's literary society. At the peak of his career, soon after publishing *The Moods of Ginger Mick* in 1916, Dennis wrote warmly to one of the brothers: 'I have never ceased to remember the good old C.B.C. and the great times I had there. What little success I have had lately is built on good, solid foundations laid in the old days in Wakefield St' (Butterss 32).

In December 1891, a few months after his fifteenth birthday, he left Christian Brothers' College to become a junior clerk in the Adelaide office of the New Zealand Loan and Mercantile Agency Company, a prominent pastoral and wool-broking firm at 19 King William Street on the corner of Gresham Street. Dennis said that he bought a couple of Dickens novels with his first week's pay. Soon afterwards he was sacked for reading Rider Haggard's *King Solomon's Mines* in business hours (Innes 8). His aunts in Norwood, with whom he had been living after leaving school, were shocked and sent him back to his father in Gladstone (Herron 13).

At the end of 1892, the family moved a little further north-west to the town of Laura, and it was here that he discovered Rudyard Kipling's *Barrack-Room Ballads* and was inspired to begin writing again. The British author's ballads, written in the voice of ordinary soldiers serving the Empire in India, appealed to Dennis, as they did to other Australian writers, and he began experimenting in what he described as 'Australianized Kipling' (Innes 8-9). On 12 February 1898, when Dennis was twenty-one years old, the *Critic*, an Adelaide weekly, accepted two of his poems: 'Comin' 'Ome frum Shearin'' and 'The Cockie's Man'.

It is striking that in these first published poems, Dennis is experimenting with language closely related to what he would eventually use in his best-known books, and also that he is exploring the themes that would be at their heart. Like the hero of *The Songs of a Sentimental Bloke*, the speaker of 'Comin' 'Ome frum Shearin'' regrets his gambling and drinking and shows considerable remorse as he returns to his wife. 'The Cockie's Man' contains the first declaration of the political views that its author was to hold passionately for decades: it expresses sympathy for the labourer, an awareness of injustice, and a plea for 'better tucker ... better pay' and 'a decent livin'' for its main character. Almost twenty years before the publication of *The Songs of a Sentimental Bloke*, Dennis's second poem in the *Critic* derives from the same egalitarian values that were central to his most famous work. The labourer says:

> I'm but a simple cockie's man—a common sort o' bloke;
> But I'm 'uman an' 'ave feelin's, just the same as other folk
> (19 February 1898, 5)

In Laura, Dennis had grown from a youth of sixteen to a young man of twenty-one and all of the nine poems that he published in the *Critic* in the first six months of 1898 dealt with aspects of being a man, as would *The Songs of a Sentimental Bloke* later. Often, as was the case in 'Comin' 'Ome frum Shearin'', there is reference to the conflict between a man's domestic duty to provide for wife and family and the delights of a wilder and freer masculine life. Frequently, the conflict is more specifically between the attraction of drinking and its destructiveness. For example, 'Resolution' depicts the internal struggle of a shearer who resolves not to blow his cheque but fails to keep this promise. 'Casey's Shanty' describes a bush pub that has sent many men to hell. In 'The Stars', at night the speaker feels guilty for his sins—'the cash gone through an' the girls I knew,/An the seas of drink I've 'ad'—but in the morning his remorse is gone.

In the middle of 1898, Dennis came to Adelaide for a holiday, and took the opportunity to meet Alf McKain, editor of the *Critic*. McKain had taken a shine to his writing and, according to Dennis, regarded him as 'the only decent versifier' in South Australia at this time ('Biographical Notes'). McKain offered Dennis what must have been some form of cadetship on the paper, but his original brief did not include writing poetry. Dennis lived with his aunts in Norwood and travelled to the *Critic*'s office in Brookman's Buildings at 71 Grenfell Street every day. Here he learnt how a newspaper functions, and probably began to produce copy, though without a by-line. Perhaps he was too tired to write verse in his spare time because no more of his poems were published until 'The Shadow' appeared in the 31 December edition, written while he was home in Laura for Christmas. After working on the paper for about a year, he 'got sick of it', he said, and decided to head to Broken Hill looking for adventure ('Biographical Notes').

During the first half of 1901, Dennis returned to Adelaide, where McKain still had a place for him at the *Critic*, and now he began to assume a more prominent role. According to Archie Martin his 'specialty' was the popular prose series, 'The Curbstone Club', which began on 27 July 1901 and continued for almost three years ('Ginger Mick's Pal', 2). It was modelled on Peter Finley Dunne's widely-syndicated pieces from the Chicago *Evening Post* in the voice of Mr Dooley, a loquacious Irish bartender. Dennis's version had several men, principally the stage-Irish character, Dinnis Madigan, discussing topical events. 'The Curbstone Club' first appeared immediately after an issue of the *Critic* which had featured a 'Pictorial Souvenir of the Royal Visit', containing no less than 49 photos celebrating the trip to Adelaide of the Duke of Cornwall and York, who was touring the country after the Federation ceremonies in Melbourne. Dennis had his main character begin with a comment on the vast interest in the royal visitor, particularly from his wife: '"Jook, Jook, Jook," said Mr. Madigan; "'tis nothing but Jook these times. I'm havin' him for breakfus', dinner, and tea, an' a thrifle at bed time to slape on"' (27 July 1901, 11).

In this second stint at the *Critic*, some of Dennis's contributions were now poems written in response to topical matters, the earliest in a genre that would be his bread and butter for most of the rest of his life. For instance, on 3 August 1901 a news item about a man felling the eucalypts on his land for railway sleepers inspired a pro-environment poem titled 'The Song of the Saw', one of countless nineteenth- and early twentieth-century parodies of Thomas Hood's 1843 poem, 'The Song of the Shirt':

> One by one did they crash to earth;
>   One by one did the kings depart,
> While I whirred and buzzed, and shrieked in mirth,
>   As I gnawed into the very heart.
>
> And lo! In the land that had known their reign,
>   The land that was verdure-clad and fair,
> Nought but the rotting roots remain
> To tell of the mighty kings that were. (10)

His first poem for the *Critic* addressing an explicitly political topic was 'When I Went fer Federation' in the edition of 19 October 1901. Its speaker had been in favour of Federation at the start of the year, but was now dismayed at the new tariffs that were causing a substantial rise in the cost of many staples (see Howell 28).

Dennis was also very keen to get his verse into the *Bulletin*, the benchmark of success for an Australian poet. In January 1901, about the time he returned from Broken Hill, he had sent that journal a contribution and the response from A.G. Stephens in the 'Answers to Correspondents' column had addressed him in unambiguous terms: 'C.J.D. Would rather kill another "Dying stockman" poem than resuscitate one which "appeared 18 years ago"' (12 January 1901, 15). In April the following year, the *Bulletin* accepted a mildly humorous prose piece, 'Essay on Cockies', which covered many of the stereotypes about these small farmers — their diet, appearance, poverty, and exploitation of their labourers (5 April 1902, 32). A month afterwards, though, another verse contribution was rejected. It was not until 19 November 1903 that he finally cracked the *Bulletin*, with a poem titled 'Urry', consisting of the instructions given by a selector's wife to her large family during a hectic day (36).

At the beginning of 1904, ructions at the *Critic* saw Alf McKain leave; he was replaced as editor by Dennis (*Advertiser*, 3 February 1904, 4). The Hon. Joseph Vardon, a member of the South Australian Legislative Council, was chief proprietor, and he could see that his 27-year-old employee had considerable ability as a writer, even if he had only a few years experience in newspapers. At the *Critic*, it was the editor's responsibility to write the political leaders and one of Dennis's earliest tasks was to comment on the inauguration of the first, short-lived Federal Labor government. In stating the newspaper's position, he was cautiously supportive, writing that the *Critic* 'sees no reason for any hysterics' about Mr Watson's rise to power and giving the new Prime Minister and his followers 'the credit for being clean-handed and clear-minded' (27 April 1904, 4). Another of Dennis's duties as editor was to attend theatrical opening nights, which he did with some enjoyment, resplendent in tails and black tie. He found the administrative tasks involved in operating a newspaper much more of a grind (Martin, 'Ginger Mick's Pal', 3).

In February 1904, Dennis published a couple of poems in the *Critic*, including 'Mornin' Magpies', about the uplifting effect of birdsong, a topic to which he would return many times in the last decade of his life (10 February 1904, 20). This material may have been written before he assumed the editorship because he found little time for verse during the rest of the year, though one issue in December contained three poems. He managed to continue 'The Curbstone Club' until the end of May 1904 and then followed that series with three similar contributions under the title 'People Madigan Knew'. The following year was even leaner, with a small number of prose pieces and only four poems in the *Critic*. His desire for recognition as a poet continued, however, and the *Bulletin* published 'Brothers o' Mine' in October 1905, a poem comparing a wealthy churchgoer's lack of charity with the generosity of a 'sinner' who spends his Sundays in the pub (12 October 1905, 39). A fortnight later the *Bulletin* contained a single stanza from Dennis under the title of 'Voice of the Bush', using the joke from W.T. Goodge's 'The Great Australian Adjective':

> 'Voice of the Bush! what doth it say?'
> Exclaimed the bard, in dreamy study.
> The bushman stared in some dismay,
> But truthfully responded '___!'
> (26 October 1905, 14)

It was a joke that Dennis would later exploit at greater length and to much greater effect in 'A Real Australian Austra-laise', beloved by generations of Australians.

He was feeling weighed down by some of the editorial tasks and wanted more time for poetry, and there may well have been tensions with the *Critic*'s board about the paper's direction. The chief proprietor shared the editor's protectionist views but they had very different ideas about social freedoms. Vardon was a temperance advocate and, at that time, president of the Young Men's Christian Association (Saunders). Dennis, on the other hand, subsequently claimed to have invented the word 'wowser' when he was editor of the *Critic* (Gye 5). In fact, the term was already in use in John Norton's *Truth* before Dennis was appointed to the editorship, but the claim indicates how incompatible his and his employer's attitudes were. Possibly intensifying tensions between editor and chief proprietor was the fact that Vardon, the minister for industry, was under attack in parliament for being associated with a journal whose aim was, one speaker asserted in August 1905, 'to deal with the seamy side of life' (*Advertiser*, 18 August 1905, 3).

Dennis and his friend and sub-editor, Archie Martin, began to discuss establishing a new paper where they would be much freer, and the idea quickly gained momentum with the input of another of the *Critic*'s contributors, the entrepreneurial Beaumont Smith. The three men formed a syndicate and began to make arrangements for the inaugural issue (*Gadfly*, 12 February 1908, 3). At first they considered a number of fairly staid names: the *Post*, the *Weekly Mail*, *Town Topics*, and *Town Talk*. Eventually, they settled on the *Gadfly*, a title appropriate to their intentions and their attitude to the world. What the trio wanted to produce was a weekly that pricked and stung, and in the process they intended to enjoy themselves. The *Gadfly* was launched at a price of threepence on Wednesday 14 February 1906.

Dennis was the editor and, in addition, produced much prose and poetry, publishing occasionally as C.J. Dennis but more often as one of Den, Klariden, Irish, C. James, Terence O'Ruddy, and various shortened forms of these (McLaren 13-19). Geoff Burgoyne surreptitiously wrote the political leaders from his desk in the South Australian civil service, under the *nom de plume* of 'G Elburg', and this gave Dennis the freedom to devote his attention to more creative contributions. He experimented with styles, exercised his considerable sense of humour, and expressed his views on many topics. As Martin noted, he 'once more wrote with enthusiasm, wrote the things he liked writing' ('Ginger Mick's Pal', 3). He had three poems in the first issue and six items in the second. Dennis worked on the *Gadfly* for its first twenty months and Burgoyne was to comment that 'his verse was the brightest feature of the paper' (9). Certainly, his considerable facility with rhyme and metre was apparent in his poetic contributions, although it is fair to say that the pressure to meet deadlines meant that the quality of the verse and prose was uneven.

Like its more famous Sydney uncle, the *Bulletin*, the paper was fiercely nationalist, and this can be seen in Dennis's own mockery of a Victorian Education Department proposal for celebrating Empire Day in schools. The Department recommended that school children undertake a series of patriotic geography and history lessons, readings and recitations, as well as singing the national anthem and saluting the Union Jack. In response, Dennis wrote 'Empiah Day', imagining questions and answers about geography and history:

> 'What is England?'
> 'Home.'
> 'Who rules England?'
> 'The King.' (Here the children prostrate themselves and strike the ground...)
> 'Who is the greatest man in the world?'
> 'The King.' (Same business.)
> ...
> 'What is the principal export of England?'
> 'Gentlemen.'
> 'Are you gentlemen?'
> 'No, we are of lowly birth and Australians.' (Here the dear children weep copiously.)
> (9 May 1906, 22)

The *Critic* prided itself on its independence, and the first leader asserted that 'Our opinions, such as they are, belong to us, and the paper is not published, influenced, or subsidised by any clique, league, political party or organisation' (14 February 1906, 4). This freedom from external influence extended to religious questions, and when the *Gadfly* was accused of sectarian bias, Martin remembers Dennis pointing out that 'the destinies of the paper were controlled by an Anglican, a Roman Catholic, a Wesleyan Methodist and an Atheist' and saying that, in his opinion, the atheist was 'the most religious of the lot' ('Ginger Mick's Pal', 4). But in spite of such assertions of independence, the *Gadfly* and its editor held a loose set of views typical of radicals and of the Labor Party in the first decade of the twentieth century.

Among the regular targets for Dennis's verse and prose were the rich and powerful who opposed, in his words, 'all forms of socialistic legislation for the betterment of the people' (18 July 1906, 6). His particular *bête noire* was the ex-Prime Minister, George Reid. In Dennis's eyes, Reid's chief crimes were his ardent advocacy of free trade and his national campaign against socialism, which coincided with the founding of the *Gadfly*. In 'Selfish Australians' Dennis suggested that Reid's motto might be: 'Australia for the Foreigner, the Fatman, and G. Reid!' (31 October 1906, 739).

In response to a pro-free trade article in the *Register* that argued for 'the healthy breezes of competition', Dennis wrote a poem titled 'Healthy Breezes', detailing the effects of free trade on working people:

> We're cold and hungry fact'ry 'ands,
>   An' we've got no work to do;
> The fac'try's shut an' ruined, but
>   Wot's that to me an' you?
> For wot care we w'ile trade is free,
>   Tho' there ain't no ghostly show
> For the fact'ry 'and in a freetrade land,
>   When the healthy breezes blow.
> (20 June 1906, 3)

Among Dennis's favourite targets were wowsers of all shades. According to Martin, it was his editor who memorably described the temperance advocate, Henry Gainford, as 'an artesian bore' ('M.', 21). Dennis had already published 'The Parson and the Play' in *Melbourne Punch*[1] but he recycled the poem in the *Gadfly*, accompanied by a series of photographs of its author, dressed as the parson. This piece tells a story about a parson who goes to a vaudeville show and is seduced by what he sees on stage, eventually hiring a pair of opera glasses so that he can get a better view of the action. It concludes with the parson declaring that 'it's better to have seen and sinned than never look at all' (27 March 1907, 1109). One of his more polished poems, 'The Righteous Man' compares public piety with what he saw as the private realities of business practice:

> Is Sunday, and the man of prayer,
> Of aspect mild and chastened look,
> Kneels in the church, and worships there,
> And bows his head upon a book;
> Reading the lesson for the day,
> He bleats devoutly
>   Let us pray.
>
> Is Monday, and the man of trade,
> Of aspect keen and crafty look,
> Sits in his den where schemes are laid;
> And bends his gaze upon a book,
> Planning the business for the day,
> He softly mutters
>   Let us prey.
>
> (12 September 1906, 640)

But as well as attacking the powerful in some of his verse and prose, Dennis was aware that the causes in which he believed needed more than just words. He was critical of the political inaction of those with radical views, perhaps including himself. In 'Us', a poem published in the third issue of the paper, he laments the fact that too many of those unhappy about politics in Australia just stand around talking about what should be

---

[1] I am grateful to Perry Middlemiss for this information.

done, instead of acting. It asserts that the Australian public is responsible for its politicians and that apathy is what enables 'the Fat Man's rule' (28 February 1906, 13).

At the *Gadfly*, Dennis liked to play the part of editor in a theatrical way, dressing immaculately and affecting a *pince-nez*. He also liked to write in green ink, a habit that he was to continue for most of his life. Sometimes high spirits got the better of him, as Martin recalls:

> Dennis, one lunch hour, instead of walking sedately down the stairs, slid down the bannisters landing at the feet of an excited old lady, who inquired breathlessly, 'Can you tell me where I can find the editor of the *Gadfly*?' With perfect gravity Dennis gave her a sweeping bow, 'Madam,' he replied, gallantly, 'I am the editor.' ('M.', 21)

At the same time, as something of a contrast to this bohemian and artistic persona, he enjoyed presenting himself as a practical man. He loved to make things with tools and to tinker with contraptions. Martin felt that Dennis could have had a career as 'a first-class tradesman', if he had not wanted to write poetry. Another trait that observers would notice throughout his life was that, although often an engaging companion, he could sometimes appear standoffish. In fact, the bohemian artist, Fred Booty, who supplied material to the *Gadfly*, joked about offering Dennis a sovereign so that he would speak to him ('M.', 21).

At work, Dennis was an erratic editor. Burgoyne describes him as 'decisive and dynamic at times' but also 'subject to moods and intervals of A.W.L.' (Burgoyne 9). The 'moods' were possibly early instances of the depression that would later trouble him; the absences without leave are explained in a letter written many years afterwards by Martin:

> His bouts were at intervals—some quite prolonged. Sober, he was very sober. The other way he was a pig but a pig with the decency to stay hid. We never knew where he was. I believe he drank alone. He hated himself for it (as he told me) and derived no pleasure from

the booze. ... I don't think he ever knew himself where he had been.
(Martin to Chisholm)

Perhaps a hint of the seductiveness of alcohol for Dennis can be seen in his first poem in the *Gadfly*'s inaugural issue, a piece humorously attacking temperance advocates for requesting a reduction in the number of hotels. Their appeal had come in the middle of a February heat wave:

> See the perspiration falling,
> Hear the beer-pump softly calling,
> Softly calling thirsty citizens to come,
> And that dry, hard feeling soften,
> Quaffing long and quaffing often;
> Ponder parson, ponder deeply, and be dumb!
> (14 February 1906, 3)

Time and again, Dennis's contributions to the *Gadfly* returned to the opposition between different kinds of masculinity, that topic which had been so important in his earliest published verse. At one extreme, he could jokingly endorse a man preferring beer to women, as he did in 'His Choice' (10 October 1906, 691). But other pieces were much less certain. A month after the paper was launched, a short story, 'On the Loose', examines the conflict between masculine freedom and the domesticity of marriage, explicitly giving voice to opposing viewpoints. Having provided positive and negative perspectives on male camaraderie and also on domestic manhood, the story finally decides in favour of the latter with the husband's sentimental declaration of his love for his wife.

Dennis's own relationships with women—apart from his aunts—were noticeably distant at this stage of his life, and Humphrey McQueen has raised questions about his sexuality (343-53). Given the accounts of his effeminacy as a youth (Butterss 26-38), such speculation is hardly surprising. Dennis's sexual preferences during these years are impossible to determine but it is clear that his closest friends from the *Critic* and the *Gadfly* did not expect him to settle into a traditional nuclear family. Will Dyson said to Dennis's wife that 'Clarrie was the last man I ever thought would get married' (Herron 64). Similarly, Archie Martin wrote of this period: 'So far as the ladies were concerned I think he was shy of them. To my knowledge he was never greatly interested in any one in particular and I confess to a slight surprise at the news of his marriage' (Martin to Chisholm). These statements might well be gently indicating at least an uncertainty about Dennis's inclinations during his twenties. Within a decade he would be blissfully happy in the early stages of his marriage.

Like most Australian satirical journals before and after it, the *Gadfly* struggled financially throughout its existence, and, as time went on, Dennis found that the day-to-day requirements of keeping the paper afloat were frustrating. During 1906, he managed to send occasional poems to the *Bulletin*, publishing six that year, but he was unable to keep this up and none appeared in the following year. In the middle of 1907, he sent a collection of his verse to Thomas Lothian, the Melbourne publisher, hoping it might be issued as a book (Dennis to Lothian). It was probably the poet Bernard O'Dowd, Lothian's first reader, who recommended rejecting it (Close 6). What Dennis really wanted was to devote more attention to writing good poetry.

He left the *Gadfly* in November 1907 to try his hand as a freelancer in Melbourne and was replaced in the editor's chair by Martin, who kept it going for a further fifteen months. The paper's financial difficulties arose largely because of the size of Adelaide—160,000 people were not sufficient to supply a regular readership for a satirical paper—and partly because of the inadequacy of the distribution networks in other states (Innes 14). The staff tended to place some of the blame on the citizens of its hometown. Dennis's own succinct assessment, much later, was that 'the *Gadfly* was born before its time and that Adelaide was the wrong place for its birth' (Herron 16). Burgoyne put it more elaborately: 'The sad fact was that Adelaide was not the field for a paper which was irreverent of the shopkeeping aristocracy of the city, and which, instead of bending the knee to Baal, poked him impudently in the ribs' (9). He is correct in pointing to a fundamental problem, which was that Percy Bird, the business manager, was desperately trying to raise advertising revenue from people who often held exactly the views that the paper lampooned. Nor can the erratic nature of Dennis's editing and his periods of absence have assisted the enterprise. But while Dennis's drinking bouts meant that others sometimes had to cover for him, his energy and his contributions gave the paper much of its humour and bite and were crucial to the many fine issues that emanated from the Currie Street office.

Dennis's literary education had begun on holidays in his grandmother's house in Norwood, and his skills as a writer were first noticed and encouraged at Christian Brothers' College in Wakefield Street. As an unformed 21-year-old living in Laura, he had gone on tentatively to submit some poems to an Adelaide newspaper. Almost ten years later, that young man was hardly recognisable. As well as having edited two metropolitan newspapers, he had honed his writing skills substantially, experimenting with a range of different accents that were good preparation for the larrikin verse he would go on to write. His earliest published poems in the *Critic* displayed the central elements that he would develop at length in *The Songs of a Sentimental Bloke* and *The Moods of Ginger Mick*: an egalitarian outlook and an interest in the conflict between domestic responsibilities and masculine freedom. In addition, although both the *Critic* and the *Gadfly* had been centred in Adelaide, each had been more widely distributed and this had given Dennis a taste of a national audience, something he found very attractive. The foundations for producing his most successful verse were in place; all he needed was the time and space in which those poems could evolve. He wrote the first of the pieces about the Sentimental Bloke and Doreen in Toolangi, a tiny town 70 kilometres north-east of Melbourne, less than two years later.

WORKS CITED

Burgoyne, Geoff. 'Hatching a Gadfly'. *Bulletin*, 22 September 1954. 9.

Butterss, Philip. '"Where a youth dreamed dreams": C.J. Dennis's Early

Days in South Australia'. *Journal of the Historical Society of South Australia* 34 (2006): 26-38.

Close, Cecily. 'Thomas C. Lothian: Lawson's Melbourne Publisher'. *La Trobe Journal* 70 (Spring 2002): 4-17.

Dennis, C.J. 'Biographical Notes given by C.J. Dennis to R.H. Croll', 6 December 1913. C.J. Dennis, *Backblock Ballads and Other Verses*, C1021, ML.

___. *The Moods of Ginger Mick*. Sydney: Angus & Robertson, 1916.

___. *The Songs of a Sentimental Bloke*. Sydney: Angus & Robertson, 1915.

___. to Thomas Lothian, 23 August 1907. Lothian Papers, MS 6026/40, SLV.

Gye, Hal. 'The Story of C.J. Dennis'. Papers of C.J. Dennis and Hal Gye, MS 6480, item 100, 1 NLA.

Herron, Margaret [Olive Dennis]. *Down the Years*. Melbourne: Hallcraft, 1953.

Howell, P.A. *South Australia and Federation*. Kent Town, SA: Wakefield Press, 2002.

Innes, Guy. 'Australia's New Poet: C.J. Dennis—a Personal Sketch'. Angus & Robertson Papers, MS 314/25, ML.

Jenkin, P.B. 'The Man that I Knew'. *Australian National Review* 4.20 (1938): 15-20.

'M.' [Archie Martin]. 'The Sentimental Bloke: Bard's Bohemian Days'. *Sun* (Sydney), 9 July 1916. 21.

Martin, Archie. 'Ginger Mick's Pal'. Angus & Robertson Papers, MS 314/25, ML.

___. to Alec Chisholm, 26 May 1944. Papers of C.J. Dennis and Hal Gye, MS 6480, item 104, NLA.

McLaren, Ian. *C.J. Dennis: A Chronological Checklist of Contributions to*

Journals. Adelaide: Libraries Board of SA, 1976.

McQueen, Humphrey. '"We are not safe, Clarence; we are not safe": Sentimental Thoughts on "A Moody Bloke"'. *Meanjin* 36.3 (1977): 343-53.

Saunders, Malcolm. 'Vardon, Joseph (1843–1913)'. *Australian Dictionary of Biography*, National Centre of Biography, Australian National University <http://adb.anu.edu.au/biography/vardon-joseph-8906/text15645>. Accessed 28 July 2013.

5 Adelaide Around 1935: Stories of Herself When Young

Susan Sheridan

Three women writers who grew up in Adelaide in the 1920s and 30s later published autobiographical novels based on that experience—Nancy Cato's *Marigold* (1992), Geraldine Halls's *This is my friend's chair* (1995) and Nene Gare's *A House with Verandahs* (1980) and *Kent Town* (1996). They write the Adelaide of this period into existence—its city shops, dance halls and cinemas, its suburban homes and schools. At the same time, they offer accounts of the class-differentiated experiences and aspirations of young girls growing up between the two world wars.

Nancy Cato was born in 1917 and lived in Adelaide until she was fifty. Nene Gare, two years younger, left for Perth when she was twenty and never returned, whereas Geraldine Halls (also born in 1919) left Adelaide at the same time and lived abroad for 30 years, returning to spend the last decades of her life here. All three are looking back at their girlhoods, decades later. What impressions of Adelaide around 1935 do their novels provide? What perspectives are attributable to class differences in their families of origin? How much correspondence is there between the youthful dreams each attributes to her protagonist and the life the writer actually led?

The title of this chapter alludes to Joy Hooton's ground-breaking study of Australian women's autobiographies, *Stories of Myself When Young* (1990), which in turn took its title from Henry Handel Richardson's memoir *Myself When Young*. Only Nene Gare's first book finds a place among Hooton's rich collection of women's life writing, as the other three titles were published later. Indeed, Gare and Barbara Hanrahan are the only twentieth century South Australian subjects featured in Hooton's study. Hanrahan is the unparalleled practitioner of 'stories of herself when young' in Adelaide. Her autobiographical fiction set in the 1940s, 50s and 60s, and her historical novels set in Edwardian Adelaide, dominate fictional impressions of those decades. Perhaps they also served as a stimulus for these three older writers to recreate the Adelaide of their childhood and youth in the 1920s and 1930s, in the novels considered here.

Compared with the best-known examples of Australian women's autobiographical fiction, like Miles Franklin's *My Brilliant Career* and Christina Stead's *The Man Who Loved Children*, as well as Hanrahan's *The Scent of Eucalyptus* and other novels, these texts are not primarily concerned to present a fictionalised account of the author's formation as an artist, despite the fact that their protagonists may share the author's sense of what was necessary to enter into independent female adulthood. Both Cato's and Halls's novels belong centrally in their chosen fictional genre, using autobiographical material to provide local colour, as well as some elements of the *bildungsroman* or novel of formation. Cato's *Marigold* involves a melodramatic family secret as well as the heroine's coming of age; it ends with her leaving home, and Adelaide. Halls's *This is my friend's chair* is another variation on this genre, where the heroine's relations with her family are paramount and understanding comes only with the deaths of her parents and of Lizzie, the family's scheming live-in companion. This longer time line involves the protagonist leaving and returning to Adelaide many times.

Gare's two books are more directly autobiographical — she claimed that she could only ever write from life, studies of the people around her (Giuffré 15). In both *A House with Verandahs* and *Kent Town* (a series of linked stories, which were published after Gare's death) Peace, the narrator, is the middle child of seven, as Gare was; but the classic autobiographical emphasis on self-formation is less important than her portrait of the whole family in their social milieu.

ON THE EDGE: *A HOUSE WITH VERANDAHS* AND *KENT TOWN*

In both *A House with Verandahs* and *Kent Town* Peace Hounslow, like her creator, is one of a large family living in a small rented house in inner-suburban Kent Town, just across the Parklands from the city of Adelaide. The father, a harness-maker, works from a shed in the yard, where he also keeps a horse and trap. The family keeps a cow in the Parklands, which has to be fetched and milked every day by the children. There is never much money, but father never misses a day at the races and 'allows himself' one hundred pounds a year betting money (*A House*, 58). Mother surreptitiously buys small insurance policies and tickets in Tattersalls Sweepstake; she even places discreet bets at the local pub, The Maid and Magpie. Just once, they have a week's summer holiday at Victor Harbor. Despite their poverty, the family's class position is somewhat ambiguous. All the Hounslow children attend East Adelaide Primary school, in the salubrious adjoining suburb of St Peters (where many cousins on their father's side live), because their mother deems the schools in Norwood to be too rough.

High school, however, is out of the question for the young Hounslows. Instead, there are night school classes or, for Peace, a year at Muirden Business College (founded in 1900, offering general education as well as vocational subjects, it still exists today). After only a year there, when she is fourteen, Peace follows her older sisters into a job as a department store sales assistant, though her mother has ambitions for her to have an office job. She is 'promoted' to the Tube Room in Myers, where 'carriers' conveyed along wires suspended from the ceiling delivered cash or account details, and a row of cashiers sent back the customer's change (*Kent Town*, 118). Money is found for a few music lessons for one sister, and some art lessons for Peace, but it is typical of the Hounslows' fecklessness that these undertakings cannot be continued—the father decides that he will not be beholden to anyone else for his children's education.

This aspect of the Hounslows' life is more prominent in the earlier novel, *A House with Verandahs*, where the focus is centrally on the family and the tumbledown house they live in. Money troubles are central but not related to the economic Depression of the period, only to the parents' bizarre attitudes to money and property: the father, for instance, refuses the opportunity to pay a minimal price for the garden area which they have been using for years for almost nothing, because he thinks it greedy of the owner to want to sell it. Peace's observations of her parents and siblings, relations and neighbours, from early childhood to delayed adolescence at 14, are made from a naïve perspective, which results in a consistently comic, often hilarious, account of the family. She and her siblings share their mother's desire for a 'house with verandahs' (rather than their cramped cottage with a lean-to kitchen and no bathroom) but no one will criticise the loving, charming, feckless father for refusing to move. The eccentricities of both parents are observed with loving acceptance.

Substantially the same story materials are re-used in *Kent Town*, but with different emphases, showing up the fictional elements in each text. *Kent Town* consists of a discontinuous narrative of short stories. It actually has more concrete references to places and events—such as the Depression and the onset of war—than *A House with Verandahs*, and is franker about sexual matters. Gare told an interviewer (Giuffré 18) that she had to leave a lot out of *A House with Verandahs* so as not to embarrass her eldest sister—things which she presumably felt able to include in the later stories.

In *Kent Town* Peace, again the narrator, is a teenager, figuring out how she wants to live her life, and so her friends at school and work are the focus of interest, not so much the family. She is curious about how other people live, like her friend Lyn whose parents don't speak to one another. Lyn is pretty, and when they go to the Saturday matinee at the pictures, or to Botanic Park on Sundays to wander among the soapbox speakers, Peace watches her attract 'boys'—though neither of them knows what to say to these creatures: 'I was resigned to never being the kind of popular that Lyn was. It didn't seem to be in me' (106). When Lyn's first boyfriend rejects her and she swallows Flytox and is rushed to hospital, Peace vows that 'never, never would I have anything to do with love and men' (111). She hates tongue kissing but loves dancing—she goes to a dance club at St Peters Town Hall and to the bigger Trinka club in town. She wonders if this is what her father meant when he told her—his only attempt at sex education—that 'you'd know when it was all right about getting close to boys. It felt all right to me when I was dancing' (123). Still, she never manages to attract anyone she likes: 'I could still only stand most boys if I looked past their ears'—but 'maybe if someone like Ramon Navarro turned up in my life ... ' (137).

When Lyn ends up married and a mother at 15, Peace feels 'panicky, as if the baby was part of a trick ... As if marriage was a trap that girls fell into. Lyn didn't look a bit happy' (141). About to turn 16, Peace is disappointed not to find, as she had hoped, 'everything spread out like, here you are, all yours' (4). She doesn't know what there is to look forward to now—friendship is still reliable, but she certainly hasn't made up her mind about 'being married' (143). In *A House with Verandahs*, however, Peace is not ambivalent. She thinks that a girl had to marry first, and then get on with living: 'Goodness knew I'd be lucky to get any kind of husband and I believed that for girls, marriage was a thing one simply had to accomplish before getting on with the real business of living' (116). Like Adelaide itself, marriage was inevitable, not a choice. It was a grounding, a means to an end, which was 'the business of living'.

Both Gare novels portray a small world, but a varied one, as friends and extended family are numerous, and all of interest to the observant Peace. Her unworldliness is a source of humour rather than angst and mystification. Both autobiographical novels are cheerful and optimistic. The details of the Hounslow family life are close to Gare's own experience, and she offers a sympathetic picture of lower middle-class life in Adelaide in the 1930s. In tone, these novels are a far cry from Barbara Hanrahan's somewhat Gothic evocations of that dimension of Adelaide life in later decades, in *The Scent of Eucalyptus*.

This kind of loving close-up was Nene Gare's trademark as a writer: she believed that 'you have to like your characters, respect them'. Her job, as she saw it, was 'trying to make people understand what it's like to be poor and what it's like to be Aboriginal' (Giuffré 16). She had made her name as a writer with *The Fringe Dwellers* (1961), one of the first depictions by a white writer of urban Aboriginal life; it was made into a film by Bruce Beresford in 1986. This book and the collection of short stories, *Bend to the Wind* (1978), were based on the author's experience of living in Geraldton from 1954 to 1962, where her husband was employed as a district officer for the Native Welfare Department. Gare had originally intended to be a painter, not a writer, and practised both arts as an adult. In *A House with Verandahs* she merely alludes to her youthful dreams: 'One did not mention ambition—there might be laughter' (135).

Adelaide Establishment: *This is my friend's chair*

The life represented in Geraldine Halls's autobiographical novel could not be more different. The author was the third of five children of a wealthy medical specialist, Hubert Jay, and his wife Dorothea von Doussa. She grew up in a large home set in extensive grounds at Stonyfell, in the

Adelaide foothills, and attended Girton Girls' School and the University of Adelaide. There she left her studies unfinished in order to learn shorthand and typing, and earned her living as a stenographer—she wanted to write and to travel. She said that the 'childhood part' of *This is my friend's chair*, her last novel, was autobiographical (Larkin).

This is my friend's chair is narrated in the third person, but is focalised by the character of Sophie, whose father, Neddy Conway, is a doctor and whose mother, Clara von Hardt, is (like Geraldine's mother) descended from German settlers of an aristocratic caste (given the 'von'). They are in all respects members of the Adelaide Establishment, except that Clara and the children are Catholics—a legacy of her Irish grandmother. The children (a boy, and three girls of whom Sophie is the eldest) go to private schools; the parents belong to the Adelaide Club and the Queen Adelaide Club, and play golf and bridge, respectively; they go to Victor Harbor for the whole summer; the children have ponies and tennis and, later, use of the mother's car to drive. The large house and garden are tended by several servants, and Doctor Conway's ageing mother has a live-in help, a woman called Lizzie.

Lizzie, though a member of a 'good Adelaide family', is impoverished. Having to accept such a demeaning post, she becomes adept at making herself the confidante of various family members and binding them to her with ties of obligation or of secrecy. Because of this, she plays a central role in the narrative. But Sophie is the central consciousness and during her childhood she is too unworldly to see this, or indeed to question anyone's motives, especially sexual and power plays. In this novel, the protagonist's naïveté creates a series of sinister mysteries which are not unravelled until years later.

Sophie is socially awkward, a reader and a dreamer, but also defensive and quick to anger—like the protagonists of so many female autobiographies. She is clannish and wary of most other children. She has no perspective on the social world except the belief in her family's superiority:

> Sophie caught these social distinctions from Clara [her mother] and could not fail to be aware of them ... They were in the Adelaide air; at least, in the purified part of it that was all she was permitted to breathe. She yearned, however, for other more spicy climes and made one friend, Janet Locke, who lived in a suburban house ...

Her mother lets her know this girl is unsuitable because, although she goes to the same school and also comes from an 'old Adelaide family', the Lockes were 'reformers' whereas Clara and Neddy were inflexibly conservative. Sophie is torn by conflicting loyalties (50). Interestingly, this means that she resists both her mother's *and* Janet's influence, and this makes her susceptible to Lizzie's friendly advances.

Family is both a sustaining and a suffocating presence in the novel. Sophie's trust in family members, including her father, is often misplaced. She transfers this uncritical admiration to her mother's friend Lady Cleever, who declares that Sophie shall marry her son Jerome. Sophie dreams of this, not noticing that Jerome is pursuing her sexually precocious sister Mary. Sir Robin Cleever impresses Sophie as having 'a mind that has been forged in the world outside Australia'—though the narrative does not support this impression (136). She angrily rejects his prediction that she will never escape her 'Adelaide society advantages', maintaining that she will not marry there but will travel the world in order to become 'someone' (139). But it is this couple who, in London after the war, introduce Sophie to the older man whom she does marry. That unfulfilling marriage connects her to European culture in a second-hand way, reminiscent of the marriage between Isobel Archer and Gilbert Osmond in *Portrait of a Lady*—a young woman with strong but incoherent aspirations is caught between the old world and the new, belonging to neither.

The centrality of family also means that we get few impressions of a larger Adelaide environment. The approach of war, and changes during wartime, are sketched briefly. Part way through the novel Sophie leaves town and makes her life elsewhere, first in Melbourne, then London.

Over the years she returns from time to time to visit the family, and to witness first the loss of the family home and eventually its destruction, making way for a new housing development. By implication, this signals the end of the Adelaide she had grown up in and the triumph of post-war suburbia—and Sophie's long-delayed 'getting of wisdom', consonant with her name. In some respects, Henry Handel Richardson's *The Getting of Wisdom* is the precedent, both for the protagonist's ambitions and her social awkwardness. In other respects, the power plays between characters create complexities, which crowd the heroine out of the foreground, and the Jamesian echo predominates.

Geraldine Halls spent most of her life between the ages of 20 and 40 travelling and living in exotic places like New Guinea and later Pakistan, Thailand, Lebanon, India and France, where her husband, John Halls, had a series of UNESCO appointments. She became known as a writer of successful thrillers, under the name 'Charlotte Jay'. Her first thriller was published in 1951, and her *Beat Not the Bones* won the Edgar Allan Poe Award from the Mystery Writers of America. Later she concentrated on 'serious' fiction, beginning with *The Silk Project*, based on her life in Thailand. This was followed by *The Cats of Benares* and *The Cobra Kite*, both set in India. She and her husband lived in England from 1958 to 1971, then moved to live in Adelaide, where they ran an oriental antiques business. In the early 1990s the novelist was encouraged by the Adelaide-based Wakefield Press, which took up her early books and republished them in its crime series. This renewed interest in her work inspired her to write *This is my friend's chair*, her only novel to evoke her childhood in Adelaide. She died just a year after it was published in 1995 (Muir).

IN THE CITY: *MARIGOLD*

Like Halls, Nancy Cato published her most autobiographical work at the end of her writing career. *Marigold* draws on Cato's experiences as a cadet journalist on the *News*, then Adelaide's evening daily paper, in the years before World War II broke out. It incorporates a couple of short stories that she wrote about those times, 'Keep it brief' and 'The age of innocence,' and may have been substantially written much earlier, for it sounds like her description of a 'satirical novel entitled Keep it Brief, concerning a newspaper called the *Standard*. ... some chapters have been published as short stories, but no publisher would take it on' (Hetherington 180).

What she adds to her memoir is a melodramatic plot about the girl's search for her lost father: he—it turns out—faked his own suicide when Marigold was only nine, and disappeared into Central Australia, where he had previously travelled in search of paintings by Namatjira and other Aboriginal artists. The traces of autobiographical realism here are that Cato's admired older brother took his own life when she was 12, and her father died soon after that (Giuffré 157). Cato herself was very interested in painting, having befriended Frederick McCubbin, the Art Gallery director, in the course of her journalist's rounds; she took classes at Adelaide Art School and later, when she was married and wanted part-time work, she served as the *News*'s art critic.

Marigold is a feisty girl reporter. She rebels against having to report on events like a domestic tiff between the chimpanzees in the zoo, and the Housewives' Association meetings, and when stuffy men in power resist her requests for stories, she engineers 'scoops' by underhand methods. She even tries a bit of sleuthing, albeit unsuccessfully, and wangles a trip inland with members of the university Geology Department to recover a meteorite. She demands a desk in the (male) journalists' room, instead of sharing with the (female) editor of the Social Pages. For her the last straw is being offered editorship of the women's magazine. She resigns rather than take it on—and besides, she has enough money saved up for her passage to Europe. 'I'm leaving the *Standard*,' she tells her surprised editor. 'I will not write any more rubbish for or about women. I am sick to death of women, and their pages, and their fashions, and their clubs and committees and associations' (173-4).

Marigold, at 18, leads a vibrant and somewhat louche social life, avoiding her mother and stepfather's cross-questioning, and experimenting with drinking (in public this always has to finish by 6pm, or 7.30 with a meal). She goes to artists' parties as well as student ones. She buys herself a little second-hand car (against her stepfather's wishes) and drives herself and her boyfriends around the hills and beaches. Susceptible to the charms of her student boyfriends, she nevertheless resists the idea of marriage—even to the one who relieves her of her virginity and with whom she eventually gets to enjoy sex.

When Marigold discovers her father, on her trip inland, he tells her that the fake suicide was the only way out of his 'intolerable' life that he could see. His wife would never consent to the scandal of a divorce. As with Halls's protagonist Sophie—though for different reasons—marriage and suburbia signify the way of life to be avoided. In Marigold's parting vision of Adelaide, it is becoming 'one enormous neat suburb'. Its streets are all straight and it is 'flat as a gridiron and nearly as hot'. Like Sophie, she longs for European scenes of gentle nature and 'ruins, ancient and ivy-covered' (177-8). As the ship steams out of Port Adelaide, she tears up pages of the newspaper and scatters them on the water. 'Life, here I come!' she announces. This style suggests Sybylla, of Miles Franklin's *My Brilliant Career*, as a literary antecedent; but her determination to make the Great Escape from Australia is more reminiscent of Teresa in Stead's *For Love Alone*.

Cato as a girl never made this great escape. Instead, she married when she was 24, and had three children in rapid succession. She had to wait another 15 years before undertaking the great overseas adventure, when she left the children in her sister-in-law's care and travelled alone to London and Italy.

Her early training as a journalist, together with her passions for travel and for historical research, are everywhere evident in her novels. Most of these are historical with a strong dash of romance, featuring wilful heroines and adventurous deeds—the best-known is *All the Rivers Run*, a trilogy set on the River Murray, about a woman artist who becomes a steamboat captain.

Cato's writing always evokes a strong sense of place, and in *Marigold* the city of Adelaide is most vividly conjured—not only the hills and beaches but North Terrace, the pie cart, the newspaper building buzzing with light and noise in a city otherwise dark, where the streetlights are turned off at 1am. This sense of place is a function both of Marigold's work as a journalist, and her eagerness to get away from her own family— strict stepfather, brattish stepsister, and mother who only wants her to behave well. So she constantly looks outwards into the wider society, away from family life. The party she attends at the house of 'two migrant Polish artists' (110) sounds like the famous Dutkiewicz parties of the post-war years (Ward 13). Adelaide is represented by the artists, journalists and intellectuals Marigold mixes with, as well as by straight suburban streets and strait-laced ways.

Despite this even-handedness, Cato must have been concerned about how the critical and satirical aspects of the book would be received locally, for she prefaced the Australian paperback edition with a note on Adelaide which begins: 'This story is set in a city which no longer exists.' She goes on to list predictable objections to 'old' Adelaide's puritan and provincial habits, assuring her readers that 'All this has changed, changed utterly': Adelaide has good restaurants, she writes, the Italians have introduced good coffee, people drink wine rather than sherry, and '*Ulysses* is no longer banned; poets read their works in the parklands. Adelaide has come of age' (v).

In *This is my friend's chair*, Sophie also distances herself from the Adelaide of her childhood, but that Adelaide is defined by her family and the family home. From the vantage point of misty Melbourne, she reflects that 'In Adelaide stars shone so close and with such brilliance, she could only suppose that no one in Adelaide had really lived. No perplexity or pain hung between the stars and the innocent earth. Adelaide was a child's city' (125-6). But this conclusion is premature—Sophie is only 18, and has much to learn about the 'perplexity and pain' that she has left behind in the family there. But the statement 'Adelaide was a child's city' is true, in the end, for her—not because the place was innocent but because she was.

It is also true for Nene Gare's Peace that 'Adelaide was a child's city': the *Kent Town* stories maintain this perspective throughout, in the narrative positioning of Peace as a naïve girl at the age of 16, looking back on her childhood. The narrative takes no later, adult critical or ironic distance from that place and time. Everything is in seen in close-up, local and specific. But though naïve, Peace is observant, and although she does not always understand what she is observing, readers can join the dots. The narrative offers a strong sense of a community, its work and its pleasures, its social links and barriers.

As for the three protagonists' dreams and desires, the class differences are marked. In many ways, Peace grows up faster than the middle-class protagonists. It may be true that ambition might arouse laughter in her milieu, but at least she has a clear idea of what independence would mean. Her perception that marriage had to precede 'getting on with the real business of living' signals that she regards independence as establishing one's own base in a relationship outside the family of origin. This may not include economic autonomy and mobility, as it does for the middle-class girls. For both of them, marriage is to be avoided in favour of seeing the world—and it's a life outside Australia altogether that beckons.

Both Marigold and Sophie believe that marriage would be constraining. Marriage—in Adelaide, at least—would tie a young woman to a place in the known social hierarchy and would prevent her becoming somebody in her own right. Neither wants to become a replica of her mother. It could be said that for the middle-class girls freedom and mobility constitute their ideal, whereas for the girl from a poor family, who works in a shop and still shares a bed with younger siblings, to establish a life with someone she could love as her parents love one another—and who could hold down a decent job—is no bad aspiration for adult life. This was all happening in the late 1930s. After the war was over, Australia would enter a period of accelerating modernity, which would somewhat level out these particular class differences in women's aspirations.

Could these experiences of growing up female have been located in any other Australian city in the 1930s? Adelaide in the 1930s was thoroughly British and Protestant, with few people of Irish descent, few Catholics, and only a small smattering of German and Italian families. In these respects it differed from other Australian capital cities. But although it was well known for its puritan legislation, which closed the pubs at six in the evening and forbade the production of Sunday newspapers, Adelaide was not alone in enforcing temperance-inspired legislation in the 1930s—though it was the last city to end it, in 1967 (Magarey 27-30). The dire outcome for Max Harris and *Angry Penguins* of the Ern Malley hoax has overshadowed the fact that during the late 30s and early 40s there was a small but thriving modernist arts scene in Adelaide (Magarey 42-3; also Kirkpatrick, Chapter 7, and Snowden, Chapter 9, both this volume). But it was a small city—312,000 in the 1933 census, whereas Sydney and Melbourne were just over and just under a million, respectively. This may well account for the novelists' sense of Adelaide's particular restrictiveness.

Adelaide was also said to be more snobbish than other Australian cities, though this may only have been a function of the small size of the Establishment, and of the famous absence of convicts among early settlers. According to Halls's portrait of the Conway family in *This is my friend's chair*, snobbery was very much a feature of their lives, drawing fine distinctions among the middle classes of this small city. At the other end of the social scale, such distinctions are equally important in Nene Gare's novels. Peace's friend tells her that a boyfriend who is an apprentice plumber is too 'ordinary' (*House*, 129), and her brother Ben warns her against going to 'cheap dances' (*House*, 131). The Hounslow family and their friends—small shopkeepers and tradesmen—are the closest we get to the working-class of the period in these stories. Their poverty is a source of comedy, not political mobilisation. In none of these novels is there any mention of the masses of unemployed people begging for work or living in tents on the banks of the Torrens or protesting against reduced rations (Moss 303-9). The novels offer unparalleled insight into some aspects of the social history of the period, but ignore others that might have pointed to the larger political scene. The Adelaide their narratives bring to life is domestic and local. It is not only 'a city which no longer exists' (Cato), or even 'a child's city' (Halls), but a city evoked from far away in time and place, where early memories are inevitably overlaid with later narratives, both personal and social.

All their Adelaides, though markedly different in physical and social locales, share a sense of the city and its suburbs as a benign, even nurturing presence—even if it is one that must be left behind. 'I mentally took farewell,' says Cato's Marigold, 'of those close and friendly hills, which seemed to curve their arms about the city on the plain' (179).

Works Cited

Cato, Nancy. *Marigold*. London: Coronet Books, Hodder and Stoughton, 1993.

Gare, Nene. *A House with Verandahs*. Melbourne: Macmillan, 1980.

___. *Kent Town*. Kent Town, SA: Wakefield Press, 1997.

Giuffré, Giulia. 'Nene Gare' and 'Nancy Cato'. *A Writing Life: Interviews with Australian Women Writers*. Sydney: Allen & Unwin, 1990. 15-25 and 151-67.

Goldsworthy, Kerryn. *Adelaide*. Sydney: NewSouth Publishing, 2011.

Halls, Geraldine. *This is my friend's chair*. Adelaide: Wakefield Press, 1995.

Hanrahan, Barbara. *The Scent of Eucalyptus*. London: Chatto & Windus, 1973.

Hetherington, John. 'Nancy Cato: Girl and a River'. *Forty Two Faces*. Melbourne: Cheshire, 1962. 177-82.

Hooton, Joy. *Stories of Herself when Young: Autobiographies of Childhood by Australian Women*. Melbourne: Oxford University Press, 1990.

Larkin, John. 'Going Straight'. *Sunday Age*. 25 June 1995. 9.

Magarey, Susan and Kerrie Round. *Roma the First: A Biography of Dame Roma Mitchell*. Adelaide: Wakefield Press, 2007.

Moss, Jim. *Sound of Trumpets: History of the Labour Movement in South Australia*. Kent Town, SA: Wakefield Press, 1985.

Muir, Marcie. 'Suspense writer hailed by the critics'. *The Australian*. 28 November 1996. 13.

Ward, Peter. 'John Bray in Adelaide'. *A Portrait of John Bray*. Ed. Wilfred Prest. Adelaide: Wakefield Press, 1997. 1-19.

6 Adelaide and the Country: the Literary Dimension[1]

Jill Roe

I owe the title of this chapter to that distinctively South Australian historian John Hirst, whose 1973 study of the changing social and political relationship between 'Adelaide and the country' from the 1870s to 1917 is one of the classics of South Australian history. In what follows, I will be concerned mainly with what literary historian Geoffrey Dutton once dubbed 'the mechanics of literature' (*Snow on the Saltbush*, part 3), and with some relevant regional writings, relevant that is to the emergence of 'literary Adelaide'. The chapter deals predominantly with the first half of the twentieth century, before the 1960s. It comes in three parts, 'the country', 'the city' and 'the country and the city'. It will aim to show that by the 1960s, there was a self-sustaining 'literary Adelaide', though the literary culture was rather more closely tied to the countryside than was the case elsewhere in Australia then and rather more aware of its links to the first peoples.

My father was a farmer. Unlike many, maybe most, farmers, he read books. Unfortunately, my recall of the

---

[1] I wish to thank Margaret Allen, the late Helen Bartley, Bridget Griffen-Foley, Beverley Kingston, Jennie Strickland and Patricia Sumerling for references and other assistance during the preparation of this chapter.

many titles that came into the house in the late 1940s and early 1950s, when I left for Adelaide, is limited. But I do remember some favourite authors: Australians Ion Idriess and F.J. Thwaites, and Nicholas Monsarrat and Elizabeth Goudge, both British writers, as well as the controversial Howard Spring.

John Roe's farm was on lower Eyre Peninsula. Thus he also read the *Port Lincoln Times* and the *Adelaide Chronicle*, both weeklies serving country readers, these being delivered by a twice-weekly mail bus to a nearby general store. For a time, he also subscribed to the Sydney *Bulletin*, a publication mysterious to a child like me with its pages of print and strange drawings.

Nor was the family neglected. At night after tea and the washing up, we would gather to read a set section of the Bible and elucidatory Notes produced by the Scripture Union, most probably provided by the Methodist (as it was then) Church. This reading supplemented fortnightly church services in the tiny tin church down the road and the Methodist Hymn Book, the latter in effect another literary experience.

As for me, the youngest of four daughters, I soon twigged that reading was a way of distinguishing myself. Although too young to understand them, I perused many of the incoming titles, most manageably those about adventure and travel. By then I was just about up to Mary Grant Bruce; and when my widowed father married an English woman in 1950, I was introduced to Enid Blyton's *The Folk of the Faraway Tree* and the Famous Five, which were enjoyable but strained the credulity somewhat, also Milly Molly Mandy and her rural village.

In retrospect, for my own literary experiences, I would attach more importance to school texts and libraries. I certainly am now surprised and pleased to think that in grades eight and nine at Cummins Area School we had texts by two South Australians, Jindyworobak poet Rex Ingamells's 1943 verse anthology *New Song in an Old Land*, and in upper level art classes, maybe for reference only, Rex Battarbee's *Modern*

Australian Aboriginal Art, an introduction to Aranda painting, which had a foreword by T.G.H. Strehlow in the second edition of 1952. I doubt that such splendid local texts would have been used under a unified national curriculum.

My memories of country schools' libraries were not so positive—too much Biggles—and many of South Australia's 800-odd small and isolated country schools were reliant on cases of books brought in by teachers, themselves poorly trained. And yet, as poet, novelist and educationalist Colin Thiele saw it, these cases of books served as 'a sort of personal travelling library [often] of quite good literary value', including, for example, *Jane Eyre*, *Robbery Under Arms* and *We of the Never Never* (Dutton 76).

Where did our reading material come from? Even now, so far as I know, there is no bookshop on lower Eyre Peninsula. However, there was, and still is, a large newsagency in Port Lincoln that stocks some titles—I recently obtained *Wildflowers of Lower Eyre Peninsula* (2001) and a follow-up volume *Quieter Wildflowers of Lower Eyre Peninsula* (n.d.) from that shop—and it would order others on request. Although there was at that time no public library either, there was a Literary Institute at the back of the Town Hall which lent books—which quite possibly delayed the creation of a local public library, as happened in many parts of South Australia, according to Carl Bridge (1986). In addition, although I do not recall this applying to us, some city bookshops, such as Preece's, offered a lending library service to country people (Bayfield 151-3). There was also always the possibility of mail order, enabling keen readers anywhere in Australia to purchase titles direct from the city, as was to be the case with Mary Martin's wonderfully exotic bookshop (Lewis). As well, boxes of books were sent to schools by the State Education Department and the Public Library on North Terrace. The Public Library also ran a Country Lending Service, through which children could be sent up to two titles per month, as requested by them or selected by librarians, a service affectionately recalled by my colleague and friend the late Dr Helen Bartley, a psychologist who began her schooling up country, at Wudinna.

By the 1940s, then, it was possible for readers to access books and magazines in even quite distant parts of South Australia. More broadly, the Hirst thesis, that the relationship between Adelaide and the country—between country and city—was more favourable to country people by the 1920s, seems to have had a bearing on the health of literary culture as late as the 1940s and 50s. Perhaps this is only another way of saying that for most of settled South Australia, the rural/urban divide was seldom so sharp as in many other parts of Australia.

It will be apparent where this section is heading: to the urban culture, to the institutions that underpinned literary Adelaide, and to the people who worked in them, including from the 1930s in radio (though that is an as yet unresearched area and must be left for another time). 'Literary Adelaide' has always consisted not only of readers and writers but also of journalists, editors, printers, librarians and book-sellers, and reviewers.

Dutton's 'mechanics of literature' ensured that by the early twentieth century, country people, if so inclined, had access to a literary culture on a regular basis. It may not have been so easy to get to Adelaide then as it is now, when at least some country people can fly there and back for the day if need be, but newspapers went out by train and bus and boat all over the State on at least a weekly basis. Even pre-plane it was not that far from Port Lincoln, for example, Adelaide was only an overnight trip by boat. Furthermore, by the early twentieth century, literacy levels were high if not absolutely universal throughout South Australia, and reading was a common pastime. As well, informal lines of communication flourished. Rural and urban families tended to travel back and forth, especially during school holidays bearing news. By the 1960s, and before then, and probably still, many country people came to the city at least once a year, to the Royal Agricultural Show, maybe twice if there was an Exhibition on, or an exciting sporting event. Naturally, some took the opportunity to stock up at the bookshops, at Beck's on Pulteney Street, for instance, long since gone but once the city's outstanding second-hand book store.

The most obvious source of information about Adelaide's literary culture was always the newspaper press. Until its closure in 1975 after over a century's publication, for most country people that probably meant the *Adelaide Chronicle*, part of the Bonython fold, and as noted earlier, a weekly (Prest, ch. 2). At first glance, the coverage may seem disappointing to the cultural historian. Dipping into a rough sequence from 1905 to 1935 and 1975, it emerges that at the beginning of the twentieth century, book reviews were rare in the *Chronicle*, and in a listing of most popular titles published in the edition for 1 April 1905, the first dozen titles were all English, beginning with *David Copperfield*. Even so, it was not otherwise all cook books and self help. Almost 60 books are mentioned in the first of April 1905 edition, and the paper carried a swag of light literature— poems, sketches and short stories such as 'Be you never so gay', by Lee Wilson Dud and 'The Elder Miss Smith's Elopement'—as it continued to do until the 1970s. And by 1935, quite lengthy reviews appeared, including of some Australian works. On 3 January 1935 there was a long review of the English classic *Goodbye Mr Chips* (1934), 'a delightful novel' by James Hilton; and the 'Book of the Week' on 4 April that year was Charles Chauvel's book-of-the-film *Heritage*, which the reviewer said all true Australians should read; there was also a note that day on *Secret China* by Czech radical Egon Kisch, whose visit to Australia in 1934 had become a *cause célèbre*. By early 1975 (10 January 1975), when the *Chronicle* was on its last legs, there seem to have been more Australian books and an even wider range of titles noticed, on war history and underwater adventures, plus local titles such as sketches of Victor Harbor.

Compared with the Saturday *Advertiser* this was still rather thin fare. Not that the *Advertiser*'s practice then was by today's standards very impressive and by now it is vestigial at best, with only a few mainly local titles noted way back in its pages. What a contrast that is with its coverage a century ago, nonetheless. In the first week of April 1905, the *Advertiser*'s

'Book of the Week' was *The Gospel and the Church*, discussing lectures on science and religion, and there were some eight book reviews, six being on fiction (but apparently none of these Australian fiction). However, there was one Australian title in the 'Miscellaneous' listing, *Steele Rudd's Magazine*, approvingly referred to as 'thoroughly Australian'. Thirty years later, in 1935, the *Advertiser* was still running lengthy reviews, but also some Australian writing (including by Ion Idriess); and by 1975 coverage of Australiana was quite extensive.

It would not be right to generalise far from such limited samplings. But from what I have seen to date, it seems that until the 1960s, the *Advertiser* was still largely metropolitan in outlook whereas the *Chronicle* remained more local, more down-to-earth. Still, it seems there was some common ground; and over time both publications paid increasing attention to Australian books.

There was also a thriving printing and publishing industry. The late 1950s saw the rise of Rigby and the maturation of Griffin Press, the latter said to be the largest book-printing company in Australia by the 1970s (Dutton 230; Dunstan). Closed in 2006, the Lutheran Publishing House, producing such classics as *Stagg of Tarcowie: The diaries of a colonial teenager (1885-1887)* in 1973, also warrants mention. Even more striking is the establishment of a bold new literary journal *Australian Letters*, by Geoffrey Dutton, Max Harris and Bryn Davies in 1957 (Wilde 63).

With so many changes in cultural dynamics since the 1960s, the literary culture of the twenty-first century is much more diverse and specialised, and the idea of a linear progression towards a common culture implicit in the earlier period would seem to be a thing of the past. But a literary culture is evidently still alive and well in Adelaide, and it has a significant history to draw upon as it continues to develop, not least in a stronger sense of a positive relationship between country and city.

For some time now it has seemed old-fashioned to talk about the country, and the relationship between country and city has been a neglected subject, by me as much as anyone. However, times are again a-changing. The Governor-General's Australia Day Address of 2011 invited us to think about underlying issues in rural Australia; and Judith Brett's *Quarterly Essay*, *Fair Share: Country and City in Australia*, suggests we should at least remember the importance of rural Australia for such simple things as food. And of all places with a relevant literary heritage to contribute, it is surely Adelaide.

I want to argue that just as effective links between country and city encouraged the consolidation of a literary culture in Adelaide in the first half of the twentieth century, so writing about 'the country' was part and parcel of 'literary Adelaide' by then. To trace the relationship, perhaps it's useful to begin with Ellen Liston, whose writings on Eyre Peninsula in the 1860s and 70s have recently attracted critical attention (Hancock). However, if it is the consolidation of literary Adelaide that is the focus here, the pivotal time comes much later, in the 1940s, with the Jindyworobaks and their associates. As Chapter 7 of this book (Peter Kirkpatrick's 'Fearful Affinity': Jindyworobak Primitivism') is focussed on that movement, suffice to note here what a timely title the founder Rex Ingamells gave its manifesto in 1938, *Conditional Culture*, and to emphasise how responsive to the most advanced contemporary cultural thinking this man from Orroroo was in calling for a closer alignment with Aboriginal Australia and the Australian experience in general. It was in Adelaide, after all, that T.G.H. Strehlow and others such as C.P. Mountford and Charles Duguid, founder of Ernabella Mission, and also in her own way, Daisy Bates, were providing new insights into the desert cultures. Meanwhile writers elsewhere in Australia were increasingly producing historical fiction, even if it was all a bit vague, and most writers had reservations. Nonetheless, as Miles Franklin recognised in ''Twas Ever Thus', an essay on a *Jindyworobak Review* anthology published in 1948 (reprinted Roe and Bettison 215-17), it was a step in the right direction (although she found Ingamells's later epic poems overwhelming).

In the 1940s, poetry was still the supreme literary genre in this country, partly a traditional position but due also to the war and a desire for succinct memorable statements, with Wilfred Frank Flexmore Hudson a leading local exponent. Flexmore Hudson was a Queensland-born country schoolteacher who came to South Australia as a boy in 1924 and died in Adelaide as recently as 1988. He produced six books of poetry between 1937 and 1959, and, with the help of his dedicated wife Myrle Desmond, published a poetry magazine entitled *Poetry Quarterly*, first from Lucindale in the South-east and later Adelaide. This attracted some leading American poets, and A.D. Hope, as well as the locals. Earlier, from 1931 to 1941, the Hudsons were located up north, at Hammond in the Flinders Ranges. Reading about their time there, and the short stories of rural life collected in Hudson's *Tales from Corytella* (1985), suggests that not much had changed 'on the margins of the good earth' (Meinig 1963) since the collapse of the farming frontier up there in the 1880s; and, as with Ingamells, the experience goes a good way towards explaining Flexmore Hudson's environmental values.

In 1943 Hudson also edited one of the Jindyworobak anthologies, which appeared annually 1938-1953 under various editors. One new voice was the previously mentioned Colin Thiele. Thiele, born at Eudunda in 1920, was another young teacher-writer, whose first books were published by Preece. Now best known for such titles as the Coorong-set *Storm Boy* (1963), Thiele went on to publish over 90 books in a variety of genres, many of them with Rigby. Of relevance here are his autobiographical fiction *The Sun on the Stubble* (1961), and the fictional *Labourers in the Vineyard* (1970), set in a farming and winegrowing community of German origin north of Adelaide. Although *Labourers in the Vineyard* is not so accessible now, due to its use of dialect, it has an authentic ring, while the film of Thiele's *Storm Boy* gave him (and the Coorong) national exposure. Thiele, who died in 2006, became one of South Australia's best-loved writers, integral to 'literary Adelaide'.

As far as Miles Franklin was concerned, of all the Jindies, poet Ian Mayelston Mudie was outstanding. This was so because of his poems not his politics, which she did not share. An early Mudie volume, *Corroboree to the Sun* (1940), she found 'intoxicating'; and despite his commitment to 'Inky' Stephensen's Australia-First movement in Sydney, from which he escaped by entering the Army, Mudie and Franklin remained close. In the South Australian's work, Franklin saw her own hopes of a national literature taking shape. With *Corroboree*, she said, Mudie had gone 'farther than any of us in capturing the spirit of Australia' (Roe 404). Evidently, with Mudie, the literary relationship between Adelaide and the country entered new terrain.

Two titles of the early 1940s may suggest something of Mudie's drive: his long poem *The Australian Dream* (1943) and the edited collection *Poets at War* (1944). *The Australian Dream*, a Jindyworobak publication printed in Adelaide, is dedicated to Mudie's son Bill, and has a cover designed by Margaret Preston. Inspired by American Stephen Vincent Benet's long narrative poem 'John Brown's Body', to which Franklin had introduced him, in *The Australian Dream* Mudie envisages the dawning of an independent Australia. *Poets at War* is, as the title may suggest, simply a collection of servicemen's writings, which in effect also celebrates the Australian spirit. The Melbourne *Age* said it was a volume every literate Australian should possess (*Jindyworobak Publications*, no page).

Considering that the final section of a collected edition of Mudie's *Poems: 1934-1944* (Georgian House, 1945) entitled 'Unabated Spring' and beginning with a poem entitled 'Onwards my people' is dedicated to Miles Franklin, it is perhaps no wonder that she was keen on his work. But nor should it be forgotten that these idealist outpourings are a young man's writings and that, like Thiele, Mudie went on play several significant roles in the literary culture of the 1960s. As outlined by Philip Butterss in the *Australian Dictionary of Biography*, he became active in writers' organisations in the late 1950s, editor in chief of Rigby 1960-1965, and an organiser of Writers' Week from its inception in 1960 to 1972. He died too soon, in 1976, his ashes scattered on the Murray River.

Adelaide-born and educated, Mudie had spent much of his time up the country, when young in unskilled jobs and in later years on the river, due to a preoccupation with river boats. Mudie's heart lay with the land; and in a way he personifies the literary dynamics of 'Adelaide and the country'. A.D. Hope may have attacked the Jindies for a Boy Scout approach to poetry, but he moderated his view subsequently, and it is hard to imagine the emergence of a self-sustaining and outward-going 'literary Adelaide' without such energy.

It is striking how few women seem to have been associated with the Jindies. New South Wales émigré poet Gina Ballantyne (1919-1973) was one. She published two volumes of poetry with Preece, in 1942 and 1943, and she edited the Jindyworobak *Anthology* in 1945. But references to her work are otherwise rare, a comment in the *Advertiser* of 17 April 1943 (p. 3) that she had contributed 'a fine poem' entitled 'Voiceless' to the quarterly *Poetry* being one. Maybe there are other women, of whom I have yet to learn. But it does not seem to matter much to either literary Adelaide or to the boundaries of ideology as outlined by Ingamells. Over time, the city has boasted numerous interesting women writers. Many of them seem to draw on country experiences, as did Ellen Liston so long ago, and later the less well-known Sarah Doudy, who died at Port Lincoln in 1932. Doudy (1846-1932), an English-born country policeman's wife, was no great writer nor was she a prolific one, but Janette Hancock (2010) has brought to light some previously unknown sketches of Aboriginal people south of the Coorong that she published under the pseudonym 'Yakunga' in the *Register* of 1938, time- and class-bound as they evidently are.

As a young reader, for me the most compelling woman writer in the fifties was Myrtle Rose White (1888-1961), again not prolific but more telling as a contributor to the rural and regional dimension of literary

Adelaide. *No Roads Go By* was first published by Angus & Robertson in Sydney in 1932 and later in numerous editions also by Rigby. I once received it as a school prize—or was it a Christmas present?—and loved it, though reading recently of her married life on a station to the east of Lake Frome gave me pause for thought. Station life as she described it was different from that of the farming community I had grown up in, yet women's experiences seemed familiar in many ways. In later life, when she became friendly with Miles Franklin through the Fellowship of Australian Writers, White lived at Glenelg and became a spiritualist (Roe 484).

An invigorating regional perspective was not limited to the urgent ideologues of the Jindy movement or challenging women writers. Mention should also be made of journalist Max Fatchen, who wrote a great deal about Angle Vale and Port Victoria on the northern edge of the Adelaide plain. He even has a slight Eyre Peninsula connection, with the islands south of Coffin Bay. Here I draw on Andrew Male's biography of Fatchen (1997). Fatchen may be regarded as a lightweight, not at all literary; however, Male is surely right, if somewhat overblown, to suggest that by the 1940s and 50s readers were beginning to appreciate the 'special hues and shades of their Outback, and the bruised baskets of winter clouds over the West Coast' (83). Apparently Fatchen felt there was novelty in the bush stories, and a spirituality about the place, even a sense in which poetic bridges had been built to the landscape by Aboriginal peoples and their Dreaming.

There was plenty of room for new approaches in the literary market place by then. A concluding title for mention, and evidence of the widening scope of writings with a rural or regional dimension, is Arthur Upfield's *Man of Two Tribes*, published by Heinemann in 1956. *Man of Two Tribes* is set on the northern edge of the Nullarbor—beyond 'Mt Singular', at what he calls 'the back door to Australia's economic secrets' (62), by which he means the rocket range. One needs more than the willing suspension of belief to go along with this fantasy, but it shows Max Fatchen was on to something with a new interest in bush stories. Even the 'wild aborigines' (sic) have a positive if constrained place in Upfield's fantasy.

To conclude, albeit provisionally: by the 1940s, the literary interchange between 'Adelaide and the country' was already extensive, and by the 1960s it was integral to the character and vitality of 'literary Adelaide'. This was not just a matter of location, *à la* Upfield, though that was important, but also of demography and cultural timing. European settlement in South Australia was by then old enough to start looking itself in the face but still in touch with the rural hinterland and aware of the survival and significance of its Aboriginal peoples.

WORKS CITED

Bayfield, Juliana. 'F W Preece', *A History of the Book in Australia*, vol. 2. Eds M. Lyons and J. Arnold. St Lucia: University of Queensland Press, 2001.

Bridge, Carl. *A Trunk Full of Books. History of the State Library of South Australia and its forerunners*. Kent Town, SA: Wakefield Press, 1986.

Brett, Judith. *Fair Share: Country and City in Australia*. Melbourne: Black Inc. (Quarterly Essay 42), 2011.

Dunstan, D.A. *Story of Griffin Press*. Adelaide: typescript, 1977.

Dutton, Geoffrey. *Snow on the Saltbush. The Australian literary experience*. Melbourne: Viking, 1984.

Hancock, Janette Helen. 'A Not so Innocent Vision: Re-visiting the literary works of Ellen Liston, Jane Sarah Doudy, and Myrtle Rose White (1838-1961). Unpub. PhD thesis. The University of Adelaide, 2007.

___. 'Writing from the Fringe of Empire': understanding the gaps, silences and underlying whiteness in Jane Sarah Doudy's literary works'. *Women's History Review* 19, 3 (2010).

Hudson, W. Flexmore. *Tales from Corytella*. Comp. and ed. from a 1940s ms. by Adam Dutkiewicz, foreword by J.J. Bray. Norwood, SA: WAV Publications, 1985.

Jindyworobak Publications. 1946. List of available and projected books. Pamphlet, unpaginated [8 pps], in my possession.

Lewis, Julie. *Mary Martin, a double life: Australia and India*. St Lucia: University of Queensland Press, 1997.

Liston, Ellen. *Pioneers: stories*. Comp. Ellen A. Harwood. Adelaide: Hassell, 1936.

Male, Andrew. *Other Times: the Life and Work of Max Fatchen*. Kent Town, SA: Wakefield Press, 1997.

Meinig, D.W. *The Margins of the Good Earth. The South Australian wheat frontier 1869-1884*. London: John Murray, 1963.

Prest, E.J. *Sir John Langdon Bonython. Newspaper Proprietor, Politician and Philanthropist*. Port Melbourne: Aust. Scholarly Publishing, 2011.

Roe, Jill. *Stella Miles Franklin. A Life*. Sydney: HarperCollins, 2008.

Roe, Jill and Margaret Bettison. Eds. *A Gregarious Culture. Topical writings of Miles Franklin*. St Lucia: University of Queensland Press, 2001.

Upfield, Arthur. *Man of Two Tribes*. Melbourne: Heinemann, 1956.

Wilde, William H., Joy Hooton and Barry Andrews. Ed. *Oxford Companion to Australian Literature*. 1985. Melbourne: Oxford University Press, 1994.

7 'Fearful Affinity': Jindyworobak Primitivism

Peter Kirkpatrick

As founder and panjandrum of the Jindyworobak movement, Rex Ingamells would have a difficult relationship with the Sydney *Bulletin*, then the nation's leading literary journal. That the Jindyworobaks had national ambitions of their own was undoubtedly part of the problem, but so too was the fact that they were Adelaide-based and so lay outside the dominant literary axis of the eastern states. In 1935, however, such ructions lay in the future, and the *Bulletin* saw fit to encourage the 22-year-old Ingamells by publishing the following poem in its 20 November edition:

> From a high hill-road I saw,
>   Against a line of low crests in the night,
> The city's glitter and the city's glare —
>   A wide white sea of light,
> Monotonously lapping round
> Dark bays and capes without a sound.
>
> Then inward swept a shadow-sea:
> Dimmed-green, night-silvered mystery,
>   With star-like red-glow here and there,
> And faint shouts of corroboree.
> (*Forgotten People*, 8)

'From a High Hill-Road' was not the first poem by Ingamells taken by the *Bulletin* that year but it was more clearly a promise of things to come.[1] That the modern Australian landscape disguises a 'vanished' yet spiritually abiding Aboriginal presence would be a constant Jindyworobak theme. Here it is explicitly signalled by that single, terminal word 'corroboree'; in later years Ingamells and his fellow poets would be much freer in their Indigenous borrowings. As well, the 'shadow-sea' which inundates the 'monotonous', significantly 'white sea of light' below is a more potent, because primeval, force compared to the superficial glitter of modern Adelaide. For, although it is unnamed, the city in the poem—a veritable city of the plain—is indeed Adelaide. This is the view from Mount Lofty.

It has been easy for critics to ignore the metropolitan origins of Jindyworobakism. The movement's nationalism, and its concern for what Ingamells called 'environmental values', led its main poets to emphasise natural and rural themes. In particular, their trademark Aboriginalism[2] —their primitivist construction of Aborigines and Indigenous culture— makes them seem decidedly anti-modern. As renegade Jindyworobak turned surrealist, Max Harris, remarked in 1943, Ingamells's poetry 'concerns itself with expressing two things so far—one, the disgusting and repulsive life of the city, Big Business and Small Emotions; and two, a nostalgic self-identification with the aborigine and the spiritual values of his life (!)' (35). Yet if 'From a High Hill-Road' seeks to dim the city's glare, modern urban life is the precondition for the poem's primitivism.

---

[1] Previously that year the *Bulletin* had published 'Far-Away Hills' (5 June) and 'An Exhortation' (3 July), a landscape lyric and a love poem, respectively.

[2] 'Aboriginalism' is a term coined by Bob Hodge and Vijay Mishra in their book *Dark Side of the Dream* to describe Western discursive strategies when dealing with Indigenous Australians; in other words, ways of speaking about and representing Aborigines, and thus 'knowing' them. It is adapted from Edward Said's term *Orientalism*, from his 1978 book of that name, which analyses the West's tendency to regard Asia and the Middle East in the troubled dialectical (and indeed psychoanalytic) terms of self and other. Aboriginalism is a useful term, not least because it serves to distinguish Aboriginal*ity* as a specific mode of Indigenous self-identification. While Aboriginalism contains primitivism as a discourse, it also exceeds it.

Ingamells republished 'From a High Hill-Road' in his second collection, *Forgotten People*, in 1936, where a companion poem, 'Colonization', revisits both site and theme with greater specificity:

> Again upon this height that Flinders named,
> > I look across the plains so changed since then.
> On gully-sides, and under gum-boughs framed,
> > Fast limousines glide by on bitumen;
> > But near me are the ghosts of tribal men
> The gumtree trunks stand up like solid gold,
> As the sun drops seaward and the day grows old.

In the preceding stanza the poet asserts 'That white man's destiny meant black man's fate':

> This is the sadness of a splendid thing,
> > The undertone of sorrow in a tale
> The undertone of sorrow in a tale. (32)

Despite its title, in 'Colonization' the supposed disappearance of the Kaurna people, the original inhabitants of the Adelaide plain, is presented as a *fait accompli*, the result, not of historical violence, but the by-product of 'a most marvellous accomplishing' that the poem also celebrates.

This is an example of what Bob Hodge and Vijay Mishra have called the 'premature elegy', which assumes 'the desired end to the "Aboriginal problem", while expressing a regret that absolve[s] the feeling person from complicity or responsibility' (42). The Jindyworobaks were fond of such elegies, so their critical neglect is hardly surprising given the central role that Aboriginal continuity has played in national debates over recent decades. Besides, the ersatz 'Aboriginality' of Jindyworobakism can seem like cultural blackface. If, in his manifesto, *Conditional Culture* (1938), Ingamells insisted that 'environmental values' came first, he also argued: 'From Aboriginal art and song we must learn much of our new technique; from Aboriginal legend, sublimated through our thought, we must achieve something of a pristine outlook on life' (264).

But how much did Ingamells and his followers really learn from Aboriginal culture, and how much did they 'sublimate'? For instance, the name 'Jindyworobak' itself, meaning 'to annex, to join' (249), is a Wuywurrung word from the Melbourne region, yet there is no evidence that Ingamells ever knew its etymology. He sourced the word at remote second-hand from the eclectic glossary at the back of James Devaney's collection of Aboriginal legends, *The Vanished Tribes* (1929), and never bothered to look any further.[3] As Brian Elliott remarked, 'Captivated as [Ingamells] was by native words ... he could also be careless with them' (xxxi-xxxii).

This chapter revisits the issue of Jindyworobak cultural appropriation in order to canvass its range and modalities. Drawing upon examples by Ingamells, Ian Mudie, Flexmore Hudson and Roland Robinson, what follows traces the complex, often paradoxical, dynamics of Jindyworobak primitivism as a distinct mode of Australian modernism. Before proceeding, though, it is useful to reflect briefly on that term *primitivism* in this context, for its roots in Western culture are deep and diverse.

* * *

As Elazar Barkan and Ronald Bush have noted, 'As for "primitives", they never existed. Only Western "primitivism" did' (2). Modern primitivism draws from ancient wellsprings of mingled fear and desire: fear of the loss of cultured restraint, of the rule of the superego, and yet a concomitant desire to shirk its tyranny in order to embrace an unmediated relationship with 'natural' impulses. Marianna Torgovnick locates an originary myth of the uncivilised and therefore savage other in Odysseus's encounter

---

[3] Sellick (108-9) also draws attention to Ingamells's casual use of Aboriginal words, and his considerable indebtedness to Devaney. Gary Catalano suggested that five 'mock-Aboriginal poems' that Devaney included in *The Vanished Tribes* 'clearly anticipated the Jindyworobak movement' (66, 69).

with the cannibal Cyclops, Polyphemus, in book 9 of the *Odyssey* (*Gone Primitive*, 23-6). Elements of the myth of the 'noble' savage, on the other hand, go back as far as the pastoral tradition, although the form in which we know it today originated in the Enlightenment, as a corollary of European imperialism. In the nineteenth century, explorers and empire builders would fill Western museums with 'native' artifacts—as well as native body parts—helping to shape the modern human sciences, and in particular the disciplines of anthropology and ethnography. In due course these same artifacts would lend dark energy to modernism's assault on the artistic institutions of old Europe—most iconically perhaps in the mask-like heads and bladed bodies of Picasso's *Les Desmoiselles d'Avignon* (1907): sex, death and cubism all rolled into one.

As already hinted, the Jindyworobaks were opportunistic rather than systematic students of Aboriginal culture. Take the Arrernte (Arunta) term Alchera or Alcheringa, 'the Dreaming', which would become a cornerstone of the movement's philosophy. In the retrospective *Jindyworobak Review* (1948), Ingamells stated he first heard the word from T.G.H. Strehlow at Hermannsburg in 1930-31, during a holiday in Central Australia that 'had begun my interest in the Aborigines' (11). In that sense, desert tourism was as much an inspiration as anthropology. Further, it seems unlikely that he had read Baldwin Spencer and F.J. Gillen's account of Alchera in *The Arunta* (1927) by the time he formed the Jindyworobaks in 1938, since it later took Ian Mudie to fully alert him to the symbolic possibilities of the term.[4]

In any event, Ingamells's early attitude towards the scientific study of Indigenous life may be gleaned from the narrow lines of '"Native Section"' from his third collection, *Sun-Freedom* (1938), which recalls a visit to the ethnographic exhibits at the South Australian Museum:

---

[4] 'The Alchera had been to me and others a subject for Australian writing. We observed that Mudie was using it as symbol, and thereafter Jindyworobak writers developed the Alchera symbol more and more' (Ingamells, *Jindyworobak Review*, 19). John Dally also points out that Ingamells's first mention of *The Arunta* is in the bibliography to his 1951 epic poem *The Great South Land* (403).

> Possum hair girdle,
> dillybag,
> bough-built gunyah,
> totem-crag
> grace the Museum's
> clean glass cases;
> with dark and sullen
> waxen faces.
>
> Lubras crouch
> on well-placed stones,
> as if they have
> life in their bones —
> and a dusky, waxen
> birrahlee [baby]
> sprawls beside
> its father's knee.
>
> Let Garaway,
> the cockatoo,
> and Buln-buln, lyre bird,
> fine to view,
> haunting still
> the bushland, make
> music for the
> dead tribes' sake. (22)

A few traditional objects placed around the waxwork figures in the Museum are a poor representation of the first Australians, their supposedly lost heritage symbolised by the lifeless model of a 'sprawling' infant. As opposed to this morbid spectacle, the wild birds still elegiacally call and — like the Jindyworobaks themselves — 'make/music for the/ dead tribes' sake'. Ingamells is now less inclined to decry the loss of Indigenous culture than to sublimate it as a resource for Jindyworobak use, notably by zesting his poems with Aboriginal words. But those words might themselves be seen as ethnographic exhibits, out of context and so lacking proper meaning.

Posed against the dead hand of science is the primitive enchantment of nature itself, all the more resonant for the absent presence of its former inhabitants, 'A pang whose tenderness cannot be told':

> How can a stranger hope to understand?
> Dark ghosts go with me all about the land.
> ('Forgotten People', *Forgotten People*, 9)

By such means, premature elegy can also be a mode of Australian gothic, transforming the landscape in *unheimlich* ways that recall Marcus Clarke's famous evocation of the 'Weird Melancholy' of the bush. On the same page of *Sun-Freedom* as '"Native Section"' appears 'Occultism':

> Scrubland-night. Fearful affinity.
> Shadows. Grim-scraggled shadows. Stark,
> contorted tree-trunks in the depths of dark.
> The whisper-shouting winds like the voices of bararangs [ghosts],
> spear-hissing threats to the mind's wan equanimity.

Here melancholy is replaced by psychic danger, the product of 'Fearful *affinity*': an odd usage, possibly recalling the obsolete sense of the word as 'vicinity', while also invoking its more usual meanings of liking or kinship. In terms of kinship, *affinity* refers to relationship by marriage rather than blood, which potentially adds a racial layer to the word choice. If Ingamells has an affinity with the Indigenous bush it is by 'marriage' — by annexing or joining, that is — rather than by consanguinity. Racial difference is further marked by the phrase, 'The mind's *wan* equanimity', now threatened by an Aboriginal uncanny firmly located in the natural world.

It is a truism in whiteness studies that, as a function of historical privilege, being white can bestow invisibility, like a magic cloak, upon the Western subject. Aileen Moreton-Robinson summarises the point:

> The discourse of primitivism deploys the Cartesian model to separate the racialised white body of the knower from the racialised discourse and knowledge produced by its mind. In this way the body, which is the marker of race, is erased leaving only the disembodied mind. Whiteness, as an ontological and epistemological *a priori*, is seductive in producing the assumption of a racially neutral mind and an invisible detached white body. (81)

If this is the case for the imperial or metropolitan white 'knower', it is not invariably so for the white postcolonial subject who, as a marker of national difference from the parent culture, may wish to be other than 'disembodied'. As Richard White showed in his classic study, *Inventing Australia*, nineteenth-century arguments for Australian cultural difference often made Social Darwinist claims about the racial purity, and thus distinctness, of 'The Coming Man'.[5] Being whiter than white brings with it another set of problems, however. In a perceptive essay on David Malouf's 1993 novel, *Remembering Babylon*, Penelope Ingram has written, 'For the settler, transparent whiteness is not a mark of power as it is for the Briton or American but rather the sign of his or her weakness, a reminder of colonization' (163).

The Jindyworobaks were all too aware of the propensity of white Australians to look and behave like 'second-hand Europeans', to use A.D. Hope's phrase, which is why Ingamells insisted in *Conditional Culture* that:

> the British stock which settled here, no matter whether in country or town, has undergone profound changes. Acclimatization has been going on in subtle ways for several generations until Australians are now a people with distinctive physical and temperamental characteristics. (246)

In this regard it is worth recalling the deep influence of P.R. Stephensen's essay *The Foundations of Culture in Australia* (1935) on Ingamells's thinking:

> Race and Place are the two permanent elements in a culture, and Place, I think, is even more important than Race in giving that culture

---

[5] See, in particular, Chapter 5, 'The National Type' (White 63-84).

its direction. When Races migrate, taking their culture with them, to
a new Place, the culture becomes modified. It is the spirit of a Place
which ultimately gives any human culture its distinctiveness. (206)

The tincture of fascism is not incidental and would strengthen over the coming years as Stephensen went on to found the Australia-First Movement—which both Mudie and Ingamells were foolish, rather than naïve, enough to join. The Jindies were not fascists; but neither did they fully comprehend the extent to which their nationalism shared the soapbox with a less liberal, explicitly racist version. Even so, they were not interested in Indigenous culture for what it had to reveal about Aborigines themselves—about a truly *other* way of being in the land, that is—but as a set of environmental markers, signs of 'Place' that would define their own 'Race'. White poets would rekindle a vision of the spirit of country, of Alcheringa, while singing sad songs above the grave of black consciousness. It was through Jindyworobak that non-Indigenous people would come to live harmoniously with their Australian environment, drawing upon the site magic of the 'dead tribes'. Their disappearance through conquest represented a lost Eden or Golden Age, whose partial recovery in the realm of art was to be the guiding hope of a radically new, and specifically white, local culture.

Numerous examples of what might be called 'white tribalism' among Jindyworobak poems can be cited, but the following passage from 'Sons', the fourth and final section of Mudie's patriotic sequence, 'The Australian Dream', presents this idea at full strength. Significantly, the poem won the 1944 W.J. Miles Memorial Competition, named in honour of Stephensen's patron and fellow pro-fascist. The poet imagines allegorical 'sons aris[ing] ... as in dream-time/dark half-gods walked the earth':

> They shall bullock their hearts free from all loves
> that mar their one great love for this their land;
> they shall scour their tongues free from all trace
> of mincing snobbery; they shall guard the earth;
> they shall give to all men property and pride;

> they shall retell the tales of vanished tribes;
> they soon shall wake us to our continent.
> Firesticks of their minds will soon relight
> the scattered camp-fires of Australia's dream;
> spears of their making will defeat all those,
> trapped in a net of treachery's design,
> who'd sell our birthright for a foreign smile;
> strength of their magic will remould each mile
> of earth and life to the Australian way.
> (*Poems*, 94-95)

For the key Jindyworobaks the poetry of Place became, necessarily, the poetry of Race. In *Conditional Culture* Ingamells was strident on this theme: 'I cannot deplore too vehemently the dangerous habit of using figures of speech with regard to essentially Australian things which call up such a flood of Old World associations as to gloze over all distinctiveness' (252). The extract from 'The Australian Dream' ticks all the right boxes: *bullock* repurposed as a pioneering verb; implied contempt for the British class system ('mincing snobbery'); bush socialism ('they shall give to all men property and pride'); reverent mention of the always-assumed-to-be 'vanished tribes', along with poetic appropriation of their firesticks and spears. Ingram offers a useful insight here:

> White Australians ... seek a cultural, national identity not because they reject the one they already have but because they feel that white Australia has not yet arrived at a definition of itself. By creating a racialized identity, then, white Australians are able to assert their difference from England, which, to many settlers, is less a benign Motherland than the source and site of their own oppression as 'colonials'. (162)

The sense that 'Australia has not yet arrived' is apparent in the title and argument of Ingamells's *Conditional Culture*. For poetry, like war, can be the continuation of politics by other means. In his polemical 'The Gangrened People' (1941), he declared:

> Australia is a land that has no people,
> for those that were hers we have torn away,
> we who are not hers nor can be till love
> shall make us so and fill our hearts with her ...
> Australia waits a race whose active bone
> will mutter the white light of her limestone rocks,
> whose blood will riot with the unreserved
> rage of the red light of her sandstone ridges,
> whose minds will know the cleansing strong communion
> of midday hush, of tree-entangled stars,
> of raucous cries on dimming lakes at evening
> and all her timeless mystery of dreams.
> (*Selected Poems*, 32)

Critics such as Bruce Clunies Ross are correct in stressing that the Jindies were not only interested in Aboriginal Australia; instead, their vision 'was offered as a truer and more comprehensive account of the Australian experience, which included the legends associated with white settlement, but placed them in a broader context which revealed their ambivalence' (Clunies Ross 61). Still, Indigenous culture remained the touchstone, and not only as an unequivocal sign of national difference. Beneath the skin of their white tribalism the Jindyworobaks were also moderns and, in the main, metropolitan poets. That their nationalism embraced primitivist elements is a product of their broader context as early twentieth-century Westerners as much as their status as provincial postcolonials. Primitivism was popular across a range of high, middle and lowbrow texts: from D.H. Lawrence's *The Plumed Serpent*, to *White Cargo* (Leon Gordon's sensational play, later a film, about miscegenation), to the *Tarzan* films starring Johnny Weissmuller. T.S. Eliot had read Spencer and Gillen, and Caroline Patey has persuasively argued that the desert imagery in *The Waste Land* was strongly influenced by their descriptions of Central Australia.[6] As Torgovnick observes:

---

[6] 'T.S. Eliot was clearly closely acquainted with ... *The Native Tribes of Central Australia* (1899) and *The Northern Tribes of Central Australia* (1904), two books since hailed as anthropological eye- and door-openers' (Patey 166).

> the creation of specific versions of the primitive often depends on and is conditioned by a sense of disgust or frustration with Western values. The primitive becomes a convenient locale for the exploration of Western dullness or degeneracy, and of ways to transcend it, and thus functions as a symbolic entity. (*Gone Primitive*, 153)

Western civilisation was in a state of almost perpetual crisis after World War I. The Great Depression was swiftly followed by the rise of fascism and a growing sense that another international war was inevitable. When, in 1941, the Augustan A.D. Hope nicknamed the Jindyworobaks 'the Boy Scout School of Poetry', did he not remember his own 1939 poem, 'Australia', where, in a classic primitivist gesture, he appealed for a 'savage and scarlet' spirit to emerge from the outback as an answer to 'the chatter of cultured apes/Which is called civilisation *over there*' (54, added emphasis)?

Jindyworobak investments in Aboriginal culture should thus be seen as responding to a general and global, as well as a particular and national, sense of crisis. Here, for example, is Ian Mudie's 'Roaring 'Forties' from his first collection, *Corroboree to the Sun* (1940):

> No longer Wahn, the crow, may keep her captive,
> no longer may he drive her back,
> back to the hollow log of prison.
> No more will her wild liberty be short,
> no more the hurricane she makes
> be brief as a child's fury.
> Gheeger-Gheeger, the hurricane, is upon us;
> the hollow log where she was captive,
> the hollow prison log, is rotted;
> she is free to devastate the world.
>
> May Yarrageh and Doura-Doura, winds that woo
> the trees and thrust new growth upon them,
> may the winds of awakening
> blow on us soon.
> (*Poems*, 24)

This is an Indigenised version of Shelley's world-shaking West Wind, here upgraded to a hurricane which, given the time of writing, represents the beginning of World War II. Mudie's Indigenous references are from the Noongahburrah of northern New South Wales, derived from the writings of K. Langloh Parker, in particular her story 'Gheeger Gheeger the Cold West Wind' in *More Australian Legendary Tales* (1898). (There's an Adelaide connection, for Parker later remarried and lived there.) In his poems written during the war, Mudie was given to calling upon natural forces to bring about apocalyptic change, but here they are explicitly evoked as Aboriginal spirits that bring about both destruction and regrowth. The poet ends by praying that Yarrageh and Doura-Doura—the easterly and northerly winds, respectively—bring an 'awakening' to Australian society as well as to nature.

Torgovnick emphasises that 'primitivism refers not just to an interest in or borrowing from indigenous groups' but 'inhabits thinking about origins and pure states'. She goes on to assert that 'the primitive is the sign and symbol of desires the West has sought to repress—desires for direct correspondences between bodies and things, direct correspondences between experience and language, direct correspondences between individuals and the collective life force' (*Primitive Passions*, 5, 8). This amplifies the special place of Aborigines within the Jindyworobak project. More potent than just a cultural annexing or joining for the purposes of spiritually awakening the nation-state of Australia, Indigenous culture offered a solution to the wider problem of modernity itself. As Tim Armstrong puts it, 'If civilization is identified with mechanisms of censorship and with debilities associated with distance from the "natural" order, then primitivism ostensibly offers a route back to the "original" and whole self' (140).

This urge is at the heart of Ingamells's concern with environmental values because, in a common primitivist move, it unproblematically conflates the Indigenous with the natural. It is refracted through romantic animism in the following passage from 'The Gangrened People':

> Sun and rock, relay me power ...
> nebulae, instruct my seeing ...
> bird and beast and tree and flower,
> grant me your brotherhood of being ...
> I am to you ambassador
> to keep the faith of vanished men.
>
> The Stone Age man in us has watched his fire
> die as the cruel heaven of desire.
> (*Selected Poems*, 31)

Ingamells invokes what Romain Rolland famously called the 'oceanic feeling'—and what Torgovnick describes as 'the idea of merging', of 'dissolved boundaries between people and things' (*Primitive Passions*, 13)—right in the middle of an intensely political poem. The desire for 'the "original" and whole self' is there too in the conclusion to Mudie's 'Corroboree to the Sun' (1940), where cleansing fire takes the place of wind:

> Let us, oh sun, take fire
> from your bright heat, let bushfires rage
> about the scrub and ranges of our hearts;
> let all the dross be burned, and, as the wattle seeds
> that crack and sprout not till a fire has passed,
> let then our hearts, our minds, burgeon at last
> in growth too strong for little minds
> and little men ever to cramp again.
> (*Poems*, 12)

Both Ingamells and Mudie had political investments and thought that poetry might bring about profound cultural change. Yet, when this finds expression in a primitivist return to an Indigenous primal state, the effect can also be narrowly existential rather than social or communal. This is another reason why the Jindyworobaks had no practical interest in the welfare of Aboriginal people. It was not only that they thought—like so many of their fellow Australians—that Aborigines were, in Ingamells's phrase, 'vanished men', a dying race. It is because they felt, *as modernists*, that they already possessed the psychic resources they hoped to exploit: it was just a matter of adjusting the mind to enchantment and getting the magic words right. In fact, it was a trick that could be performed without any reference to Aborigines at all. In 'Nostalgia' (1949), Flexmore Hudson possessed the spiritual reserves to be in two places at once, both Melbourne *and* the outback:

> I caught my tram and took my seat
> in Swanston Street, in Swanston Street,
> and I was then a water-hole
> staring at a sorrel foal
> and two galahs, with wings full spread,
> on a red-gum branch above his head.
>
> At Prince's Bridge, at Prince's Bridge,
> I had become a quartzy ridge
> watching the sheep on a plain below,
> purple sheep in the afterglow,
> and horses racing to drink at a trough
> and frightening gusts of magpies off ... (23)

The title of Roland Robinson's 1962 collection, *Deep Well*, says it all, being a place both in the outback and in the mind—if not the mind itself. Robinson wrote poems that feature Indigenous people and, in *Altjeringa* (1970), would go on to make respectful verse translations of legendary stories told to him by Aboriginal informants. Nevertheless, in his most mystically-charged lyrics, he followed more conventional Jindyworobak practice, in which Aborigines remain an absent presence. Here is 'Dark Ridge', first published in the *Bulletin* in 1953:

> Clench, verse, that image, clear
> against death-wounded day:
> ridge with spear and spear
> in sudden, grim array.

> Call across that sky's
> wound the barbed spear-flight
> of swans whose urgent cries
> reach caverns of the night.
>
> Your demon there define,
> who, for an instant on
> that final dark skyline
> stands, burdened, then is gone.
>
> Clench, verse, that image yet:
> the journeying birds and man,
> grim ridge in silhouette
> since the world began.
> (*Deep Well*, 32)

Apostrophising his own act of writing, Robinson urges it to hold 'clear' the image of flocks of swans in flight, because behind it stands the haunting shape of an Aboriginal warrior, briefly glimpsed in the outline of a ridge, whose 'spears' they are. Yet the effect of this revenant figure is not exactly uncanny, perhaps because his appearance is too stage-managed within the poem's tight verse-structure and self-referentiality, or perhaps because he is insufficiently *other*, being '*Your* demon there', and so a ghostly version of the poet's own imagined natural, indeed poetic self—his *daemon*—at one with the landscape. Yet, to reprise a phrase of Ingamells, it is a 'Fearful affinity' that the speaker feels with this figure. Because of these 'spears' the day is now 'death-wounded', returning the world to 'grim' and primal darkness. The natural man is not, it seems, inevitably benign. As Robinson concluded in 'Mopoke' from *Altjeringa*,

> Where does imagination start
> but from primeval images
> in man's barbaric heart? (72)

The ultimate irony of all primitivism is that there's nothing 'primitive' about it, if by that term we refer to ancient or traditional human societies. The 'primitive' in primitivism is a largely modern invention, and it empties its object at the very moment of invoking it. The effect on the Jindyworobaks' nationalist agenda was effectively to disarm it, as issues of what was truly, deeply Australian became inexorably merged with broader questions of modernity itself. Though white ventriloquism of Aboriginality continues, the Jindies were themselves short-lived, their unifying energies having dissipated several years before the movement's annual *Anthology* ceased in 1953. By then, 'environmental values' had dispersed into the wider pastoralism of Australian verse in that period. Which is not to say that some of their core obsessions failed to survive into their later careers, as Robinson's example clearly shows.

White tribalism remained a theme for Ian Mudie, most conspicuously in his humorous crowd-pleaser, 'They'll Tell You About Me' (1952). This is a poem that self-consciously constructs itself from fragments of other texts—it 'samples' them—as a kind of national collage. As a compendium of myths, folk tales and well-known historical incidents we are, as good Australians, meant to understand every reference as part of our cultural heritage and so share in the communal joke about one man, the speaker, who is somehow all, a sort of Everyman:

> If you'd like to know more of me
> inquire at the pub at Tennant Creek
> or at any drover's camp
> or shearing-shed,
> or shout any bloke in any bar a drink,
> or yarn to any bloke asleep on any beach;
> they'll tell you about me,
> they'll tell you more than I know myself.
> After all, they were the ones that created me,
> even though I'm bigger than any of them now
> — in fact, I'm all of them rolled into one.
> (*Selected Poems*, 33-4)

Despite its stated inclusiveness, the poem contains no Aborigines, virtually no women, and only the German explorer Ludwig Leichhardt to represent non-Anglos. Mudie's composite Australian is a slightly more progressive version of the white frontiersman, and for well over a century there has been a place marked out for this figure in our culture. The tone throughout is therefore comic, a yarning 'tall story'. But I have always been puzzled by its ending, which is paranoid and defensive:

> For anyone to kill me he'd have to kill
> every single Australian,
> every single one of them,
> every single one. (34)

What anxiety feeds this implied fear of genocide? What, or who, was the assumed threat in 1952? Communism? Or it is rather that the history embodied in the poem silently recalls another 'vanished' people, a people that the poem itself—and Jindyworobakism in general—is content to make disappear?

When not booming his hopes for national greatness, in his early poetry Mudie would entertain the prospect of the extinction of white civilisation in Australia, as in 'Urgent is the Need' (1943):

> Urgent is the need before destruction
> envelops our listless minds,
> urgent is the need for building
> here this permanent dream,
> this oneness with environment,
> this people-spirit,
> this spirit of the Land,
> this permanent idea
> fused to a permanence
> of nationhood.
> (*Poems*, 66)

Without the didacticism, this anxiety later finds an objective correlative in the colonial ruins of 'Sitting Room, Strzelecki Homestead' (1954):

> When [the house] was closed the sand crept to the windows,
> leant its shoulder against the glass,

> crashed through, and trickled slowly in
> upon the carpet (bought for a city bride)
> until the pattern was hidden, and the chairs
> were set paddling in its sterile anonymity,
> and muted were the sounds of the feet
> of the ghosts that once laughed there,
> mated on the other side of the wall,
> planned vast flocks, with fruit trees
> near the bore, and vegetables beside the overflow.
> (*Selected Poems*, 38)

As a memorial to colonial hubris, with its concluding picture of 'the iron pyramid of roof/still protruding from the hand-smooth sandhill', the poem could almost be an Australian 'Ozymandias'. Given the apocalyptic strain in Mudie's earlier work, it might also be read as another kind of premature elegy, this time for white Australia. Which is why the poet expresses such fearful affinity with the site. Drowned in a sea of sand, the old house—'the last homestead/to hold men's voices along the Strzelecki Track'—echoes Ingamells's vision in 'From a High Hill-Road' of settler culture being swept away by an atavistic 'shadow-sea'. But this is no poetic wish-fulfilment, as the last lines of the poem offer a bitter allegory:

> where once dreams saw great flocks grazing,
> ... now the only living moving objects
> are the fluid mirage, the flowing, blowing sand,
> and a sad and stunted rabbit racing to nowhere,
> pursued into the mirage by a dingo shadow. (39)

Pastoral dreams of settlement, of fixity, have been supplanted by 'the *fluid* mirage', into which runs a feral rabbit—a rabbit of whiteness, if not a white rabbit—pursued by the Indigenous threat of 'a dingo shadow'. Note, though: a dingo *shadow* rather than a flesh-and-blood dingo. Unable or unwilling to engage with Aborigines as a living culture, too often the Jindyworobaks themselves started at primitivist shadows on a race to nowhere.

Works Cited

Armstrong, Tim. *Modernism: A Cultural History*. Cambridge: Polity Press, 2005.

Barkan, Elazar and Ronald Bush. 'Introduction'. *Prehistories of the Future: The Primitivist Project and the Culture of Modernism*. Ed. Elazar Barkan and Ronald Bush. Stanford: Stanford University Press, 1995. 1-19.

Catalano, Gary. 'James Devaney'. *Quadrant* 45.9 (2001): 66-9.

Clunies Ross, Bruce. 'Survival of the Jindyworobaks'. *Kunapipi* 31.1 (1981): 56-63.

Dally, John. 'The Quest for the Jindyworobaks'. *Meanjin* 39.3 (1980): 399-405.

Elliott, Brian. 'Introduction'. *The Jindyworobaks*. Ed. Brian Elliott. St Lucia: University of Queensland Press, 1979. xvii-lxvi.

Harris, Max. 'Dance Little Wombat'. *Meanjin* 2.2 (1943): 33-5.

Hodge, Bob and Vijay Mishra. *Dark Side of the Dream: Australian Literature and the Postcolonial Mind*. North Sydney: Allen & Unwin, 1991.

Hope, A.D. 'Australia'. *A.D. Hope: Selected Poetry and Prose*. Ed. David Brooks. Rushcutters Bay: Halstead, 2000. 54.

Hudson, W. Flexmore. 'Nostalgia'. *Jindyworobak Anthology: 1949*. Ed. R.G. Howarth. Adelaide: F.W. Preece, 1949. 23.

Ingamells, Rex. *Conditional Culture*. 1938. *The Writer in Australia: A Collection of Literary Documents 1856-1964*. Ed. John Barnes. Melbourne: Oxford University Press, 1969. 245-65.

___. *Forgotten People*. Adelaide: F.W. Preece & Sons, 1936.

___. 'Introduction'. *Jindyworobak Review: 1938-1948*. Melbourne:

Jindyworobak, 1948. 9-29.

___. *Selected Poems*. Melbourne: Georgian House, 1944.

___. *Sun-Freedom*. Adelaide: F.W. Preece, 1938.

Ingram, Penelope. 'Racializing Babylon: Settler Whiteness and the "New Racism"'. *New Literary History* 32.1 (2001): 157-76.

Moreton-Robinson, Aileen. 'Whiteness, Epistemology and Indigenous Representation'. *Whitening Race*. Ed. Aileen Moreton-Robinson. Canberra: Aboriginal Studies Press, 2004. 75-88.

Mudie, Ian. *Poems: 1934-1944*. Melbourne: Georgian House, 1945.

___. *Selected Poems: 1934-1974*. West Melbourne: Thomas Nelson, 1976.

Parker, K. Langloh. 'Gheeger Gheeger the Cold West Wind'. 1898. *Australian Legendary Tales*. London: Bodley Head, 1978. 121-3.

Patey, Caroline. 'Whose Tradition? T.S. Eliot and the Text of Anthropology'. *T.S. Eliot and the Concept of Tradition*. Ed. Giovanni Cianci and Jason Harding. Cambridge: Cambridge University Press, 2007. 161-73.

Robinson, Roland. *Altjeringa: and Other Aboriginal Poems*. Artarmon: A.H. & A.W. Reed, 1970.

___. *Deep Well*. Sydney: Edwards & Shaw, 1962.

Sellick, Robert. 'The Jindyworobaks and Aboriginality'. *Southwords: Essays on South Australian Writing*. Ed. Philip Butterss. Kent Town, SA: Wakefield Press, 1995. 102-15.

Stephensen, P.R. *The Foundations of Culture in Australia: An Essay Towards National Self-Respect*. 1935. *The Writer in Australia: Collection of Literary Documents 1856-1964*. Ed. John Barnes. Melbourne: Oxford University Press, 1969. 204-44.

Torgovnick, Marianna. *Gone Primitive: Savage Intellects, Modern Lives*. Chicago: University of Chicago Press, 1990.

___. *Primitive Passions: Men, Women and the Quest for Ecstasy*. Chicago: University of Chicago Press, 1997.

White, Richard. *Inventing Australia: Images and Identity 1688-1980*. St Leonards, Vic.: Allen & Unwin, 1981.

8 The Athens of the South

Alison Broinowski

'One is inclined', Patrick White once wrote to his publisher in England, and by 'one' he meant himself, 'to think of the Adelaideans as being advanced because of a handful of progressive individuals one knows.' Among the 1960s progressives he had in mind were Harry Medlin and Max Harris, and Geoffrey Dutton who had been carving a niche for Australian literature in the University of Adelaide's English Department. These Adelaide rebels, realising early what White had to offer, faced down conservative resistance to *The Ham Funeral*, *The Season at Sarsaparilla*, and *Night on Bald Mountain*, and got them successively premiered there in 1961, 1962 and 1964. Thus White, who would come to represent Australian literature to the world, appropriately took centre stage at the Union Theatre in the University of Adelaide, not in one of the venues of the Adelaide Festival, which had rejected him. Later, in a more favourable climate of opinion, Jim Sharman commissioned *Signal Driver* for the 1982 Adelaide Festival, and included the opera *Voss* in the program as well. Premieres in Adelaide followed for two less well-known White plays, *Netherwood* in 1983 and *Shepherd on the Rocks* in 1987. White enjoyed Adelaide, not only the theatre but also the dry air that was good for his asthma, the Central Market where he could buy better wurst, cheeses, herbs, fresh fruit and vegetables than in

Sydney, and an atmosphere that he found 'peaceful and civilised' (Marr 15-17). And so it still is, even if the Union Theatre has gone, and much of the intellectual ferment that swirled around it.

But, and with White a *but* always loomed, he found Adelaide in other ways 'terribly starchy and reactionary'. It was, in the view of White's biographer David Marr, an arrogant country town run by big men, 'knighted governors — the brewers, generals, bankers and newspapermen' (Marr 13). Adelaide had prospered from tin and wheat, recovered from the Depression, enriched itself again from wool and wine, acquired a car industry and an oil refinery. These were the achievements of the 'big men' of Adelaide, and the current generation, White's antagonists, were the beneficiaries. They sat on the board of the Adelaide Festival, in their armchairs at the Adelaide Club, in the members' stand at the Adelaide Oval, and they sat even more firmly on anything that was not in their view 'acceptable' and 'in good taste'. What White found was a divided city.

The Adelaide men sat as squarely, if not quite as permanently, as Sir Samuel Way sat then and still sits on his plinth on North Terrace. One of his most illustrious successors, John Bray, described Way, the Methodist law clerk who rose without a university degree to become Chief Justice, Lieutenant Governor, and Chancellor of the University of Adelaide, as a diligent and principled lawyer, though he was no great jurist, and unadventurous. But he was an English migrant whose commitment to Adelaide was as solid and enduring as the mansion he owned, Montefiore, overlooking the square-mile city of Light. When Beatrice Webb met him, Way seemed to her a

> grizzled, bearded little man, insignificant in features, voluble and diffusive in speech, with more authority than dignity in his manner; he neither pleases nor impresses ... At first he seems a fussy little Methodist ... [But] presently you discover that he is both good and wise. With intimacy one learns to appreciate his wide experience of men and things, his large-minded cultivation and above all his

continuous application in advancing what he believes to be right'.
(Bray)

What Bray and Webb both recognised in Way was an Adelaide man, complacent and self-satisfied, but always hard-working and imbued with a social conscience, a salt-of-the-earth citizen, a Freemason, who sought to improve services for orphans, destitute boys and unmarried mothers, united three factions of quarrelling Methodists, and brought a commonsense approach to the law. After Federation, Way was as concerned to preserve appeals to the Privy Council as he was mistrustful of Australia's newfangled High Court. He had a house overlooking Port Noarlunga to the south of Adelaide, he introduced Shropshire sheep to the colony, and he farmed them at Kadlunga. Propriety was bred in him, and proprietorship too. Way was well-read: he left his vast library to the University and his letter-books to the Mortlock Library of South Australiana. Having introduced full wigs and scarlet robes to the Supreme Court, and worn them on formal occasions at the University, Way might not have been pleased to know that in the 1950s law students would install a chamber pot on the plinth under his stone armchair, or that engineering students would contrive to elevate a toilet bowl to the top of the Scots church spire opposite. But he as their Chancellor and Chief Justice would probably have approved when eventually another statuesque chair would be erected on North Terrace (of more modest proportions than his) and that its occupant would be Roma Mitchell, the State's first female silk.

Such an Adelaide man might well have been familiar with arrangements in Athens in the fifth century BCE (though Way would certainly have called it BC) and would have approved of them. Under Pericles's enlightened leadership, unprecedented innovations occurred, the elite lived modestly and a majority of Athenians owned their own land, the people were sovereign and governed themselves by public debate, in an assembly where the word of the poor counted equally with that of the rich. Payment for jurors was introduced, men without wealth were allowed to hold public office, and public funds were spent to transform illiterate men into voting citizens. There were opportunities for aspirational men, just as there were in early Adelaide. But education was not wasted on women or slaves. Cities of Light had their limits then, as they would still have centuries later.

The Professor of Classics when I was an undergraduate at the University of Adelaide was John Trevaskis, an enthusiast for his subject who, like Samuel Way, had come from England and would spend the rest of his life in Adelaide. His untimely death occurred before he could finish his life's work on Athens under Pericles. In Athens between about 480 and 400 BCE, the plays of Aeschylus, Sophocles, Euripides and Aristophanes were performed; Herodotus and Thucydides wrote their histories; Sophocles and Hippocrates laid the foundations of modern philosophy and medicine; and Phidias led the way for many sculptors and architects. The brilliance of this city-state, the birthplace of democracy, was what the enthusiasts had in mind when they daringly called Adelaide the Athens of the South. Like Trevaskis, Bray, who was a classicist and poet, as well as a leading jurist and Way's biographer, appreciated the cultural flowering that established Athens as the leading *polis* of the fifth century Mediterranean world. Quite different to Way the staunch Methodist, these too were Adelaide men, who also contributed to creating something like Athens in Adelaide. Thanks to the musician John Bishop, the littérateur Geoffrey Dutton, and their friends, Adelaide was the first Australian city to have a writers week, and a biennial arts festival; Adelaide's restaurateurs claimed to have invented fusion food, and wine bars that were civilised places; good design stores flourished; in due course Adelaide acquired a gay Premier.

Adelaide people never fail to remind others that South Australia was not a convict colony but a free enterprise settlement, founded by the austere, principled men whose names—Gouger, Pirie, Hutt, Wakefield, Currie, Hindley, Hindmarsh—identify the streets and squares of the square mile city of Light, many of its protestant churches too, and even the suburb of Wayville. Torrens gave his name not only to the little, dammed-up river, but to a land title system that set the world standard. Religious non-conformists fled Germany in the nineteenth century and, being used to inland settlements, they built and gave their names to neat Lutheran towns like Hahndorf in the hills and Seppeltsfield in the Barossa Valley, dug their cellars and planted their vines. Italians and Greeks followed, showing Adelaide what could really be done with produce in a Mediterranean climate.

People from many other countries have continued to enrich the mix, although you wouldn't necessarily know that from the look of much of the tourist publicity, nor indeed from Adelaide's literature. The conventional narratives about Adelaide tell barely the half of the story. The creative potential of the place is immense. What about a play about the inner workings of a bikie gang? Why not a doco about poaching abalone on Yorke Peninsula? Or stories about what's buried beneath all those derelict stone chimneys in the Clare Valley and who built them? Is it too late for some memoirs of the wartime detention camps for Japanese, Germans and Italians at Loveday? One of the few writers of fiction to capture the look and feel of today's Adelaide is Patrick Allington. Not only does his novel about Cambodia, *Figurehead* (2009), include a compellingly visualised Australian rules football game between Port and Norwood, but it also has this description of the Cabbage and Slug, 'a traditional English theme pub' in an alley off North Terrace:

> [It had] imitation wood paneling, plush red carpet designed to hide ale stains and the blood of soccer hooligans, a framed copy of an eighteenth-century map of Lincolnshire, a red telephone box complete with an 'Out of Order' sign, and a portrait of W.G. Grace above the fake fireplace. (Allington 188-9)

It's hardly tasteful but it's not threatening either. You can almost *smell* the Cabbage and Slug. Even though the decor is so fake, its genuineness stands out like a beacon in comparison to the duplicitous murk of Pol

Pot's regime and the post-war Vietnam from which Ted Whittlemore, Allington's clapped-out journo in the novel, who has spent his career habitually patting the wrong underdog, returns unwillingly to Adelaide. For Ted, viewing Kensington's straight, manicured, suburban streets, Adelaide in 1992 is relentlessly quiet and 'about as far from the action as he could imagine'. And that's before he reaches the Concertina Rest Home (Allington 169). Yet Ted leaves you in no doubt: he is quintessentially an Adelaide man.

At intervals in Adelaide from the earliest times, propriety and comfortable conformity have collided with the disturbing and strange. When William Lane founded the New Australia movement in Brisbane in 1892, one of his first stops for recruiting colonists was in Adelaide. Already disillusioned with the sixty-year-old colony they had, off they sailed to Paraguay, hoping to found another workingman's paradise. They pursued six principles: common-hold (a Lane invention that was anti-commonwealth), brotherhood [sic] of English-speaking white people, life-long marriage, teetotalism, and adherence to what Lane called the 'colour-line' and 'communism'. Not surprisingly, the settlement soon split between those who subscribed to Lane's abstentionist, racist, discriminatory rules and those whose preferred paradise was somewhat more earthly.

No sooner had the New Australia defectors left than another challenge roused the Adelaide men to defend their principles and practices. The suffragist movement of the late nineteenth century had spread from England, Scotland, Ireland and the United States to Australia, where Louisa Lawson, Catherine Helen Spence and Vida Goldstein became household names in calling for votes for women. Less widely known were the Adelaide sisterhood, including Mary Lee, Rosetta Birks and Mary Colton. From its foundation in 1876 the University of Adelaide had taken women students, and women were admitted to degrees from 1880, although concern persisted about female medical students observing dissections. Faced with conservative male opinion, particularly in the upper house of parliament, it was not until December 1894 after a late-night debate about votes for women that South Australians joined their enfranchised sisters in New Zealand and two US States. As well, to their own surprise, they became the first women in the world to be permitted to sit in Parliament (Jones). Until 1901, those rights extended to South Australian Indigenous women too. Among the women's male supporters were familiar Adelaide names, the big men of their day, Stirling, Downer, Kingston, Playford and Magarey.

I was reminded of the conflicted Adelaide character, and how big men take positions on both sides, when I found a framed document on the wall of an ex-South Australian friend, bearing his grandfather's signature, together with those of the heads of all the churches in Australia and of the Chief Justices of all the States. It was dated 11 November 1951, Remembrance Day, and was headed 'A Call to the People of Australia'. The worthy gentlemen signatories declared at the beginning, 'Australia is in danger, abroad and at home'. Abroad at that time, we were loyally following our allies into the Korean War, so that was presumably the external danger they meant: but at home, they warned, we were also threatened, by moral and intellectual apathy. Citizens had a duty, they said, to take an active interest in public affairs and defend the community against 'evil designs' that were not specified, but that appeared to imply communism. The big men called sternly for 'community of thought and purpose' and 'restoration of the moral order'. They also mentioned 'mind and muscle', which seemed to envisage the bosses like them, and the workers, engaged in a joint effort against a common, nameless, present danger. Pericles, it occurred to me, would have been proud to send such a rousing statement to all the male citizens of Athens, if he'd had the ABC to broadcast it.

The Call's concluding line resonated: FEAR GOD, HONOUR THE KING. The moving force behind that injunction, and the whole document, was Sir Edmund Herring, a Victorian Rhodes Scholar, lawyer and distinguished soldier in two world wars, who, like Samuel Way, had become Lieutenant Governor and Chief Justice in his home State. In the inter-war years, Herring had also been a Commander in the White Guard, a shadowy organisation of ex-service vigilantes committed if the need arose to act in defence of Australia against communist subversion. It famously appeared in *Kangaroo* (1923) where D.H. Lawrence renamed it the 'Diggers' Club'. In 1953, long after his White Guard days but fresh from broadcasting the Call and still going strong, General Herring led an Australian contingent to Queen Elizabeth's coronation.

The New Elizabethan 1950s have retrospectively been regarded by some as Australia's golden age and by others as a near-death experience. People deemed to be incapable of assimilation were still unable to enter the country and so were certain ideas. In those slow, starchy days, specified words could be prevented from reaching people whom the authorities (policemen, particularly) deemed would be offended or corrupted by them. Robert Close and Georgian House had been prosecuted when *Love Me Sailor*, published in 1945, was found to contain 'obscene libel'. Close served 10 days of his three-month sentence, left Australia and didn't return for 25 years. In stitched-up 1950s Australia, Florence James and Dymphna Cusack had to expurgate *Come in Spinner* before it could be published. In two Australian States, actors in *Norm and Ahmed* (1968) were prosecuted for uttering *fuck* on stage. *Lady Chatterley's Lover* was banned for what was then called explicit language, and, later, the same fate befell *Tropic of Cancer*, *Tropic of Capricorn*, *Portnoy's Complaint* and *Lolita*. Official South Australia was not alone in its moral outrage, and in this as in so much else, it was faithfully following the British standard of respectability. Philip Larkin later described the period poetically:

> Sexual intercourse began
> In nineteen sixty-three
> (Which was rather late for me) —
> Between the end of the *Chatterley* ban
> And the Beatles' first L.P.
> (Larkin)

In the 1950s and early 1960s, Adelaide's then only university taught neither Asian Studies, Asian languages nor Creative Writing, all the things I wanted to know about. The very existence of Australian literature had been doubted by the British Professor J.I.M. Stewart, when he lectured instead on *Kangaroo* at the University of Adelaide in 1940. In my day, the Vice Chancellor was British, and so were all but one of my professors and most of my lecturers. They taught in gowns, and addressed young women as 'Miss' and young men by their surnames. We responded with 'Professor' and 'Doctor'. Weekly Latin tutorials, one on one with Professor Trevaskis, were character-building ordeals of the intellect. A Scottish professor, who taught philosophy in cricket flannels, took delight in fixing his sceptical eye on the nuns in the class and deconstructing (as we did not then say) the case for miracles and the existence of God. The best of them were awe-inspiring teachers, and so wrapped in their specialisation that they seemed unable to imagine any other life. When some of us wondered what we should do with our Arts degrees, their response was, in effect: why do you ask? You do Arts for Arts' sake.

A solitary non-Anglo lecturer delivered a course entirely in French called *Civilisation*. He took us on a rapid tour de France, beginning with painted caves, glancing in passing at Gothic cathedrals, racing on to neoclassical theatre, through Revolutionary fashion and philosophy, slowing the pace to appreciate the nineteenth century efflorescence of music, opera, architecture and science, and giving us the rounds of cuisine as well. The peloton sprinted on, descending through art that Said had not then branded Orientalist and authors whom Barthes had not yet declared dead, down Haussmann's wide avenue to a glorious finish line.

That was the gown side of North Terrace. Similarly on the town side, Adelaide's standards were largely imported from England, as were the manners and the accents of its aspirational citizens. Our passports stated we were British subjects. For all of our young lives, we had been ruled by Robert Menzies (later Sir Robert, who gave us Commonwealth scholarships, and wanted decimal currency to be called the 'Royal'), and by Premier Tom Playford (later Sir Thomas, who built Elizabeth, gave us Holdens and the River Murray pipeline), though Don Dunstan's star was rising. News Limited published a mere local tabloid. Max Harris, cultivating modernism in *Angry Penguins*, was hoaxed for it by two reactionary poets. Geoffrey Dutton, bringing republican ideas back from Kansas, and courting Russian writers, was expelled from the Adelaide Club. The locals, patriotically flushed by the coronation and a succession of royal visits, called this the New Elizabethan Era. The monarchical mindset has not died: in 2012 Murdoch's *Australian* loyally hailed the Queen's sixtieth year as Australia's Head of State with an editorial headed 'Second Elizabethan age adapted to the modern era' (*Australian*, 4 June 2012, 15).

Ladies of Adelaide, mimicking the Queen, wore hats and gloves and were barred from most professions. When women worked, they got 20 per cent less pay and were usually sacked or made 'temporary' on marriage. Roma Mitchell, who graduated before my time, was not admitted to Law dinners and had to stand behind a curtain to listen to the speeches. When she became a QC, and was refused a bank loan, she bought her first house with cash (Magarey). Respectability was pasted over sex, religion and politics like a fig leaf. Divorce and illegitimacy were socially disgraceful, private detectives lurked with cameras, and erring spouses were penalised in the courts. Still to arrive on the scene were Anne Summers and Robyn Archer, 'free love', the Pill, and Rhodes scholarships for women, let alone gay pride and AIDS.

We Arts students had heard of Simone de Beauvoir but not yet of Betty Friedan or Germaine Greer. We could quote Ovid and Montaigne but had yet to read all of Patrick White; we were more familiar with Freudian psychoanalysis, French existentialism and *Animal Farm* than with the Australian Libertarians. Rumours of an entity called the 'Sydney Push' reached Adelaide, but were typically dismissed by the Athenians of the South as what one expected of the 'Eastern States'. This was how all but a few courageous rebels fended off dangerous influences from beyond the Adelaide horizon. Being British, or at a stretch, 'Continental', was safe: for South Australians in full cringe, it helped to have achieved acceptance Overseas. Among the colony's early settlers, doughty whalers, Cornish tin miners and German sausage makers, there had been free thinkers, who had fled from other cringing societies. But many of their descendants, the parents of my generation, were ground down by two world wars and a depression, and seemed cowed by the Cold War. They aspired merely to educate their children, pay off their houses, and have one overseas trip in a lifetime. An uncle who travelled abroad more than most used complacently to reassure us, on his return, that 'Australia's the best country in the world'.

My family had Arthur Mees's children's encyclopaedia in ten volumes, which I read from cover to cover while listening to the Argonauts. It contained nothing about Australia, and I didn't know where all those Greek boats' names came from, but Mees and the ABC contributed to the mares' nest of randomly assembled ideas that were my education. My questions about what it all meant, and my search for the answer to everything, gradually subsided into accepting that both were impossible to find, though for some years I continued to search in libraries for them. In those days, Adelaide had a children's library in the old stables behind the Institute on North Terrace, which introduced many of us to the English classics, though it banned Enid Blyton and W.E. Johns. Adelaide also had excellent, independent book shops like the WEA, the Argonaut, and Mary Martin's, from which for many years Max Harris sent his booklist all over Australia and the world, and kept me supplied with books in remote places. Independent publishers existed too, like Griffin, Wakefield, and Rigby, in whose shop I had a job in university holidays selling stationery and could use my staff discount to buy the Oxford complete works of English poets, one by one. In the summer afternoons I used to retire to the hot attic above the shop and read the proofs of low-brow novels for Rigby to publish. A Croatian woman once brought in a manuscript, painfully typed in hesitant English, about the experiences that led to her joining what we now call the diaspora. I still regret deciding that it wasn't worth editing for publication, and I wonder what became of it: that was too many years before Anna Funder.

Four forces combined to crack open the carapace of literary Adelaide: the Adelaide Writers' Week, *Australian Letters*, *Australian Book Review* and the Adelaide Festival of Arts. We owe them, as Patrick White recognised, to Geoffrey Dutton, Rosemary Wighton, Max Harris, Mary Martin, John Bray, Ninette Dutton, and their friends, supporters and successors. Adelaide then felt confident to pioneer Fringe theatre in Australia, State film funding, World Music, the Ring Cycle and the Festival of Ideas. The fact that these institutions were created in Adelaide and are still with us makes the 'Athens of the South' claim sound less self-congratulatory. Adelaide still produces world-class artists in several fields, and still attracts distinguished people who become residents, like J.M. Coetzee, Brian Castro and Claire Roberts, or who return to live, like Nicholas Jose, Ivan Shearer and Robyn Archer. The Creative Writing program at the University of Adelaide owes its success to several of them. The schools are still good, pleasant houses are still affordable. Some who don't live in Adelaide continue to be drawn back to visit, and are tempted to stay.

Yet the stitched-up, xenophobic Adelaide remains a counterpoint or a reverse magnet to all that. Inward-looking smugness drives daring creativity away and resentment festers about those who leave. A city nervous about its future is tempted to invest undue optimism in schemes whose rewards may turn out to be minimal. The Monarto decentralisation project was one such example for South Australia; the Ghan railway, uranium and nuclear power, the O-Bahn, and pandas at the Adelaide Zoo are others. In the 1990s, the proposal to build a Multifunction Polis with Japanese funding and technology as a science and leisure city of the future attracted Australian enthusiasm and criticism in roughly equal measure. A vague suggestion from Japan's Ministry of International Trade and Industry in 1987 ignited a fuse that ran from State to State and through numerous committees and consultancies, ending with the Federal Government choosing a site in waste land north-west of Adelaide. This was not what the Japanese seeking a 'silver city' for retirees had in mind, and it was much too far from the Gold Coast. The result was disillusionment and bitterness all round (Mouer). A city does better by playing to its strengths, not to its dreams of avarice, and art and culture, design and creativity, education and a civilised lifestyle are among Adelaide's long-standing talents.

Adelaide's founding principles were sound, and its periods of renewal inspiring. The danger of propriety is that over time it can make people petrified of change and difference, and can petrify their ideas in stone. Festivals of Ideas notwithstanding, difference is not an easy idea to sell in Adelaide. A blog writer, Malcolm King, in December 2011 likened 'Adders' to a bee in amber, rare and beautiful, small and perfectly formed. But he observed, apparently from personal experience, that its people are still sitting in the same chairs as they were 25 years ago, running a 'closed shop' into which employers take only the people they know, suspicious of anyone new, and thus practising 'recruitment apartheid'. Even the arts, King complained, have lost their hypodermic capacity, and he accused Adelaideans of using art 'not as a vector to explain our place in the world, but as a psychological crutch to shore up dashed dreams and tattered ideals'. As the best and brightest flee, qualified people are being poached by the mining States, and net annual emigration from South Australia prevails over new arrivals. Adelaide, he concluded, is slowly dying. In support of this prediction, King cited an essay on provincialism by Pierre Ryckmans (the writer Simon Leys): 'Culture is born out of exchanges and thrives on differences. The death of culture lies in self-centredness, self-sufficiency and isolation' (King).

Athens was, of course, the birthplace of democracy, and the centre of the Mediterranean world, but as a city-state that concentrated upon itself, and deliberately sought to be sufficient unto itself, it eventually became dangerously isolated from its Delian neighbours. Freedom was for men, no one else. Athens produced dramatists and historians whom we still read, but the words of women and slaves were not deemed worth the trouble and expense of recording on papyrus or carving on stone tablets. Adelaide under Don Dunstan may have been the closest the city ever came to Athens under Pericles, the ideal Athens of the South. Even then few knew that as usual, the United States was ahead of Australia: the title had already been claimed since the 1850s by Nashville. In Adelaide today, and for that matter Nashville, literary voices of both genders and many backgrounds are no longer silenced by convention or censorship, even if writers now have to seek more innovative means of publication to get read. Both Athens and Adelaide have historically sought the freedom of the human spirit, and created civilised cities, yet citizens of both are now leaving. Athens is now struggling, and faces a worse economic future than Adelaide. If the claim about the 'Athens of the South' is to apply to Adelaide, it needs to draw on its considerable strengths for a revival of prosperity, certainly, and self-confidence, as much as modern Athens does.

WORKS CITED

Allington, Patrick. *Figurehead*. Melbourne: Black Inc., 2009.

Bray, J.J. 'Sir Samuel James Way (1836-1916)'. *Australian Dictionary of Biography*. Vol. 12. Melbourne: Melbourne University Press, 1990.

Jones, Helen. 'Votes for Women', condensed for the Women & Politics website by Dr Helen Jones from *In her own name: a history of women in South Australia*. 1986. Adelaide: Wakefield Press. Rev. edn, 1994. <http://www.slsa.sa.gov.au/womenandpolitics/vote>. Accessed 26 June 2012.

King, Malcolm. 'Adelaide — Athens of the South's long, slow decline'. *On Line Opinion*, <http.//www.onlineopinion.com.au/view.asp?article=13015>. Accessed 25 June 2012.

Larkin, Philip. 'Annus Mirabilis'. *High Windows*. London: Faber and Faber, 1974.

Magarey, Susan and Kerry Round. *Roma the First: A biography of Dame Roma Mitchell*. Kent Town, SA: Wakefield Press, 2007.

Marr, David. '"So much of our life in it", Arrogant Adelaide and the theatre of Patrick White'. *Australian Book Review* (Melbourne) 341 (May 2012): 12-17.

Mouer, Ross and Yoshio Sugimoto. *The MFP Debate: a background reader*. Melbourne: La Trobe University Press, 1990.

9 Max Harris: a Phenomenal Adelaide Literary Figure

Betty Snowden

Max Harris was an exceptional and charismatic presence both in Adelaide and beyond. His significant contribution to Australian literature included founding and co-editing several literary journals, publishing his own poetry, enthusiastically encouraging other peoples' writings, contributing in several publishing ventures, initiating bookselling strategies, warring with the publishing world, prolific journalism, and persistent confrontation with a traditionalist establishment. This chapter seeks to emphasise the significance of his long and energetic involvement in the literary life of the city and the nation.

Maxwell Henley Harris was born at Henley Beach, an Adelaide suburb, in 1921. His childhood was spent in Mount Gambier in the southeast of South Australia and in that small town he gained his greatest formative influences. His imagination was filled with a profusion of local myths and he was later instrumental in directing Melbourne artists Arthur Boyd, Sidney Nolan and Albert Tucker towards their own consciousness of an environmental mythology.

Harris won a three-year boarding scholarship to the prestigious boys' private school, St Peter's College in

Adelaide, where his first English teacher was John Padman, a critical influence. Padman recognised Harris's literary talent and took him under his wing, introducing him to modern British, US and European literature. Harris read and absorbed the work of writers such as W.H. Auden, T.S. Eliot, Graham Greene, Christopher Isherwood, Louis MacNeice, Henry Miller, George Orwell, Stephen Spender, Dylan Thomas and Virginia Woolf. Harris's publishing career began with poems in the student St Peter's College magazine, where he wrote under the pseudonym Victor (his father's name) and also H.H.M. (Maxwell Henley Harris backwards). He left school mid-year in Leaving Honours due to his father's restricted financial means, but continued his studies alone, working at the *News* by day as a cub reporter and studying in the State Library in the evenings. For his efforts he gained the Tennyson Medal for English Literature in 1938.

In 1939 he enrolled at the University of Adelaide to study Arts and Economics. There he lived life at a dizzying speed, becoming involved in everything that sparked his interest. He quickly gained notoriety as a rebel poet, critic and editor, revealing an exceptional intellect and a passionate and profound political idealism. By age 19 several of his poems had been published in literary journals, and he had won the University's Bundey Prize for Poetry.

Harris was precocious, cutting a dash in black shirt and white tie, while he held court in the university refectory with something of an Oscar Wildean affectedness. He was often hounded, criticised and humiliated for his difference. John Hetherington records:

> That period was an unprecedentedly exciting one in Adelaide's intellectual history, and Max and his friends, as champions of new concepts of thought and self-expression, were under suspicion by orthodox groups. One day, some of them including Harris, were seized by their opponents, frogmarched to the nearby Torrens River and flung into the water, clothes and all. It was not, however, a total victory for the reactionaries. Harris still remembers with pleasure

the sight of a group of his own friends hurtling towards his attackers, who were presently gasping and spluttering in the Torrens beside him. (Hetherington 216)

His writing also suffered bitter, conservative assaults: two particular instances were to have lasting effects. The first was in 1943 when he published *The Vegetative Eye*, a novel written in a surreal stream-of-consciousness manner. It was not a masterpiece; indeed, it was not easy to read. Conservative poet and academic A.D. Hope, who hated and feared modern literature, relished the opportunity to review it, using this first book from a young writer as an opportunity to deliver a venomous and scathing attack. Hope's review, entitled 'Confessions of a Zombi', was published in a 1944 issue of *Meanjin* and began:

> 'THE VEGETATIVE EYE' reminds one of a one-man band. It is a book about Mr. Max Harris, the well known Manager of the Educated Womb, written by Mr. Max Harris, published by Mr. Max Harris, and advertised with fearless praise by Mr. Max Harris in Mr. Max Harris's journal *Angry Penguins*. Nearly all the characters in the book turn out to be Mr. Max Harris, too ... It reads like a guide to all the more fashionable literary enthusiasms of the last thirty years. Mr. Harris doesn't miss a trick. ...
>
> All this suggests that the writer is in that delightful stage of adolescence at which the discovery of literature is apt to awaken in immature minds a conviction that, unless they immediately convey their discoveries to an ungrateful world, nobody will ever know that such writers as Joyce, Dostoyevsky, Baudelaire and Swift ever existed ... (Hope 44-7)

The review was so damning, and the reaction by readers so unenthusiastic, that regrettably Harris never published another novel.

The second major assault was the 1943 Ern Malley hoax. Harris always maintained his conviction of the poems' literary merit, despite the evidence that they were deliberately concocted verse. The question is: once he knew that the poems were put together for the purpose of humiliating him and decrying modern poetry, did he maintain this stance to save face or did he genuinely value the original creative poetry? He has certainly been well vindicated considering the current almost 'cult' interest in Ern Malley.

The real tragedy of Ern Malley is that we lost a fine lyric poet. Before the hoax Harris had published two poetry collections: *The Gift of Blood* in 1940 (aged 19) and *Dramas from the Sky* in 1942. Both were well received. Harris's published poetic output ceased for nine years after the event and he never regained his earlier confidence. During the rest of his life he produced only three collections, each 12 years apart, and these were published privately: *The Coorong and other poems* (1955), *A Window at Night: selected poems* (1967) and *Poetic Gems* (1979).

In the late 1930s Adelaide society was deeply conservative in its thinking about the arts, in the social behaviour it condoned, and in its politics. The Adelaide establishment ruled. Modernism had not yet reared its ugly head and the war was about to begin. Yet within the younger members of society, a group of literati with new ideas was emerging. In the realm of poetry, the Jindyworobaks began the changes. Harris became interested in the Jindyworobaks and their push to move Australian poetry from its colonial confines into a more indigenous or 'national' form, discarding British overtones. At only 17, he joined the movement with fervour. He was initially excited and stimulated, pleased that the movement had taken a step away from Australian bush ballads. Later he acknowledged that it 'had an overall significance as a coordinating and liberating factor' ('Critical Extracts', in Elliott 270).

It was the Jindyworobak Club that published Harris's *The Gift of Blood*. The book received mixed reviews. In the *Bulletin*, James Devaney singled him out: 'Max Harris is by far the most interesting of the Jindyworobaks ... his experiments are interesting ... the young Dylan Thomas is doing the same thing in England'. The comparison with Dylan Thomas would no doubt have pleased Harris immensely. Elsewhere, Devaney saw him as 'a great literary artist in the making' (*On Dit*, May

1940, 2). Another reviewer was more mixed: 'Max Harris has a strong poetic sense, a depth of feeling, and skill with words. Some of the phrases in his assorted poems are striking and original. What else there is to Max Harris as a poet cannot yet be seen — not by this reviewer, at any rate, for much of the meaning of the poems is unintelligible' ('Bodleian'). However, his poetry often aroused more criticism than it did praise. 'So young, so green, so what?' cried J. Alex Allen, while an outraged correspondent of Melbourne *Bohemia* wrote: 'Max Harris needs a sound spanking' (*On Dit*, May 1940, 2).

The poem 'Mad Jasper' from *The Gift of Blood* made such a positive impression on a fellow university student, Edgar Woods Castle, that he retained a memory of it throughout his life (Castle interview):

> mad Jasper stood poised on the skyscraper wall
> and felt this the moment to end all
> the desires he'd never get,
> to leap from his life's concrete parapet,
> He watched the silly dawn arise,
> the trams creep up the hollow hill,
> the railway's mass of glassy flies
> snouting out of the morning's chill ...
>
> In anguish mad Jasper loosened his grip
> and established one true relationship.
> ('Mad Jasper', 30)

Harris soon became dissatisfied with the Jindyworobaks, distrusting what he saw as an obsessively 'nationalist' writing. With his knowledge of British and US writers and poets, he wanted to see Australian literature move towards a more European modernism. His own poetry reflected, and was influenced by, British and American poets.

As a precocious 18-year-old, with all of youth's idealism and arrogance, Harris contributed an article to the Melbourne-based journal *Bohemia* entitled 'I am an anarchist — so what?'

> Artistically I am an anarchist. I am 18. Many people immediately put two and two together and get the inevitable 5 as result. Which is really no more than saying that it is much easier to let your prejudices blurt out the result for you and hope for the best, than test a new way of thinking, a new approach to Australian poetry ... That no poet can expect his work to live if he writes in a form which has outlived its usefulness, which is decadent and leaves people cold ... The poet must also be a craftsman before he can be a great poet ... he cannot carve a Colossus from a splinter of jarrah. ('I am an anarchist—so what?', 12)

Underlying this message is the assumption that Harris was himself already a craftsman, ready to carve his great Colossus. However, he was also attempting to say that poetry needed to change, to reinvigorate itself in a modern idiom.

Charles Rischbieth Jury and J.I.M. Stewart were English lecturers and tutors at the University of Adelaide when Harris was an undergraduate. They had both been educated at Oxford University. Jury was a classicist and poet, and Stewart wrote crime fiction in his spare time. Poet, children's writer and educator Colin Thiele remembered those days in tutorials with Harris:

> There were four of us in the English tutorial: Max, Mary Martin, myself, and another fellow ... Once every four weeks we were expected to speak for an hour about our paper. On one occasion Max spoke on Keats's letters. I will never forget it. Max gave what I believe was one of the most brilliant dissertations that I ever heard from a student. He talked about French poetry and the French Symbolists, and Dostoevsky and Yeats. I don't remember clearly enough to know how he was going to stitch this altogether and equate this to Keats's letters. The Prof. sat back under a halo of smoke from his pipe. Max finished with a brilliant peroration and then there was a great silence. Finally the Prof. came out of his halo and said: 'Most interesting paper Mr Harris. Now what about Keats's letters?' (Thiele interview)

Thiele greatly admired Harris: 'Max was quite extraordinary. His reading was phenomenal and he had an incredible memory' (Thiele interview).

ANGRY PENGUINS

The first radical literary magazine produced at the University of Adelaide was *Phoenix*, published by the Student Union from 1935 to 1939. The editorial introduction to the first issue stated: 'No need for apologies, it is time to change' (Unknown author, *Phoenix*, 3). When the printing of the 1939 issue was under threat for financial reasons, the University's Vice-Chancellor sent Sam Kerr to Jury for assistance. In an ABC radio talk that Jury gave in the 1950s entitled *Life and Letters in Adelaide* (Miles 3), he recalled:

> I thought then, and still think, that, qualitatively it was by far the best literary document produced by young students that I had— have—ever seen. It contained among other things a fair amount of early Max Harris; two of Donald Kerr's poems; and three of Paul Pfeiffer's poems ... (Miles 3)

In the preface to *Phoenix*, Jury talked of the journal's 'atmosphere of modernness that I like.' He singled out Harris's poem 'Boat-Train': 'it has rhyme, but not continuous rhyme; and reason, but its reason is not rational. It is a selective treatment of a particular stream of consciousness; and this is unified partly by means of the situation in which it occurs, and partly by a prevailing mood' (Jury, 'Preface', 15).

After the final 1939 *Phoenix*, students pushed for a replacement journal. Elliot Johnston said that 'Max and Sam Kerr were very strong and outspoken members of the Arts Faculty committee and that both had a great deal to do with the publication of the new journal' (Johnston interview). It is commonly believed that Harris founded *Angry Penguins*, but this is a myth. The truth is that after the demise of *Phoenix*, at an historic Annual General Meeting of The Adelaide University Arts Association on

7 April 1940, it was proposed that a sum of £3.3.0 be granted towards an annual literary magazine to replace *Phoenix*. An editorial committee of seven was appointed, comprising 'Messrs. D.B. Kerr & M.H. Harris as the editors, with Messrs. P.G. Pfeiffer and G. Dutton, and Misses M. Swan, A. Hogben and J. Murray as sub-editors, with Mr. Jury as patron'. This full editorial team has never been mentioned in any discussion of the journal. The men are all well-known but the women sub-editors were Hilda Mary Swan (known as 'Mollie'), Alison Hogben and Judith Murray. Mollie Swan was a poet whose poems were published in *Angry Penguins* no. 1, 1941. She had also been one of the three editors of the 1939 *Phoenix*.

The title of the new journal, suggested by Jury, was taken from a line in one of Harris's poems:

> We know no mithridatum of despair
> as drunks, the angry penguins of the night,
> straddling the cobbles of the square,
> tying a shoelace by fogged lamplight.
> ('Progress of defeat', 60)

Jury wrote about Max Harris and Paul Pfeiffer's work in a piece entitled 'Two poets'. He devoted most of the space to a detailed critical analysis of Harris's poetry, confessing to not fully understanding it but praising its originality and flashes of brilliance:

> Form and a decent degree of clarity seem to me to be the most important virtues in poetry after rhythmical and imaginative power. Max Harris has all of them by snatches, and the last two of astonishing quality; yet he cannot sustain any one of them for long at a time ... [His] sense of form is still in process of being worked out; his material, it appears, is sometimes insubordinate; his expression is often superbly assured and splendid ... His way of thought is still a mystery, one supposes in some measure even to himself. There are passages of glorious beauty scattered all through his work, side by side with the strangest crudities ... It would be misleading to call Max Harris simply a romantic, for romanticism in the narrower

sense of that work is not what he aims at. As to what he does aim at, I dare not pretend I have a satisfactory understanding of all his ideas, for he would show me up. (9-12)

The elder statesman and poet concluded: 'These remarks ... are written in acknowledgement, and as an indication that I have perceived what is happening in Adelaide, and to Adelaide' (16).

After *Angry Penguins* no. 1 was published early in 1941 (not 1940 as previously thought) the Arts Association ceased the journal's funding. Dutton, Pfeiffer and Kerr enlisted in the RAAF in 1941, and Harris continued as sole editor of issues nos 2-3, funded by subscriptions and assistance from Jury and Stewart. *Angry Penguins* no. 2, 1941, was published, but not funded, by The Adelaide University Arts Association. In the second issue Harris wrote 'We thank those people who have offered this book such violent opposition, such pitiful prejudices, that this production became imperative and therefore possible' (8).

For the third issue in 1942 Harris was again the sole editor, the journal now dissociated from The Adelaide University Arts Association. He acknowledged his chief supporter, writing 'What is of value in this magazine is dedicated to Charles Rischbieth Jury, than whom few people have done more for Australian culture' (3). He also thanked Professor J.I.M. Stewart and John Reed of the Melbourne Contemporary Arts Society who had provided financial support.

After the publication of the third issue, Reed, a solicitor and wealthy arts patron, invited Harris to Melbourne to discuss the idea of working together on *Angry Penguins* no. 4. Reed offered financial support and suggested that the journal should include a visual arts section and that he himself be the arts editor. In *Angry Penguins* no. 2 Harris had already introduced visual content with images by James Gleeson and Sidney Nolan, including the latter's famous *Woman and tree*. In *Angry Penguins* no. 3 (1942), Harris had published memorable images by Melbourne artists, Albert Tucker and Arthur Boyd, and Adelaide artists, Doug Roberts and

Dave Dallwitz. In the fourth issue (late 1942), Harris remained the 'editor and proprietor' with John Reed as collaborating arts editor. The journal was still based and published in Adelaide. Reed introduced an even larger visual component with critical art reviews, adding the works of V.G. O'Connor, Noel Counihan, Ivor Francis and Bruce Williams. Harris fully endorsed these additions that changed *Angry Penguins* 'from a literary journal to a literary and art journal proper' (*Angry Penguins* 4, 1).

Harris ran an office in Adelaide, travelling frequently to Melbourne where he joined the lively scene that centred on John and Sunday Reed at Heide. Harris's passion to publish the work of others and his own poetry continued unabated. With Reed he championed the Melbourne group of young modern artists. This group of painters later assumed the title *Angry Penguins*, eclipsing the literary association.

The two men also set up Reed & Harris, a publishing firm that operated from 1943 to 1946. Reed & Harris took over the publication of *Angry Penguins* in Melbourne for issues 5-9 from 1943 to 1946 (two issues in 1944). Other Reed & Harris titles included Peter Cowan's novel *Drift* (1944), Geoffrey Dutton's first book of poetry *Night Flight and Sunrise* (1944), psychiatrist Reg Ellery's *Eyes Left! The Soviet Union and the post-war world* (1943), Harris's *The Vegetative Eye* (1943), Cynthia Reed's *Lucky Alphonse* (1944) and Alister Kershaw's second book of poetry *Excellent Stranger* (1944). They published the Ern Malley poems: *Ern Malley: The darkening ecliptic* in 1944 and also *Angry Penguins Broadsheet* from January to December 1946.

MARY MARTIN BOOKSHOP

In 1945, one of Harris's fellow university students and close friends, Mary Martin, opened a small bookshop in the Brookman Building. Harris moved to live in Melbourne in November. The following year, knowing that Harris was tired of working for Reed and that the Ern Malley affair had dampened their spirits, and also that his wife and baby daughter were in Adelaide, Martin invited Harris to join her in running the bookshop. Harris resigned from Reed & Harris and returned to live in Adelaide in October 1946. Reed & Harris and *Angry Penguins* closed shortly afterwards. The shop was already at its third venue: a tiny place in Alma Chambers near the Stock Exchange, crammed with books and offering coffee to customers. It was a lively buzz of Adelaide literati and a place for browsing and talking about books with Harris and Martin.

Over the next four decades, with his extraordinary entrepreneurial flair and real desire to sell books, Harris expanded the shop into an Australian and Pacific mail-order business with stores in four Australian capital cities during the 1970s, and New Zealand and Hong Kong briefly in the early 1980s. The company was the first really entrepreneurial bookseller in Australia: the first to introduce remaindered books into the country, visiting British and American book publishers' warehouses to search for titles that could be sold cheaply in Australia; the first to run a mail-order service; the first to introduce quality art books into Adelaide; and the first to introduce discount sales and Sunday trading. Today Harris would have run online sales at discounted prices, with free mail service. I believe that he would even have approved of e-books, and the use of iPads and mobile phones in the cause of reading.

From 1950 to 1962, Harris wrote and printed *Mary's Own Paper*—better known as *MOP*—a monthly paper filled with news of cultural Adelaide and of new book titles. This little magazine became extremely popular not only for its information but also for Harris's witty and perceptive remarks about local cultural events and people gossip.

In 1950, concurrent with *MOP*, Harris began writing his famous monthly Mary Martin Booklist through subscription membership. This was the first mail order catalogue for a bookseller, detailing new titles with brief descriptions and offering bargain prices. It became immensely popular with subscribers throughout the country, including the far reaches of country outposts.

AUSTRALIAN LETTERS 1957-1968

In 1957, Harris founded *Australian Letters*, a literary journal providing short stories, poems and articles by Australian writers. He invited Geoffrey Dutton and Bryn Davies to be joint editors; both were English lecturers at the University of Adelaide at the time. Rosemary Wighton later joined the team. While the journal was aimed at an international readership, its content, unlike *Angry Penguins* and *Ern Malley's Journal*, was to be entirely Australian.

At the time that Harris founded his new journal there were five literary journals that had all been established during the 1940s: *Southerly*, *Meanjin*, *Overland*, *Quadrant* and *Westerly*. As of 2013, these journals are all still being published. Journals such as the Jindyworobaks *Venture*, the Melbourne *Bohemia* and Cecily Crozier's Melbourne *Comment* had disappeared by this time, along with *Angry Penguins* and *Ern Malley's Journal*.

Susan Sheridan has noted that *Australian Letters* was 'eclectic in the best sense, but not narrowly avant-garde' in the manner that *Angry Penguins* had aspired to (Sheridan 276-7). In her comprehensive discussion of *Australian Letters* and post-war modernity, Sheridan concluded that the journal 'was ahead of its times' (276-7).

In *Australian Letters* October 1960, Harris and Dutton pioneered a remarkable series of collaborations between poets and artists. Artists were commissioned to illustrate, or rather respond to, a set of poems by different poets. Harris's own contribution was six poems entitled 'The Circus and other poems', with accompanying images by Arthur Boyd. Harris had a preoccupation with death that revealed itself in many of his poems. 'Dim the Green Hope', one of the poems in this group, has a refrain 'There is no bride but death':

> Dim the green hope in your young eyes,
> For there is no bride but death. (27)

Some of the other brilliant pairings were Judith Wright/Clifton Pugh, Douglas Stewart/Donald Friend, David Campbell/Russell Drysdale, Geoffrey Dutton/Lawrence Daws, Randolph Stow/Sidney Nolan and James McAuley/Leonard French. There were altogether 18 collaborations between 1957 and 1964.

Australian Book Review 1961 to 1974

In 1961, while *Australian Letters* was still in full swing, and with Geoffrey Dutton and Rosemary Wighton, Harris founded *Australian Book Review*, another major Australian literary journal. It became the first and only Australian journal to focus entirely on a critical examination of new Australian literature. The opening editorial read:

> There is an imperative need for a publication such as 'Australian Book Review'. The Australian community is developing an eager interest in the slow but sure maturing of our national culture; and there is no lack of a potential readership for Australian books. ... Fortunately, there is no shortage of critical intellect in Australia. Amongst writers, high-level journalists, and University staff there are critical minds sufficient to sustain the highest standards in 'Australian Book Review' ... (2)

In 1963 Harris wrote: 'I suspect I am abnormally interested in socio-cultural diagnostics. From my point of view there should be as many magazines and groups of magazines as there are convulsive changes in a culture itself' ('Angry Penguins and after', 9)

Harris and Dutton were contrasting characters. Dutton was highly social with seemingly endless renowned and influential connections. He hailed from a privileged and wealthy background: a vast pastoral country property and homestead, and the landed gentry. Harris, from working-class origins, was not given to flaunting connections. He was averse to social pretension and shallowness. In his early life he was outgoing and flamboyant, although he and Von always preferred smaller intimate gatherings of friends rather than large parties. In later life, Harris and his wife gradually retreated into an almost hermit-like existence, refusing most invitations out. Harris was deeply devoted to Von and to his daughter Samela and two grandsons, Ryder and Sam. He kept his family extremely private. Dutton was a man-about-town: charming and irresistible. He became the front-of-house person for their journal and publishing ventures, while Harris was the ideas man. These poured out far too rapidly for him to act upon them all.

Dutton published his poetry frequently. Harris kept much of his in a drawer. Dutton was an academic. Harris was somewhat anti-academia. Yet they formed a formidable team, sharing an immense enthusiasm for literature and the desire to encourage, promote and publish the work of Australian writers and artists. Harris initiated a series of four annual publications of the best of Australian poetry from 1958 to 1961. These were published by *Australian Letters* at the Mary Martin Bookshop and selected by Robert Clark, Dutton, Harris and Ian Mudie (*Verse in Australia*).

Harris contributed to Writers' Week at the Adelaide Festivals, often chairing panels. Harris, Dutton and Harry Medlin organised staging the premières of three of Patrick White's plays by the Adelaide University Theatre Guild at the University's Union Theatre, when these had been rejected by a conservative Adelaide Festival Committee. Patrick White had sent *The Ham Funeral* (written 1947) to Dutton to read in 1961. Dutton passed it on to Harris who immediately recognised its worth and insisted that it must be performed. The play was a huge success. Two years later, in 1962 they staged *Season at Sarsaparilla*, and in 1964 *Night on Bald Mountain*. Despite his rejection elsewhere, these three plays firmly established White as a serious Australian playwright.

In 1961 Harris assisted in the founding of Penguin Australia, and in 1965 of Sun Books with Dutton and Brian Stonier. Sun Books was dedicated to publishing Australian writers in paperback editions. Harris was appointed literary editor and adviser for both publishing houses. Early titles for Sun Books included Geoffrey Blainey's *The Tyranny of Distance*

(1966), which is still in print, and the David Campbell-edited anthology, *Modern Australian Poetry* (1970). In 1968 they published a hardback copy of *The Vital Decade: 10 years of extracts from Australian Letters*, which was a summary of the writings produced in the previous decade in the journal.

Breaking the British and US publisher's stranglehold over the Australian publishing industry—known as the Traditional Market Agreement—was another significant cause to which Harris devoted his considerable energy. It was abolished in 1976.

The Critics and 'Browsing'

In 1962, Harris chaired a panel for the ABC TV program *The Critics*. It was the first literary critical discussion program in the country and took place fortnightly in different capital cities over a period of ten years. Harris saw the purpose of *The Critics* as 'contributing to a furtherance of the craft'. *The Critics* discussed books, films, plays and cultural events. Those on the panel were from various cultural spheres, always erudite and well informed. On the final program Harris included Tom Brown, Russell Drysdale and Morris West.

Harris analysed his fellow humans with a knife-edge precision, acuity and wit, ignoring protocol and unafraid of the dead establishment. This is particularly notable in his regular weekly column entitled 'Browsing' written for the *Australian* from its fourth issue in 1964 for 27 years until 1991. He took to what he described as 'poppy lopping', writing about many famous Australians often in a brazenly critical way. Two articles that were particularly harsh, yet highly amusing, were his pieces on Robert Menzies and Dame Nellie Melba. However, he wrote admiringly of many others, including Doc Evatt and printer Bob Cugley. Many saw Harris's vocabulary and clever use of language as pompous and even arrogant, but most enjoyed his wit and word skill employed to squash pretension and conversely to applaud excellence and integrity. He wrote on anything and everything with humour, irony and his own brand of humanism and intelligence. Above all he wanted his audiences to face the issues of a narrow, prejudiced Australian society. He relished stirring the pot, often making enemies in so doing.

Conclusion

From 1943 Harris published one novel, five books of poetry, and three collections of pieces from his 'Browsing' column. These collections were *The Angry Eye* (1973), *The Unknown Great Australian and other psychobiographical portraits* (1983) and *The Best of Max Harris: 21 years of Browsing* (1986). He also contributed hundreds of poems, short stories, articles and reviews to numerous journals and poetry collections throughout his lifetime, including, in the early days, *Jindyworobak Anthology*, *Bohemia*, *Venture*, the *Bulletin*, *Comment*, *Angry Penguins* and *Angry Penguins Broadsheeet*, and continually in other literary journals: *Direction*, *Meanjin*, *Overland*, *Quadrant*, *Southerly*, *Westerly*, *Voices*, *Australian Quarterly* and *Nation*. He also published poems, articles and reviews in *Australian Letters* and *Australian Book Review*. He was an insatiable reader and writer. After working in the bookshop all day and meeting with his friends after work to discuss everything under the sun he still found the time to write and to edit and to publish with enormous energy and zeal. Through his 'Browsing' column he did his best to make his readers think seriously about current political, social and cultural issues.

Harris was awarded an AO for his services to literature in 1989. In 1993 he received the University of Adelaide's prestigious Alumni Award from the Cornell Chapter representing the Arts and the Performing Art 'in recognition of profound contributions made to cultural creativity as the founding father of Australian modernism in the Arts'. He died in Adelaide on 13 January 1995, aged 73 years.

Max Harris was one of Australia's finest men of arts and letters, as distinguished poet, writer and journalist and as renowned publisher and bookseller. He was also responsible for promoting and furthering lively and relevant critical debate in the environment of new Australian modernism, for which he was a key and consistent proponent. He rose to the challenge of defying the establishment and exposing narrow-mindedness. His was a keenly felt, often controversial presence on the Adelaide literary and cultural stage.

WORKS CITED

Bodleian. 'Leaves from the latest book'. Source unknown, 1940. Max Harris Papers, Barr Smith Library Special Collections, The University of Adelaide.

B.V. 'A new note in Australian poetry'. Source unknown, 1940. Max Harris Papers, Barr Smith Library Special Collections, The University of Adelaide.

Elliott, Brian. Ed. *The Jindyworobaks*. St Lucia: University of Queensland Press, 1979.

Harris, Max. 'Boat-train'. *Phoenix* (1939): 15.

___. 'I am an anarchist — so what?' *Bohemia* (July 1939): 12.

___. 'Mad Jasper'. *The Gift of Blood*. Adelaide: Jindyworobak, 1940, 30.

___. 'Progress of defeat' VIII. *The Gift of Blood*. Adelaide: Jindyworobak, 1940, 60.

___. 'Introduction'. *Angry Penguins* 2 (August 1941): 8.

___. *Angry Penguins* 3 (1942): 3.

___. 'Introduction'. *Angry Penguins* 4 (1942): 1.

___. 'Editorial'. *Australian Book Review* 1.1 (November 1961): 2.

___. 'Angry Penguins and after: a contribution to our literary history'. *Quadrant* 7.1 (1963): 9.

___. 'Dim the green hope'. *A Window at Night*. Kensington Park, SA: Australian Book Review, 1967. 27.

Hetherington, John. 'Max Harris: Middle age of a boy prodigy'. *Forty-two faces: Profiles of living Australian writers*. Melbourne: Cheshire, 1963. 214-19

Hope, A.D. 'Confessions of a Zombi'. *Meanjin* (1944): 44-7.

Jury, Charles Rischbieth. 'Preface'. *Phoenix* (1939): 15.

___. 'Two poets'. *Angry Penguins* (1940): 9-12.

___. Transcript of a radio talk: *Life and Letters in Adelaide, 1950s*. Charles Jury Papers, Mortlock Library (PRG/20/20/2 pp. 7-10), quoted in John Miles, 'Beautiful Sammy'. *The Independent Weekly*. 28 August-27 September 2005. Features, 3.

On Dit 10.10. Tuesday 14 May 1940. 2.

Miles, John. 'Beautiful Sammy', *The Independent Weekly*. 28 August-27 September 2005.

Sheridan, Susan. 'Australian Letters and postwar modernity'. *Australian Literary Studies* (April 2008): 276-7.

Unknown author. Editorial. *Phoenix* 1935, in John Miles, 'Beautiful Sammy'. *The Independent Weekly*. 28 August-27 September 2005. Features, 3.

Verse in Australia 1958: a yearly collection. Selected by Robert Clark, Geoffrey Dutton, Max Harris and Ian Mudie. Da Costa Building, Adelaide. *Australian Letters*, 1958.

Verse in Australia 1959: a yearly collection. Selected by Robert Clark, Geoffrey Dutton, Max Harris and Ian Mudie. Da Costa Building, Adelaide. *Australian Letters*, 1959.

Verse in Australia 1960: a yearly collection. Selected by Robert Clark, Geoffrey Dutton, Max Harris and Ian Mudie. Da Costa Building, Adelaide. *Australian Letters*, 1960.

Verse in Australia 1961: a yearly collection. Selected by Robert Clark, Geoffrey Dutton, Max Harris and Ian Mudie. Da Costa Building, Adelaide. *Australian Letters*, 1961.

INTERVIEWS

Edgar Woods Castle, 27 June 2007.

Elliot Johnston QC, 15 July 2007.

Colin Thiele, 4 May 2003.

10 Geoffrey Dutton: Little Adelaide and *New York Nowhere*[1]

Nicholas Jose

It ought to be impossible to talk about literary Adelaide without due mention of Geoffrey Dutton (1922-98). As a prime mover of Writers' Week and the Adelaide Festival of Arts, and founding co-editor of *Australian Letters* (1957–68) and *Australian Book Review* (1961-), both magazines based in Adelaide, Dutton was central to the city's post-war cultural initiatives. He was associated with the University of Adelaide, where he studied for a year before enlisting (another magazine, *Angry Penguins*, appeared controversially there that same year, 1940) and later taught. He was one of the English Department's lively cohort of writers and scholars who were enthusiastic about Australian and other 'new' literatures.

From Adelaide, Dutton played important national roles too, as editor at the newly formed Penguin Australia, co-founder of Sun Books, publisher at Macmillan and editor of the *Bulletin*'s literary supplement. He served on

---

[1] I am grateful to Tisi Dutton, Robin Lucas and John Thompson for help with this essay, and to Cheryl Hoskin, Special Collections Librarian, Barr Smith Library, the University of Adelaide.

influential committees and boards, including the Commonwealth Literary Fund and the inaugural Australia Council. Dutton was a bold and astute editor, as shown in the commemorative volume he co-edited with his Adelaide friend and colleague Max Harris to showcase the achievements of *Australian Letters*. That book, *The Vital Decade: Ten years of Australian art and letters* (Sun Books, 1968), includes pairings of work by leading artists and poets of the day, Sidney Nolan with Randolph Stow, for example, and Clifton Pugh with Judith Wright. It also includes the famous piece Patrick White wrote for the magazine, 'The Prodigal Son', one of the best of all Australian essays. Christina Stead's novella *The Puzzleheaded Girl* first appeared there, as did Peter Carey's first published story. Another success in those years was *The Literature of Australia* (1964), a multi-authored survey under Dutton's editorship that sold some 60,000 copies for Penguin Australia.

Dutton was writing all this time too. In the course of his life he published more than 40 volumes of poetry, biography, criticism, fiction and non-fiction. In an obituary for the UK *Independent* the critic Clement Semmler suggested that Dutton's 'contribution to Australian letters was probably unrivalled in his generation' (Semmler). 'It was thanks to the inspiration of great editors like Geoffrey Dutton that book publishing truly came of age in this country,' concurred University of Queensland Press editor Craig Munro in *Southerly* (7). Such claims are well-justified.

Yet generations come and go, and Dutton's reputation has fallen into the shadow that can immediately follow a literary life, as neglect prepares the way for eventual reassessment. It would therefore be more than possible in 2013, fifteen years after his death, to talk about Australian literature, and even literary Adelaide, without much more than a passing reference to Geoffrey Dutton.

The sheer scope and variety of Dutton's activities complicate the task of evaluating his contribution, both as cultural figure and as writer. Dutton's autobiography *Out in the Open* (1994) provides much useful material, but complicates even further the intersections of life and art. Dutton's life is also inextricably linked to Patrick White's, which we know largely through the filter of David Marr's magisterial biography (1991) and follow-up edition of White's selected letters (1994). In that reconstruction, after White's break with him in 1982, Dutton becomes a warning negative example. Dutton's informed assessment of White's behaviour, based on years of close contact, has been overshadowed by Marr's White's bilious purging of Dutton and what he called 'Duttonry'. 'You're vile, vile, vile', Nin Dutton (Dutton's first wife) remembers White saying when she rang around this time to help with a housekeeper (Marr, 'Life', 615; 'Letters', 562; Dutton, 'Out', 456). It was a pattern for White to repudiate old friends—Barry Humphries, Lawrence Daws, Brett Whitely among them—especially if they had a new partner.

A different approach to reconsidering Dutton can be found by looking to what he does best as a writer—his poetry. Dutton was first and last a poet (Jose; Munro). In this chapter I draw attention to an important missing piece in that body of work by discussing Dutton's last substantial poem, *New York Nowhere*, which was published posthumously a few weeks after his death in 1998. It appeared in a limited collector's edition of 175 copies with etchings by John Olsen, photographs by publisher Robert Littlewood and a CD of the poet reading the work. It has not been reprinted since. The volume was expensive to buy. Only a few libraries purchased copies. The Barr Smith Library at the University of Adelaide has a copy presented by then Vice-Chancellor Mary O'Kane in 1999 as the Library's 2,000,000[th] book: one of the 20 extra deluxe copies bound in emu skin (!) that sold for $3800. While the book may be consulted in the library, photocopying and scanning are made difficult by its size and value, not to mention copyright issues. This evidently desirable rare volume has seldom surfaced on the secondary market—perhaps more because of the value of Olsen's etchings than the mystique of Dutton's poem. A more accessible edition of *New York Nowhere* was originally envisaged, but it didn't happen for a range of reasons, including the author's demise.

The painter Jeffrey Smart commented when the poem was published that his friend would need no monument because he had already written his own (Barclay). Dutton died of a final stroke in Canberra on 1 November 1998. This last book was posthumously launched at the Olsen Carr Gallery in Sydney on 9 December that year. At the time critics suggested that the poem would 'lead to a re-evaluation of Dutton's output' (Usher). A similar enthusiasm hailed the work as 'possibly the longest poem in Australian literature' (McCulloch, 'Testament'). At some 900 lines, it is longer than Bernard O'Dowd's *The Bush* (1912) but not as long as *The Great South Land* (1951) by Rex Ingamells, *Captain Quiros* (1964) by James McAuley or *The Dunciad Minor* (1971) by A.D. Hope, to name some other outlandish creations. It is also modest compared to the proliferating verse novels of the 1990s, including works such as Dorothy Porter's *The Monkey's Mask* (1994) and Les Murray's *Fredy Neptune* (1998) that use poetic personae with a sophisticated ambition quite unlike Dutton's. 'Some thirty verse novels [were] published in Australia since the mid 1970s, the number accelerating through the nineties into the turn of the millennia', notes critic Christopher Pollnitz, who discusses Murray and Porter in this verse fictional context (229). But *New York Nowhere* is decidedly not fiction.

A limited edition has limited reach. Today, in a changed technological era, a poem that is unavailable in digital form may as well not exist. That has been the fate of *New York Nowhere*, which does not appear in Sydney University's online Poetry Library with Dutton's other poems, and has minimal citation on the AustLit database. This may be an effect of Dutton's faded reputation, or it may be a contributing factor to that eclipse. Its absence makes the arc of the poet's work incomplete. For the poets of Dutton's generation, late style was often radically different from early and middle, reflecting marked personal, social and artistic shifts. The end reveals a trajectory of new starts in the work of David Campbell and Rosemary Dobson, for example. In Dutton's case, such understanding has been denied. Only now as *New York Nowhere* becomes accessible to a new audience can it take its place in a re-reading of Dutton's poetry as a whole, as a recapitulation, a lost key.

* * *

The book's full title is *New York Nowhere: Meditations and Celebrations, Neurology Ward, The New York Hospital*. Dutton found himself there in mid-1995 after he had a stroke while travelling with his wife Robin Lucas by train to New York from Toronto, where he had been invited to read at the prestigious Harbourfront Readings. He suffered hallucinations, partial loss of vision and other temporary disabilities, but, in the words of his medical specialist, he 'dodged the bullet', partly thanks to a mini-stroke a year earlier. With recovery underway, he was discharged and able to return to Australia. In a letter of 23 July 1995 from his home in the Glasshouse Mountains, he wrote to his daughter Tisi of ideas for poems coming out of the episode. Two years later he got together with Melbourne art publisher Robert Littlewood and the special edition eventuated. John Olsen offered to contribute etchings as a kindness to an old friend. Littlewood's photographs document the making of the book and the people involved, as the publisher came to know the older writer and his zest for life, though Dutton was still suffering some effects of the stroke. Lucas, identified in the book only as 'she who comes', plays an important role in the poem. Her daily presence at Dutton's bedside in New York had helped the patient's recovery. She had played a life-saving role, and Dutton intended to dedicate the poem to her.

It is hard not to agree with John Olsen's remarks at the launch that the experience in New York 'enabled [Dutton] to review his life in quite an extraordinary way' (McCulloch). Media attention at the time concentrated on the personal circumstances that enveloped Dutton's life after the poem was written—like 'something out of *A Midsummer Night's Dream*', according to Olsen—and may have clouded its reception

(McCulloch, 'Testament', 'Poet'). A new approach begins by reading the poem on its own terms as a work of literature.

* * *

New York Nowhere is in 47 free verse sections of varying length, a discontinuous monologue set in the New York hospital ward that dramatises the goings-on around the poet in the present, and also inside the poet's mind as he tries to make sense of what is happening, ranging back over his life, to other scrapes with death, other moments of extremity, other places and times, even as he moves forward to partial healing and an eventual, tentative release back into the world.

The characters in the drama are deftly, vividly present: Richard and Danny, the young fellow inmates; the doctor; the nurse; and 'she who comes'. The speaker is a biographically recognisable Geoffrey Dutton, and key incidents from the autobiography *Out in the Open* that he published the year before this stroke, in 1994, and in other earlier poems, recur in epitome, stripped to expressive essentials. The speaker is a literary man who weaves his text through with literary allusions, personalised and sometimes hermetic: his 'silent anthology of dead friends' (*New York Nowhere*, XXI; hereafter cited by section number only).

'It came out of nowhere,' says young Richard at the start, referring to his brain tumour (I). The poet takes up the idea of 'nowhere', the blackness or chaos from which life is created and destroyed, and develops it in an extended set of metaphors with knotted, even confused, variations, as it becomes a therapeutic process: 'The healing is slowly coming out of nowhere' too (XLVI). Along the way the darkness proves 'fertile', but not without humiliation and vulnerability. The poem is fractured, characterised by lateral association and oblique connection, a chequerboard, a crossword, a game of snakes and ladders that nonetheless holds to a determination to communicate. Accordingly, its idiom is mostly plain-spoken. This 'nowhere', contrasted with 'somewhere', takes form through a set of contrapuntal oppositions: the present with the past (a childhood memory of working with a blacksmith; a plane crash in wartime Papua New Guinea); here (a clean white hospital/prison) and there (remembered natural environments); inside and out on the street; the self and the world; black and white; death and life; the Black Prince and a White Angel. It is ironic that New York, the ultimate cosmopolitan city, should here be the Nowhere, while distant Australia is this man's Somewhere, though also another kind of nowhere, as he notes, when it is conceived as *terra nullius* (XXXVIII). The poem follows the elliptical lines of such traverses, which are the speaker's way of seeing and being. As with the stroke, strange pathways occur in the brain. Often he returns to rustic lore for understanding: in XVI he compares himself to a white gum that suddenly falls from eminence, a widow-maker with the telltale line of termite dust where the branch has dropped from the trunk. 'You could say it had designs on me, then spared me,' he muses, seeking pattern in the apparent randomness of things.

The poem is conscious of its literary avatars in its quest for meaning in extremis: the poet Rilke, writing in terminal illness; Robert Lowell, institutionalised and confessional. Francis Webb's 'Ward Two', an earlier Australian hospital sequence, provides a close covert intertext. In his introduction to *The Literature of Australia* Dutton had written that Webb 'seems to have become central to Australian poetic consciousness' ('Literature', 9). There are those seekers of self-knowledge in prose, Montaigne and Johnson, both afflicted with ills of the flesh. At times Winnie in Samuel Beckett's *Happy Days* comes to mind, immured in sand as she searches for 'that memorable line', except that Dutton's memory is good, his literary fragments betoken survival, and his tone, surprisingly, is one of winnowed optimism:

> Maiden in the mor, Merry Margerete, midsomer flowre,
> Piers and Harry, the ploughmen, the shearer with the bony hands,
> She who walks in beauty, or the one in the barge's throne,

> Or that dusky woman, so ancient hardly human, or Cook's officers,
> Yawning languidly on deck, right by the reef,
> Or Andy gone with the cattle, or the colt from old Regret,
> Or cruel girls mocking with their mother's eyes.
>
> Fragments that are not ruins, even if I am. (XXI)

A note glosses the collage of allusion in these few lines: Anon, Skelton, Langland, Gerard Manley Hopkins, 'Click Go the Shears', Byron, Shakespeare, Rider Haggard, Kenneth Slessor, Henry Lawson, Banjo Paterson, David Campbell. And, not necessary to reference, line 430 of Eliot's *The Waste Land*, 'These fragments I have shored against my ruins'. It all comes back.

One of the work's most intriguing aspects is the way it at once disables and enables itself: 'Here I am, a writer, who cannot read or write' (XII). This condition licenses a concentrated, disrupted, circling approach, with apparent false starts and indirections that nonetheless eventuate in a shapely story, from arrival at to departure from the hospital, across a few days and nights—a persistent argument, a new expressive synthesis.

The argument is about the power of the imagination to create the world from 'fertile chaos', as contrasted with the capacity of hallucinations out of nowhere to occupy that same darkness with distorting or deceiving effect. An old literary debate between 'fancy' and 'imagination', primary and secondary (in Coleridge's usage), is given a new twist. The hallucinations induced by the stroke torment the poet, getting in the way of both the generative blackness of nowhere and any hope of seeing clearly, again or for the first time. These hallucinations are conveyed in the language of a 1940s apocalyptic poem in section I. In section III the poet invokes Blake's 'vegetative eye' as a way of trying to distinguish hallucinogenic vision from true sight. Although Max Harris is not mentioned by name, *The Vegetative Eye* is the title Harris gave to his first novel, written in an overwrought surrealist vein that Dutton finally rejects.

* * *

The discipline of actuality, of fact, as grounding for imagination is a pervasive concern through Dutton's writing, as he seeks the writer he truly is. His biographies of Adelaide's founder William Light and the explorer Edward John Eyre bring out this strength, as do those fine poems about the world outside himself, such as 'Theberton Hall, 1955', about Light's childhood home in England. *Founder of a City* (1960) is a sympathetic account of Light (1786–1839) as a genius who must continuously battle the odds, and the mixed hand fate has dealt him. Dutton appreciates Light as a Regency figure, part Romantic, part rationalist, whose defeats are part of a larger triumph. The biography defends Light through a persistent winnowing of fact and speculation. Such balance, wryly acknowledging failure and compromise in near-impossible situations, characterises Dutton's affection not only for Light but for Light's legacy in Adelaide, compromised as it is, for South Australia, for Australia. Light named his Adelaide property Theberton in memory of the peaceful place in rural England where he spent his boyhood. Thanks to a misprint the name was spelled wrongly on subsequent maps. For Dutton that epitomises the shifts that inevitably occur, not a tragedy, but an irony for the historian to savour:

> And William Light would laugh to find misspelt
> The name of Theberton he gave his hut,
> — Now rows of houses with their front doors shut,
> A respectable suburb known as Thebarton,
> In Adelaide, a city he had begun
> Three years before his death, and got no thanks.
> ('New', 37)

Light was philosophical, sure of his own rightness: 'I leave it to posterity ... to decide whether I am entitled to praise or blame' for siting the city as he did ('Founder', 288). The biographer is no less sure in his critique: 'Theberton Cottage [Light's house] was demolished in 1926, despite the protests of the few South Australians who cared about one of the precious relics of their history' ('Founder', 280). Light's fight for his vision of an improved, even ideal society and his realism about the degree by which that vision would fall short are emblematic, in Dutton's version, of the lot of all Australians who, like himself, take on the burden of building and enhancing their world. The ambiguity of actuality is necessary to the task, in the same way that the facts of Australia will always resist the fiction.

That became a seam of tension between Dutton and Patrick White. When he read and liked *Founder of a City*, White speculated on a possible play about Light and the other personalities involved in establishing Adelaide. He asked Dutton: 'Have you anything of the theatre in you, or aren't you sufficiently dishonest?' (Dutton, 'Out', 241-2). White was on to something. The answer is that Dutton's work explores the relationship between actuality and fancy, the world and the individual, in a way that gives weight to honesty. Plays were about the only literary genre Dutton didn't attempt, and he came to think that the dishonesty of theatre had corrupted White and his work. Dutton had moved to have White's *The Ham Funeral* produced in Adelaide in 1961 after it was rejected by everyone else, including the Adelaide Festival committee. He was less happy when the success of that production launched White into a career as a playwright at the expense of other, better things. 'I have often wished that I had never asked him to send me that script of *The Ham Funeral*; the theatre, as he had told me before we met, is a dishonest business', Dutton later wrote ('Out', 248). In the unsparing exchanges when they fell out in 1982, it was White's seduction by the young and charming theatre crowd and the gratification of opening night applause that Dutton most deplored: 'the theatre gave him warmth but dishonesty to his own artistic conscience' ('Out', 458). In relation to the publication of White's discarded novel fragment *The Hanging Garden* (2012), David Marr puts a similar argument, blaming Adelaide, with Dutton as its agent, for luring White into the theatre to the detriment of major new fiction. 'Now we can see *Signal Driver* [the play commissioned by Jim Sharman for the 1982 Adelaide Festival, the same year White and Dutton fell out] for what it is: consolation of a kind for a fine novel lost' ('So much', 16).

When Dutton and White first met, White thought they might have been related—fellow Australian aristocrats. White was tempted to move to Adelaide with Manoly Lascaris to live with the Duttons, as family. But this was a version of himself that White later sloughed off. When Dutton, encouraged by Murray Bail, published a tribute on White's seventieth birthday that revealed their shared past and background, it was the last straw. The offending piece is relatively innocuous, but it touched a nerve. It embarrassed White, exposing the sentimentality behind the author's savagely satirical mask and showing up his recent memoir *Flaws in the Glass* as artfully selective. White protests too much: Dutton emerges as the truth teller in the relationship.

No less than White, Dutton was publicly courageous in his stances: his republicanism; and his embrace of Soviet poets, such as Yevgeny Yevtushenko, at the height of the Cold War. He was proud of his Jewish ancestry, and regretted the way White had cast off his Jewish friends ('Out', 28, 458). 'In recent years it has been painful to observe you becoming ever more vain, intolerant and authoritarian, even descending into rabid anti-Semitism', Dutton wrote to White the year they broke off relations ('Out', 456-7). A wounded White complained to composer Richard Meale: he 'says I am swollen with vanity ... anti-semitic into the bargain ... it's a relief to be free of Duttonry' (Marr, 'Letters', 563-4).

* * *

If his deepest impulse was to praise, Dutton did so weighing the negatives. 'The biographer must ask, "What is the truth?" and stay for an answer', he writes ('Out', 192), though his own autobiography does not always do so.

By *New York Nowhere*, he is able to ask himself Montaigne's question, '*Que sçais-je*' ('What do I know?'), and quote Yeats on choosing 'perfection of the life, or of the work', knowing that flaws in one can reflect flaws in the other, while final judgment hangs in the balance (XXIV, XXXV).

Dutton's poetry gains from being grounded and disciplined. It finds its best idiom when it incorporates qualities from prose, when it is observant, considered and conversational. In *New York Nowhere*, where any praise must overcome extremes of negativity, matters of form and style press with new urgency, as the poet expresses his own disintegration. Utterance breaks apart and is reforged.

Francis Dutton, the poet's eldest son, shrewdly observes that 'even though he was in his 70s when it was written ... the autobiography was premature' (McCulloch, 'Poet', 3). Key incidents in *Out in the Open* recur in *New York Nowhere* in abbreviated, abstracted form, as distilled metaphor. The autobiography is an attempt to put things on the record. It provides rich material for cultural history and some personal stuff that is embarrassing in its seeming candour and its unexamined omissions. Exculpatory arguments run throughout, with the author's mother and with other women in his life, with 'little Adelaide', and with White, all entangling proxies for the writer himself, his worse or better angels: Australian Republican vs Queen Adelaide. As apologia, *Out in the Open* comes with a perplexed sense of emancipation, before the even more perplexing twists and turns of the journey to New York's nowhere and back.

The poem, by contrast, convincingly generalises, by compression and self-reflexivity, from the personal to the metaphysical and broadly human. In the autobiography, for example, the poet recalls an image 'out of my mother's readings to me from the myths of ancient Greece' of 'Pallas Athene coming down from the sky with her robes streaming, spear in hand and the Gorgon's head on her shield. When I heard of her severe beauty and her blue eyes I identified her with my mother, who could be very severe' ('Out', 32). Dutton's attitude towards women is one of the uncomfortable things in the autobiography. In the later poem this image is transmuted into an evocation of the hallucinations induced by the stroke:

> Flies Athene ... the severe sword warrior, fully armed ...
> Widening from black nowhere to black nowhere,
> With the resolute Gorgon's head on her shield ...
> ... leaping now in the sight behind my closed eyelids.
>
> Exquisite tyranny which needs no eyes to see. (I)

Mother, *ewig-weiblich*, the eternal feminine, knowing and powerful, becomes a form of oppressive illusion within the self.

Other scarring experiences are similarly transmuted: hymn-singing at boarding school, where Dutton felt his mother had abandoned him (VII); a wartime stint in jail that taught existential lessons (V); and the multiple miracle of surviving that plane crash in the New Guinea jungle at the end of the war when 'some invisible trap in the clear sky ... hit us' ('Out', 127; *New York Nowhere*, IV; also 'The Volcano'; 'New', 34-36). Near-death is answered by saving love, where love remains an ambiguous mystery.

New York Nowhere is a last love poem for the unnamed 'she who comes'. An unnamed White surfaces here too. *Out in the Open* tells a story of White's near death by drowning at Rocky Point on Kangaroo Island in 1968, when his gumboots, the wrong footwear for the occasion, filled with water and he was sucked into the blowhole at a favourite fishing spot. Nin Dutton plunged in to save White, and Dutton and a male friend hauled him out: 'Above his mute mouth his blue eyes, alarming at any time, had the look of a man being buried alive. ... From then on, that spot was known as Patrick's Hole' ('Out', 359). The resistless, saving love evoked in *New York Nowhere* awakens that distant memory as pure image:

> Love in the spring between the black rocks,
> Love in the stream homing to the sea. (XIV)

Rocky Point was a touchstone of 'purity and honesty' in a slippery world for Dutton ('Out', 273). It inspired White's story 'Dead Roses' that appeared in *The Burnt Ones* (1964), dedicated 'to Nin and Geoffrey Dutton'.

If Dutton's writing is at its best when it rests on the prosaic ground of actuality, it is especially strong when it engages with the particular places to which he is so deeply, if resistantly, attached. His poem 'An Australian Childhood' (1967) records an upbeat overcoming of any melancholy of alienation from the more glittering centres of culture that his privileged kind might once have felt:

> And when my mother played Chopin, the door
> Let out the notes to sing where they were born,
> Paris, Majorca, Vienna or Warsaw;
> Not a grace-note fell on Booleroo or Quorn.
>
> But now, far off, doing eighty down the freeway,
> I wait at memory's lightning for the thunder
> Of names I grew from, my roots then as today
> In Nuriootpa, Tanunda, Eudunda and Kapunda.
> ('New', 80-1)

This good-humoured engagement with the ground in which he had grown, including his family, especially his mother, and the property at Anlaby where he grew up and later lived, and, at a more distant tangent, Adelaide, continued after he got away to Queensland, in apologetics and reassessment in prose and verse as his perspective changed. Yet he could only keep going, finally to New York where the closeness of death took him all the way back to 'little Adelaide', where fear had been a frisson, a creative pulse:

> I'm a student again, in little Adelaide,
> And the beaky, humorous Professor's lecture
> Suddenly becomes sonorous in the hushed theatre,
> As he begins to read Dunbar in his native Scots, with the Latin
> Refrain: '*Timor mortis conturbat me ...*'

> At seventeen, it meant more to me than cemeteries,
> Even more than the war, some ten years old ... (XXXIV)

New York Nowhere is the accomplished last work of a rare poet. It can be understood in terms of the limitations, and the struggle against limitation, that shape Dutton's best art. Part of that is a way of making his own experience emblematic while keeping it ordinary. Without that honest discipline, which can perhaps be thought of in terms of the flat grids and long clear vistas of the places of his beginnings, he was nothing.

Geoffrey Dutton was a wanderer, a promiscuous litterateur, a friend to too many, a public figure who wore too many hats, and a distinguished poet. In the last decade of his life, after leaving South Australia, he happily occupied a string of different habitats with Robin Lucas. *Out in the Open* concludes with a section called 'To the Glasshouse Mountains, 1983–93'. The *New and Selected Poems* he published in 1993 concludes with the sequence 'Moving to the Glasshouse Mountains'. Ending both books is the poem 'Little Testament' (the title is Villon's), written in 'the sixty-ninth year of [the poet's] age': 'I go north and say farewell to frost' ('New', 225). He didn't know then that a journey much further north lay ahead, to New York Nowhere, which would intensify the poetic renewal that is already evident in the 1993 selection, in 'Aboriginal Dance, Hooker Creek', for example, where Dutton writes: 'we are a continent of dust/ And not until we learn to live with dust/ Will our skins be clean' ('New', 199). *New York Nowhere* is a poem of determined, roundabout return to life.

WORKS CITED

Barclay, Alison. 'Poet's Corner'. *Herald-Sun*. 20 August 1999.

Dutton, Geoffrey. *Founder of a City: The Life of Colonel William Light*. Melbourne: Cheshire, 1960.

___. *New and Selected Poems*. Sydney: Angus & Robertson, 1993.

___. *Out in the Open: An Autobiography*. St Lucia: University of

Queensland Press, 1994.

___. *New York Nowhere: Meditations and Celebrations, Neurology Ward, The New York Hospital.* With etchings by John Olsen. Central Park, Vic.: Lytlewode Press, 1998.

Dutton, Geoffrey. Ed. *The Literature of Australia*. 1964. Ringwood, Vic.: Penguin, 1976.

Jose, Nicholas. 'A Wise and Gracious Garnering'. *Voices* 3.4 (1993): 100-2.

McCulloch, Susan. 'Final testament to a life no holds bard'. *Australian*. 9 December 1998.

McCulloch, Susan. 'The Poet, His Wife, Her Boyfriend, His Mother: The Long Goodbye'. *Australian Magazine*. 12 December 1998.

Marr, David. *Patrick White: A Life*. Sydney: Random House, 1991.

___. 'So much of our life is in it'. *Australian Book Review* (May 2012): 12-17.

Marr, David. Ed. *Patrick White: Letters*. Sydney: Random House, 1994.

Munro, Craig. 'Geoffrey Dutton (1922-1998)'. *Southerly* 58.4 (1998): 6-7.

Pollnitz, Christopher. 'Australian Verse Novels'. *HEAT* 7, new series, (2004): 229-52.

Semmler, Clement. 'Obituary — Geoffrey Dutton'. *Independent*. 25 September 1998.

Usher, Robin. 'Artsbeat'. *Age*. 9 December 1998.

New York Nowhere:
Meditations and Celebrations, Neurology Ward,
The New York Hospital

Geoffrey Dutton

I

In the ward the two young men with bandaged heads
Lie beside me, opposite me, where we
Are drawn up like parked cars whose owners have lost the keys.
Richard, Danny, fit young guys, runners, footballers,
Tripped in mid-stride by tumours in the brain,
They call softly to each other across the ward.

"It came out of nowhere, I was riding high,
Everything going right for me. When *wham*!"

"Yeah, same here. At the New Year's Eve party
She asked me 'Has it been a good year for you?'
I said 'Honey, don't you stand too close to me,
The lightning might strike you.' That's how good it was.
Then this thing hit me out of nowhere."

The same with me. After the good reading at Harbourfront,
At ease in the train from Toronto to New York,
By the flick, flick, flick of the May-green trees
At ninety miles an hour along the Hudson,
Suddenly a red-hot drill bored into my skull
And the flickering vertigo of the flashing tree trunks
Disappeared into black nowhere
With a bang-ache splitting the rhythm of the rails,
And in the nothingness of my vision, behind my closed eyelids,
Flashed cadmium comets with cobalt tails,
Exploding viridian planets, streaks of alizarin
Strapped with ochre, cerulean fishtails,
Rainbow windmills flicking, acid lemon rockets
Spraying crimson lake, hyacinthine loops,
Auroras of anguish across the black universe of my brain.

I laid my bursting head on the sanity of my wife's lap,
Knowing all this, but nothing of what it was,
Just hanging onto my wife's strength until Penn Station,
A taxi, the blur of the streets, night,
And the brilliant interventions of hallucinations,
Going, coming, never a lasting star.

We carry black nowhere around inside us
And out of it comes the clot, the crab,
And what had been the faithful heart
Pumped the blood that formed the clot that felled us.

There's no warning at all, no 'Beep beep'
Like a reversing truck. You're just hit.

And that great black nowhere of the brain
Exists in an unsafe home of bone,
And all the transmitting is internal, not like
Radio waves entering a house of glass and concrete,
Sparking out from a wired steel tower.
Just a softness seen only by surgeons.

For those of us who are hallucinating
Every man is his own Zeus,
And out of our heads, whether opened
By Hephaestus' axe of pain
Or in drugged sleep by the surgeon's buzzsaw,
Flies Athene, not the goddess of wisdom and weaving,
But the severe sword-warrior, fully armed,
Riding a host of galloping lights and shapes
Widening from black nowhere to black nowhere,
With the resolute Gorgon's head on her shield
By which only Zeus was not turned to stone,
But whose glaring eyes and snaky hair
Are leaping now in the sight behind my closed eyelids.

Exquisite tyranny which needs no eyes to see.

II

I lay on a trolley in the hospital corridor for hours.
After all, this is a teaching hospital
And we patients are necessary laboratory rats.
So every now and then a student
(They look like doctors, but are nervous),
Would come, do the same tests, ask the same questions.

They demand, we stagger and forget.
I can't do the dolly-walk, heel to toe,
But I know my name, Mum's maiden name,
The time of day, the day, the month, the year.
What loads of detail we carry around!

But the third time one asked me the name
Of the President of the United States,
It sparked a feeble rebellion, and
I replied, smartarse, "Who's the Prime Minister of Australia?
And in answer to your question, Doctor, Hillary Clinton's husband".

He didn't speak, but he liked being called Doctor.

Then the top doctor, with his circling, clicking fingers,
"Tell me when you can see them, when you can't",
And his rubber hammer, does all the tests over again.

He's the neurologist, a distinguished Professor,
But also a straight-shooting New Yorker.
He shows me the CAT scan, the black cloud's fearsome
Turmoil across the grey valleys of my brain.

"Well, Mr Dutton, ya dodged the bullet.
Y've had a severe stroke. Ya should be dead,
Paralyzed or speechless, but it went for your eyesight,
That's why ya can't see anything on ya left,
But ya'll improve, it will get better."

Then he points again to my brain.
"Ya see that tiny little black channel there?
That's what saved ya, how ya dodged the bullet."

I remembered, maybe a year before, in Queensland,
In the evening pouring my wife a whisky.

I missed the glass by the width of a glass.
Fool. Sat down to read the paper.
Couldn't see the left hand side of the page.
It wasn't there. Held up my hands.
Couldn't see the one on the left.

After the local hospital, the CAT scan, the doctor
Pointed to a tiny little dark channel
Across the soft walnut surface of my brain.
Maybe the first tributary of the Styx.

He said "You've had a mini-mini-stroke".

So now in New York Dr Coronna says
"It was that tiny little channel that saved you.
The massive stroke ran down it
And left you without your left vision,
Instead of dead, paralyzed or dumb".

So it was the illusion that saved me.
The illusion that the whisky was going into the glass.

How words lead us on too!
'Illusion' originally meant 'mockery'.
Indeed, the whisky sprawling over the bench
Did mock me with an empty glass.

But if you search further, you find 'illusion'
"Distinguished from hallucinations.
Illusions must always have a starting-point
In some actual impression, whereas
A hallucination has no such basis."
So the whisky not connecting to the glass
Was an actual, single impression, not the multitudinous
Hallucinations crowding out of black nowhere.

Then Dr Coronna points to the X-ray of my heart.
"The lefthand side of your heart's like an English muffin."

Giggling, I answer "We call them crumpets". "Ya do?"

III

Surely it's something that would appeal to William Blake,
That what I am seeing dazzlingly in hallucinations
Has nothing to do with my undamaged eyes,
For the vegetative eye is only a messenger
And is not needed for all these whizzing vanes.

Yet waiting in nowhere, there is always somewhere,
That somewhere where something is waiting,
Or worse, coming. The one certainty, out there,
Is the Black Prince of Nowhere, whose dominion
Has always been the endless night enclosing
Those tendrilly white dreams of eternal life.

It could be any time, banal as a holiday,
In the Broad Arrow Cafe in the beautiful ruins
Of Port Arthur, where, after the shooting, a fireman
Who looked in, said he thought the people sitting
Around the tables were having tea and buns.
It came out of nowhere, and the gunman maybe
Thought they were in prison and he was setting them free,
His trigger finger the nod from the Commandant.

Black nowhere, unperturbed by stars
Of knowledge, love or hate or fear,
And the dive into it is also the sliding over of night
Where the chemistry of darkness embraces the crystals of day.

IV

The way it came out of nowhere to Danny and Richard
Hit the nonchalant immortality of youth ...
When you're young and swift in doing,
Not even knowing you're 'the cream and crown of all',
When you're like a green tree bending in the breeze
By the stiff, grey, ringbarked trunks,
And there's no thought, in your warm covering, of a future axe.

And even when, in an aeroplane with a broken wing,
Near the volcano, I was spinning down to the jungle,
To certain death, then hit the trees – and lived,
Was but to pause, take a few breaths,
Shake yourself like a wet dog, and walk out.

For the Greek poet, 'Health is the best that Heaven sends;
next, to be young amongst one's friends ...'

The arrogance of health means no harm;
if there's a secret fault, it's safe in nowhere.
But 'nothing's more imminent than the impossible'.

Dear old Grandfather Age with his attendant
Family of pain and itch and falter, makes slow
Approaches where for youth it's clear hot or cold.

V

Once I was in another prison, of black stone,
And through the bars of the tiny window
Through which the old lags said it was better not to look,
Even if you'd managed to climb that high,
There was the sky, the air beyond the walls, in which
I was not allowed to fly. The inane burble of a pigeon,
The clap of its wings taking off, the sound of freedom.

In a locked cell, the slightest sound outside
Goes over the walls, an escaped prisoner,
While in the towers the armed guards see nothing.

And when the cell tapped you on the wrist with stone
It was only a dumb kind of cruelty.

If someone were to write a history of cruelty
How universal it would be –
The thrilling spectacle of Imperial days,
Gladiators, dying for the pleasure
In the eyes of stone, of men of girth and hue,
Much the same as those who later laid
A barbed wire wreath on the brows of our century.

The warder's boots echoed from the steel walkways,
Sometimes they stopped, and there was a slight scrape
As they shifted the cover on the peephole in the steel door,
And for a moment, in solitary, one wished to be left alone.

Here in the ward the white is germ-free but not quite kind,
And there is no blue at all, let alone sky,
And each anchored bed is a little steel island.
All the more reason to treasure what's left on the mind.

VI

We're members of the world's greatest club, The Sick,
From which no one is blackballed, no one can resign.
Though the fees are often huge, in its halls
Jews and Blacks and derros are all welcome,
Nobody cares which way you vote,
Whether you slobber in your soup, shit your bed or yell
Like the damaged man in the curtained end of the ward,
Who is screaming again and again "God, I have sinned,
I declare my sins unto the Lord,
God be merciful to me, a wretched sinner, God pardon me".

Et le Bon Dieu dans son fauteuil de nuages
fait BOUM, doesn't give a fuck,
Way up there in the off-limits blue.
God it seems, is the Nowhere without nowhere.

VII

I lie in silence, remembering the hyms at school,
'Praise my soul the King of Heaven, to his feet thy tribute bring...
Praise him for his grace and favour to his children in distress...'

Please, Dr Coronna, bring Him the tribute
Of the CAT scan, with its black smear of damage
Lurched across the pale valleys of my brain.

But I do try to praise, for if we do not try
To offer our souls to someone we remain in nowhere.
I think of Rilke, dying of leukemia,
(Although, of course, in 1926, not knowing what it was),
Uncannily saying his sickness came from the marrow
Of his bones, writing an elegy for Marina Tsvetayeva,
Only six months before his death,
'*So unschuldig sind Götter, sie warten auf Lob wie die Schüler.*
Loben, du Liebe, lass uns verschwenden mit Lob'.
'So innocent are gods, they wait for praise like schoolboys.
Praising, my love, let us be lavish with praise'.

VIII

We hang on more to life, with death in the room,
Because it's life itself that is hanging on.
Life can wait for centuries to declare its survival,
Like grains of wheat in an opened Pharaoh's tomb
That are still prepared for the humble process of growing.
But there's also that other life in a jar of rice,
The weevil working in dryness to turn it into dust,
Or the moisture of maggots boisterously wriggling
In the underside of flesh, out of reach of the sun.

Survival is also a reappraisal of the ugly.

IX

Now behind some other blue curtains, another man
Is shouting "**I need** you, **I need** you, **I need you**".

Me too, buddy, though she's a different 'You'.

The stern black nurse you always obey,
Though really she's so gentle, is now saying to him,
This man who had a tumour cut out this morning,
"You know, what ya goin ta do, honey,
You'se goin ta roll over, real slow now – there".

In the air-conditioning the striped blue curtains flutter
Like a fibrillating heart. All's heart and brain here,
Absolute rulers of the territories of limb, tongue or eye.

Arrogant in our health, yet we were born to squirm.
I'm haunted by a cliché phrase: "Running on empty".
The gauge reads zero. I'm emptied out.
But the engine keeps running, fuelled from somewhere.

How ironic then that a drip goes into my arm
To thin my blood and purge the hallucinations,
Like a car sucking from a pump at a petrol station.

X

I'm thinking how much worse it is for her than me;
She's alone in New York, yet not quite alone.
I could have left her all alone by dying.
And if living, how much of me will she have?
A brain-damaged, thin-legged, dependent creature?

XI

The eloquent city preaches gospels of ugliness and waste.
The West Side is across a whole world,
Central Park a green Atlantic.
Some little verses sail to me like Columbus' ships,
Across four or five hundred years:

'My lefe ys faren in a lond –
Alas! Why ys she so?
And I am so sore bound
I may nat come her to.
She hath my hert in hold,
Where-ever she ride or go,
With trew love a thousandfold.'

Yet at the same time TV singing jingles haunt me,
Unwanted rubbish washed up on my lonely shore,
And barging unasked into memory comes the sort of person
Who always crosses threads on a toothpaste tube.

XII

Here I am, a writer who cannot read or write.

Although it's often a life of being ignored or crushed,
There's a wholesome humility about being a writer
As well as the reckless vanity of trying
In a field where others have already done so well.

I wonder if engineers look at the Pond du Gard
Or the Golden Gate Bridge, and think they'll try even harder
With their thumping logs over a dry creek bed.

You just have to say to yourself like Tolstoy
'I'm beginning a new exercise book
as though in a new state of mind'.

Here there are no certainties, only 'dusty answers'.

XIII

Yet there **is** a certainty, if spared from accident,
The certainty by which I live today,
For which I live as long as I'm allowed to live,
That she will walk into the ward
Some time today.

I couldn't tell you, with any certainty at all,
Which way she's walking across Central Park,
Which two trees her path's passing between,
But it's more certain than Park Avenue
That life will begin again when she walks into the ward.

XIV

Love in the spring between the black rocks,
Love in the stream homing to the sea.

In hospitals or in prisons of steel and stone
The flesh of lovers turns into body count,
Proximity is probing or palpating,
Or finally sliding a lump onto a trolley.
Nothing flows out of fingers or lips.

With lovers, however, the slightest touch together
And they stick like Velcro, hiss when they're torn apart.

Gandhi was nervously right: 'Something tells me
That every touch, be it ever so superficial,
Is bound to lead to the eruption of animal passion.'

But that's also love, which is not always white cotton.

XV

Hospitals, those white camps of humility
For the prisoners. For those in charge,
From the mean to the revered, power.
And they're in cahoots with your very own weakness,
So you betray yourself, and cannot get out of yourself.

Oh to be free amidst the randomness of life,
To wander like Antony and Cleopatra through the streets
And note the qualities of people, or like Walt Whitman
Be one of a crowd in Broadway or on Brooklyn Ferry!

Instead, there's this clean continuum
Where we miss the strangeness of things,
Mysteries like the migration of birds, natural noises.
Somewhere on a long, empty beach there are
Little wave shushes, the chirring and whingeing of seagulls.

Or somewhere there's a silence, as never here,
A magic island in the sleeping lake's embrace.

XVI

Or I could be far away near a whipbird in Queensland,
Stumbling through the bush, flicked by supple boughs
Or by dead branches digging in with twigs,
Spider webs across the eyes,
Ticks dropping on skin, sidling into hair…

A kookaburra hits the grass and ground, and flies
To a bough, shaking its head, something in its beak,
A little lizard? A beetle? A worm? Whatever, down it goes,
Rippling the neck-feathers, like a little wind on grass.

Kookaburras are silent when they drop on a worm,
They are not hunting when they laugh and wake serious humans,
Who can also fall from whatever eminence
Silently as the white gum they call the widowmaker,
They prey of what was hidden, dust under the skin.

Out in the open! A natural grassy clearing.

Bare feet safe here. On the cheeks, a brush of breeze.

One night I was pursued to bed by laughter...
Two kookaburras in the stringy-bark by the house,
A short walk in air away. In later daylight,
Hanging out the washing on the hoist,
I was suddenly enveloped in leaves and boughs
And cracked on the skull, knocked flat, by a thicker branch.

Up again, I followed the white trunk
Thick as my thigh, back to the stump, eighteen paces.
There was just a thin rim of wood, filled with termite dust.

You could say it had designs on me, then spared me.

A couple of paces to the right, and I'd have had
The full weight of the trunk right on my head.

At such times you shake a bit, and then move on,
The way a golden grevillea leaps as a scarlet
Honeyeater takes off, then swings, slowing, up and down.

XVII

Here in hospital all's designed to be so caring,
Even if the nurses never answer the bell you're told to squeeze.

One longs for the indifference of Nature,
The rain-shrouded mountain which will not grieve,
The cutting rocks which will not grow softer in the dawn.

Wouldn't it be great if a nurse's cap were suddenly
Barbarous as a pineapple's stiff headdress.
We might be in colour, individual, alone.
But here privacy's about as likely as a solitary ant.

So, by lying here, so close to death and deaths,
We populate our solitariness ourselves,
And discover that all our precious lives have sprung
From this fertile nowhere in that ancient chaos
Seething around all the time inside us.

XVIII

You get to be a believer, all right, in hospital.

Nowhere might just be friendly, starred with love,
And the barbarians, for all their cruelty, might be
Galloping in to freshen up the decaying Empire.

Despite the trolley that just went by,
The possibility of renewal is all around us.
As out in nowhere there is neither guilt nor shame,
So we're absolved from what comes out of nowhere.

Danny and Richard are not responsible
For their white bandages of humiliation and pain.
Maybe in their parentage there could be some blame
Although not because of shameful actions.

All of which makes it no less hard
That we're in prison without having been found guilty.

XIX

'Be absolute for death; either death or life
Shall thereby be the sweeter...' But, Duke Vincentio,
There's not a soul here, I think, but gasping
Opts for life, being so close to death.
Here's the time, the place, for honesty,
But not that easy kind of facile pessimism,
An intellectual oneupmanship
That's only possible for those who've had
A good breakfast. What's best is a guarded optimism,
Coming with a dented tin bowl of starch and ricewater.

Lowell, who tried so often for the whole,
Quoting Gramsci added up the halves of things,
'Optimism of the will, pessimism of the intellect'.

Not bad. But maybe it's just as well
Richard and Danny are not intellectuals.

XX

Danny is hanging on, but alas he can't let go.
Pain grown out of fear is no less pain:
Opposite me in the ward the doctor and the physio
Are trying to persuade Danny he has to start
Using his limbs again. The operation was a success.
He's OK. But when they ask him to flex his leg
He squeals, just like a wounded rabbit,
He can't help it, he cannot move it.
He squeals as they turn him and try to get him to stand.

We try not to notice. He squeals again, this time
Like an old tram's steel wheels being forced round a corner.
He cries "But it **hurts** if I move my legs, it **does**, it **does**",
And patiently they go on reasoning with him,
"Danny, you're **all right**. There's nothing wrong with your legs,
You **must** move your muscles, otherwise they'll wither".

Danny squeals again, they go away, will try again.

Richard is always laughing, although after his first operation,
The bandages still on his head, they found bits of the tumour
Still there. He's just had a second op.
He's long time been a famous rich lady's chauffeur.
He gently dented her Continental. "I'd never done that before,
That's how they found out. It was the tumour did it.
I just never saw that fire hydrant on the right.
I feel terrible about the Continental.
Maybe I shouldn't drive Mrs F. again".

She sends him delicacies, hothouse grapes,
Figs from Turkey, olives from Spain, he offers them to me.
His phone is always ringing, often it's her
Saying of course she'll have him back again,
But he worries what might happen. "What if there's still a bit there?
Like they missed that bit the first time they cut me."
Then he laughs, and says, "Sure, I'll be OK".

His phone rings again, it's his brother. "Hi Ted – I'm fine…"
Thank God Danny hasn't got a phone.

XXI

In this enormous city no one rings me,
I have no visitors, only she who comes,
But even she can't be here all the time,
So I call up old absent friends
In memory and answer them back.
The Bell Telephone Company's making nothing out of me.

True, I have my eyes although they cannot read for me.
But there are still lots of people in my damaged brain
Whose living voices I never was able to hear.

While the hefty ward sister shouts at her colleague
I lie here with my silent anthology of dead friends,
Maiden in the mor, Merry Margarete, midsomer flowre,
Piers and Harry, the ploughmen, the shearer with the bony hands,
She who walks in beauty, or the one in the barge's throne,
Or that dusky woman, so ancient hardly human, or Cook's officers,
Yawning languidly on deck, right by the reef,
Or Andy gone with cattle, or the colt from old Regret,
Or cruel girls mocking with their mothers' eyes.

Fragments that are not ruins, even if I am.
Some of the lines, the verses, come out tangled;
Better remember books than lovers
Who flee from me that sometime did me seek
With naked foot stalking in my chamber.

XXII

There is only one that matters to remember,
And her feet are maybe now, this minute,
Coming towards me across Central Park,
And she is weighed down like a Third World
Hospital visitor, with edible food, clean clothes.

XXIII

Outside the walls, the eye of day
Will have gone under the lid of night,
That familiar blackness, pledged by stars.
But here the moons and comets swirling in my night
Come from the brain's nowhere. It makes no difference
To them whether my eyes are wide or closed.
There is a busy muteness here.
A shrouded trolley goes by on rubber wheels.

It would be better to die in a grassy paddock,
To be left there as a host for hawks and crows,
A nest for blithe maggots, to give birth to life.

There is never quite darkness in this place,
In the muttering nights of hospitals where nothing is ever
Quite still; not even us. Although we're parked
We're moving out of the nights and into the days,
Empty, undriven, but moving, like cars
Being delivered, clamped to the rails of the truck
But still flexing their springs at the bumps on the road.

XXIV

Somewhere there is the country
That is still ourselves, but the border of which
We have to transgress, even though we have no visa,
In order to look anew at our exiled selves.

How to know oneself but not become self-centred...
Then remembering one who was so often right:
'*Que sçais-je?*' For nowhere is always
Too vast to know, let alone all the little somewheres.
But here's still the *essai*, the trying, to abide what it teaches.
And I would like to talk to the great Doctor,
The lexicographer, 'harmless drudge',
About stoicism, for instance, for he suffered much
From pain and even more from '*tristis et atra quies*',
While still managing to say 'The great remedy
which Heaven has put in our hands is patience'.

But patience is not for that other religious man
In the next ward, still begging God to forgive him,
Wanting Him to hurry and accept all those sins
Growing silently as tumours, but not out of nowhere.

When we're sick it's not only the healthy who can help,

The sick and suffering set us a new perspective.

'The greatest misery of sickness is solitude.'
So the worst in prison are put in solitary.
I'm sad for Danny's squeals, but in a way grateful.
Richard's phone calls are not for me,
Especially if I'm trying to sleep, but at least
There's a voice connected to a world outside
And not cut off by the trolley with the sheet.
What a paradox it is, that in health,
In that outside world, we long for solitude,
And the worst curse of hallucinations
Is the gaudy, gross populating of nowhere,
So that even with our eyes shut we are not alone.

XXV

There can be no healing without a wound.

The stroke's black scar, the doctor says, will heal.

In the clear, sunny day the smoke was incongruous.
There was a bushfire coming, out of sight,
It popped with a harmless sound like tennis balls.
But then the air turned liquid above the flames.

In Queensland, after the bushfire,
We found a python's skin, perfect from eyes
To vent, glittering on the sullen black ground.
The snake was somewhere else by then, renewed, shining.

XXVI

I listen to old Joe across the ward. His nowhere's on the right.
"He come out of nowhere, the kid, the kid on the light bike.
Outa the empty street on my right. He was a week dying.
I know, don't tell me, I know it wasn't my fault.
But I know, don't tell me. I know I done it".

XXVII

The New Yorker in the white coat, serious as ever,
But dropping his humour, repeats the reprieve,
"In four to six months your sight should improve.
So ya should get better".

So I lie here with the words "I will get better.
I **will** get better…"
In the fluttering rhythms of my fibrillating heart,
I use these keys to hit the slack strings of my brain,
Like the piano-tuner's patient, tuneless search
For the right tension that's being in tune.

The irregular pulse is still the beat of life.
The words still have the same meaning,
Let's hope the meaning is not only words,
Though words are never static, they're the pulse too.

Then there's the impotence of facing the ceiling
As you're wheeled down corridors and into lifts,
And then the inevitability of nurses' hands
And waiting for those impatient gods, the doctors.
But they can't get at the words hiding in nowhere.

XXVIII

I am fourteen or so, in the workshop,
Learning about the ways of steel from old Mick,
Whizzing the handle on the fan of the forge
Till all the coals glow from red to white
And then hammering the rosy steel
On the anvil with its rhino horn, and then the drill
And the oily, smoking curlings from the prone, holed steel,
While the belt slaps on the high pulley.

I'm thirsty. The clank of the iron-handled pump
By the underground tank pulls a cold fall of pure water
Soon rimming the enamel cup. I drink, fill another for Mick.

XXIX

The simplicities of remembered work can still bring succour,
Here, where no work can be done, by hand or brain.
Dostoevsky in Siberia thought that if it were desired
To reduce a man to nothing, the most atrocious
Punishment would be to make him work
At something absurd, absolutely useless.

When I was in the black prison of stone,
Every day, in the yard, prisoners
Were put to work, building little walls
Of brick and mortar. Next morning they were told
To knock them all down and start again.

As there were not walls enough around them.

XXX

At such times, there, or here, it's best
To remember the body, its diurnal work,
Even when it's nearly been destroyed.

My heartbeats sound in my head, pillowed on the bed,
Like an old one-lunger in a rusty boat,
The single piston hammering the cylinder
From a loose throttle, fast, quicker, slow,
But steadily making a plodding progress
Through the sea, with twin bow-waves curling,
While the one white wake fans widely.

XXXI

After so many trials, why are there still
So many errors, with all that accumulated wisdom?

The first gourmet who fine-chopped
Oleander leaves and tossed them in a salad
Died in considerable discomfort – while his silly sheep
Knew all about oleanders, gave them a miss.

XXXII

Mostly out of here, in far countries,
Most of all in the one I call home,
My thoughts fly slow as a flock of ibis
Going from the swamp by the bridge to some other
Succulent mud, to search in with long curve of beak.

But my body stays here, lean from distress.
In four days I've lost fourteen pounds.
That old stuff about how in every fat person
There's a thin one crying to get out –
How do you know you'd want to meet that person?
Nevertheless I'm listening now, I'd rather like to hear
A fat resident laugh in my structure of bones.

XXXIII

There are many countries I love, but that's a different
Kind of memory, one with surface roots
That pull easily, even without a cyclone.
'This life abroad', said Christina,
'Unclasps all my contacts with life'.
How much more so this half-life in hospital.
If there were windows there might be trees
And if there were trees there might be birds,
But even in Central Park they'd not be mine,
Though the rocks and earth might be, being universal.
Yet what a fearful portent it would be if black cockatoos
With their dragging, funeral flight and graveyard cries,
Made a slow appearance over Central Park.

XXXIV

I'm a student again, in little Adelaide,
And the beaky, humorous Professor's lecture
Suddenly becomes sonorous in the hushed theatre,
As he begins to read Dunbar in his native Scots, with the Latin
Refrain: '*Timor mortis conturbat me…*'

At seventeen, it meant more to me than cemeteries,
Even more than the war, some ten months old,
More of the slow warning of the black cockatoo
Mingling with the reminders of the cathedral bells.
But I was young, and it was only an idea,
More of a *frisson* than an insinuation of fear –

Your death would come some time, maybe welcomed
By unimaginable age, from inside your body,
Out of some starless night of nowhere,
Though even for the young there could also be a range of somewheres,
Grey bullet, black drowning, white avalanche,
Or even a golden sandfall like a whispering hourglass.
Or merely a buzz, a mosquito from bad air.

XXXV

'Perfection of the life, or of the work.'
Yeats had never read Rilke's German almost the same:
'Denn irgendwo ist eine alte Feindschaft
zwischen dem Leben und der grossen Arbeit'.
'For somewhere there is an ancient enmity
between the life and the great work'.
In the German, just one letter between anywhere
And nowhere, *irgendwo, nirgendwo,*
That little letter 'n', so nice and neat,
Also the gateway to a wilderness of negations,
Nein, nichts, niemals, niemand,
No, not, never, no one,
Also the hammer-clang of loneliness and death,
Of King Lear's helpless repetitions.

But the words keep slithering down the rope
Of the alphabet, and without words
No message will be allowed through.
While they are breaking us we are already making more,
Saving us with choirs of celebration, '*Freude, Freude…*'

XXXVI

Between somewhere and somewhere the programmes can go wrong,
Those Five Year Plans, the Chairman's new agriculture
That led to millions dying secretly in famine.

Yet we're so obstinate, if allowed to survive.
Our nowheres, too, make gibber deserts of plans.

But how the stones shine! Though they provide
Neither food nor drink, the desert dew falls nightly;
If you're thirsty you can catch it in plastic sheeting.

XXXVII

I am not blind, but I cannot read,
And all on the left of my vision falls off into space.

How lucky, then and now, there's a library in my head,
Albeit lots of the books are a bit incongruous,
Like *Hiawatha*, a poem about what we called
Red Indians, which our German governess
Taught my sister and me. It's more than sixty years ago
But I can still remember the hypnotic trochees:
'On the shores of Gitche-Gumee,
Of the shining Big-Sea Water,'
The rhythm opening visions of unknown waters and forests –

It didn't hurt my little brain to learn so much by heart,
Now scorned as rote, but it's a habit I've never lost,
So now there's that unlocked library
Behind the prison bars of my eyes,
And I have good conversations with the dead.

It's kind of them to give us their immortal comfort,
And also to be a sort of cattle-prod
To this inert body stuck in the race,
For they're also an aim, a tall sign of winning,
Like the original meaning of the word 'steeplechase'.

XXXVIII

Our nowhere is vaster than the universe
And its stars, planets, invading meteors,
It's immune from telescopes, neither of space nor time,
And its ruler, the Black Prince of Nowhere, he knows
He'll get you, he's immune from revolution.

Yet inside us there is also a country which was really *nullius*,
No dusky trees turning into people;
We settled it with memory, words, sights, sounds,
The geology of Now, rocks in the earthy years.
Though Nature often tried to eliminate us.

We have a remedy for all those injuries.
The imagination. With it we are gods,
We have the shaping power. In dreams
The imagination is taken prisoner –
Dreams, however much, healthy or sick, we need them,
They are invaders of our own black nowhere,
By being so inventive, so exact.
So we wake up having lost it, still unable to see,
Unless they are found again by the imagination,
Letting us walk in medieval gardens,
Giving us pleasure domes and sacred rivers.

New York Nowhere

Even in this whitelocked prison, sights and sounds

Can be conjured up, roads, paintings, symphonies,

But never a scent or stink, neither wattle blossom

Nor the graveyard stench of a too-long-wet dishcloth.

Hidden in scents, say rosemary or mown grass,

Are also the swiftest conduits of longest memory.

But in hospital or prison that current is never switched on.

A twig of rosemary leaves, astringent, dry,

Would instantaneously make me a child again,

In my mother's garden by the sea, rosemary hedges

Along the tight brick paths, and from over the fence

The untidy smell of seaweed twisted with gull-cries.

Yet here in this antiseptic, sterile ward,

I had the worst dream I've ever known.

Never had I caught a scent in a dream before.

There was a tall man, dead a week or so,

And I could smell nothing but his green flesh.

It held me like the scent of my own death,

And I turned to the man next to me, who was not Richard,

In the mud, in the trenches, in the First World War.

XXXIX

I'm happy to submit to the indignity of the drip
If it chases out those comets and shooting stars
And leaves my imagination free to grow from nowhere,
Although imagination tangles dangerously with memory,
For imagination is the power that has no boundaries,
While memory is tagged with landmarks, seamarks,
Some leading to a happy place, others
Losing us in endless mangrove swamps,
Boots sucked by mud below horizontal boughs
While crocodiles' eyes rise like little islands
Above the still water of the estuary.

Dreams being also enemies of imagination,
Are so seductively similar, but heedlessly given
To the passive prisoner in the bed of sleep,
Whereas the imagination is out and active.

It's a bit like the leading out from sex in love,
The release that's also a liberation,
For in love there's no warder peeping through the door.

XL

But we must always be wary of the fear in imagining,
Especially those who work alone, and with words.
'No one is so easily frightened as a writer.'

And there's a further danger for a poet
Who's had the fortitude to lift off, having first
Escaped the tyranny of real things,
Hoping to fix it more securely in the abstract,
To be confined to the chase of pure form
As vision is closed off by hallucinations.

That's when the past beckons most seductively.
But the past's for explaining, not for yearning.

Fortunately, at seventy-three, I'm too old
For nostalgia, that leaching disease of foolish middle age –
Not that old age can't be foolish too.
Where did I put it? What was I going to do?
Those endless straw trivialities
That fill sheds but couldn't feed a sheep in a drought.

XLI

I remember how lovely that soft-flanked sandhill,
Unmarked by the prints of lizards or birds,
High as a waterfall, but quite still,
And the children taking it by surprise, like a fortress, from the back,
Flying, diving, rolling, yelling down it,
Their bodies releasing little avalanches.

The purity of the sandhill was violently vandalized,
But a few days later the returning wind
Had sculpted it smooth again with whispers of sand;
It's not often that wounds heal so perfectly.

Healing – the silent, unwilled healing,
The cuts that are healing in Richard and Danny's sleep –

One morning, in my vision, on the left, maybe
The black emptiness will have retreated
Just a little, 'ealing' become 'healing', 'he' 'she',
Though the latter could be a bit confusing without
Some glimpse of a further meaning to crack the code.

XLII

I've been lying here in The New York Hospital for four days
And no one's made my bed, let alone changed the sheets.
After three days without a wash
I ask the ward sister if I could have one.
She roars "Watcha wanna wash?"
"Me," I plaintively reply. "Nurses is busy.
I'll getcha some water." She disappears,
Comes back with water in a steel basin
Which she dumps by my bed, and goes. I wash bits
Of myself and sort of dry them with Kleenex.

The bed alone costs more than a night in the Plaza.

In that bed all day, I'm remembering incongruous
Tips for sleeping out in the bush, where the nights are icy –
My mother: "Always dig a hip-hole on hard ground."
An old opal miner: "Sleep between two fires,
But mind yer don't roll into one of 'em."

XLIII

Hospital beds are narrow, and a bit hard,
But definitely a big improvement
On the lean straw palliasse in the prison cell.

Our own strength, coming out of nowhere,
Will help us to open the cell door, then the gates,
And there's the vast city, which was always there,
And the long crowds that are not shortened
By you recognizing someone you didn't particularly
Want to see. The city makes no demands on you,
You're not slotted into suburbs or country towns, where
The baby sits like a little emperor
In his pen, and the lone mother manages
While the absent husband is slid into a filing cabinet.

The city is in the mind, inside it, inside us,
Fertile chaos is given back to us.

The best thing, when the hallucinations go,
Is that I can see again with my eyes closed,
Creating worlds again from the chaos of nowhere,
And when you have suffered you can see certain things
Which in happiness are hidden behind impressionist landscapes.

Dreams and imagination can now meet,
Hardening reality for different ends.
Someone, even the beloved, can now stiffen
In the darkness the prisoner's slack flesh again.
So in the nightly drift towards extremities
When Eros was always locked out, Thanatos admitted,
We can now pass like radio waves through concrete,
Past the nurses who neutrally administer
All rites save those that make man and woman one.

XLIV

Now the time is coming for my release, if not pardon.
I am nervous of many things, but most
Of what the man in the white coat warned me
Was certain to come, as it seems it always does
To those whose brains have been damaged, that out of nowhere
The black dog will be unchained, call it
Depression, dejection, either way it's down,
Down into useless insignificance,
A black pool to drown in, just waiting,
As if the wounded brain were taking its revenge
Instead of accepting the healing and the scar.

XLV

Yesterday Danny walked. It began slowly
With a whimper. But no squeal. Just cautious feet.
We all cheered. Danny and the helpers smiled.

This was also the day when Mrs F. herself
Came to see Richard, swirling a scent
Of Joy (by Patou) and an elegance of Paris
Into the cold white bones of the ward.
"Hi!" she said to me, with a smile all for me,
"Do you mind?" as she had to turn her back on me to talk to Richard,
"The Continental's ready and waiting for you,
Richard, and so are we. Hurry on out!"

On such days optimism wags its tail,
Lollops around the ward and licks our faces.

XLVI

You never feel so foolish in hospital
As on the day you're allowed to leave,
When you're wearing your ordinary clothes again,
Reflecting that, often, Western man's
Most colourful clothes are his underpants, unseen.
Sitting on the edge of the bed, waiting to go home.
These are indeed my own, familiar clothes,
But I'm not the same person who last wore them.

This does not worry her when she comes to lead me home,
For she inhabits both spaces, the somewhere
At the time, and the timeless nowhere I carry inside me,
And she performs the miracle
Of returning me to myself.

The one who stumbles on her arm is already renewed.

When there's nothing to be, to see, nowhere to go,
They usually say you're driven back on yourself –
But yourself has to be someone to go back to,
Not for those little or seemingly big achievements,
But for love, something drawn out of nowhere
To an assenting boldness somewhere within us,
Like the bold upward stare of a desert flower
Right into the dangerous face of the very sun,
And the flower keeps open-eyed and is not blackened.

Yet there's a rich irony to my returning vision,
That I can see the right hand side of everything,
But it's through a shroud of white mist, like flying through cloud,
The brilliant droplets glittering so I have to wear
Dark glasses – out of black nowhere, a white cloud.

I am walking out, out into the great city.

The healing is slowly coming out of nowhere, allowed.
If our great remedy is patience
Then death also can be indulgently patient,
However often there's a contemptuous flick
That switches off a short life or a long.

Maybe the Black Prince of Nowhere likes
A bit of spirit in his subjects. Since we are all
His, why should he be in a hurry to have us?
Maybe he's amused, looking at our white prisons,
That can release the damaged back into life
Along the corridors where shrouded trolleys
Are blindly going the other way.

There are no limits to the room within me, even
In the white prison there was waiting a fertile darkness.

XLVII

Walking on her arm through the normal streets
New York Nowhere becomes Out to Anywhere.
The city's lights flash and tremble, but are not fearsome,
It flows, stops, honks, accelerates to the sky.

But Anywhere as well as Nowhere is inside us.
It is only in ourselves we can rebuild,
While all around us people are falling apart,
The pedestrians who seemed to be whole.

After we have survived, blithe Anywhere
It is not. Remember the doctor's warning
Of the waiting dark pool fit for drowning in,
Flecked with the cold chips of stars.

Walking, and on her arm,
Nowhere has not been No, and in what we are seeing
Neither of us is blocking the view.
We have seen too much for that.

But what am I doing
With all this talk of 'I' and 'You' and 'We'?
How selfish are the sick!
Yet on the helicopter ladder from the wreck
It's hard to think of anyone else.
Later you find self-help is only a stage,
And 'stages of development do not repeat themselves'.
Love, too, though unhalted, still moves by stages.
We must prepare ourselves, especially in love,
One day, far out in the spinifex desert,
To see just one ear-tip of happiness,
A kangaroo propping over a sandhill.

You need the other. But what if the other
Is exhausted, used up? Think about this as you walk
Through the uncaring city on her arm.

Though the sleeping batteries are there inside us
We can't turn ourselves on like a torch.
All we can do is hang on
And mumble about inner resources
Until one day Danny is dancing
And Richard is driving the Continental.

How lovely and leading are the streets to Anywhere!
And beside us is that unexpected ally, time.

Though the Black Prince rules us creatures
He is powerless to prevent
The sun rising in the Anywhere of time.
Daylight! The White Angel allows
Dead trees to be surrounded by seeds,
The ocean to be washing the dirty world,
And doesn't look down on the trivial,
Is even happy to be 'silly like us'.

The Black Prince is a solitary fellow,
He has no friends, only desperate supplicants,
No ordinary followers praise his company,
While the White Angel delights in love and friendship,
Sympathy without a single purpose of the ego.
Time flows with the White Angel,
The Black Prince is left with gravestones.

To be spared is something. Give praise.
It's early to be sure of joy. But in time
The sun also comes Out of Nowhere.

Meanwhile the greatest mistake is to think
We will no longer be tortured, out in Anywhere.
Here in New York Anywhere
You have to let go her arm
And walk alone. Don't drag her down.
Love is neither hallucination nor illusion,
But a constant learning in how to see clearly.

The White Angel's way past the black pool
Is beyond the doctor's warning.
As if Eurydice were leading Orpheus,
Only she will not look back,
Nor he, being led into the day.

11 A Coffee With Ken: Ken Bolton's Adelaide

Jill Jones

In a recent review of one of Ken Bolton's latest books, *Sly Mongoose*, his friend, the poet Pam Brown, writes:

> Ken can often be seen walking down a city street in Adelaide, frowning slightly, (possibly from the glare of a bright sunny day, possibly with the *frightful weight* of thought) whistling fragments of tunes to himself, heading from his job at the Experimental Art Foundation to a favourite, or rather, familiar, yet never cool nor trendy, café for lunch. There he might jot down some notes while waiting for his plate of mezes. Those notes, in spidery indecipherable-to-anyone-else handwriting, will end up as poems ... (Brown)

The title of one of Bolton's more recent works, *At The Flash and At The Baci*, name checks two, now apparently defunct, Hindley Street cafés where this note jotting often occurred. Although Bolton's work features many references to specific acts of Adelaide city living, a sense of a 'literary Adelaide' is largely absent, though a visual art scene is central. As Bolton himself has said about his move from Sydney to Adelaide in the 1980s: 'Adelaide is an easily negotiated town & I liked it. I took almost no part in its literary life, but the art scene was genuinely interesting. What Adelaide offered me as a writer was anonymity' (Cook 53). In this chapter, I want to walk around in my own poet's way two things operating here: how a writer's sense of place may feature in their work, and more peripherally, the way a writer from elsewhere negotiates Adelaide.

It was partly through Pam Brown that Ken Bolton came to Adelaide. He stayed and she left. Brown was working at the Experimental Art Foundation (now the Australian Experimental Art Foundation) around 1980, 1981 and, according to Bolton, persuaded the EAF to give him a residency there over December 1981 (Minter). He ended up getting a job as the EAF's offset-printer and, from that time, did various kinds of work at the Foundation. He has been running their bookshop, Dark Horsey, for many years, as well doing various forms of art criticism in everything from the *Advertiser* to serious art journals such as *Photofile*, *Art and Text* and *Art Monthly*, much of it recently collected in a book of art criticism, *Art Writing: Art in Adelaide in the 1990s and 2000s*.

This chapter mainly refers to Bolton's more recent work, from *At The Flash and At The Baci* onwards, but there is reference to Adelaide in Bolton's poems from the 1980s onwards: names of people, venues, streets, and so on. With *At The Flash and At The Baci*, for instance, the local is announced specifically by the book's title and the book begins by explicitly dealing with an Adelaide setting, in the first lines of the poem, 'Home Town':

> Driving into work while
> Cath reads about driving around London
> & wondering when will I next write a poem
> or whether to just work on *Gwendolyn*
> a poem of John's & mine & maybe I should
> it is half mine, I drop Cath off, do a
> U-turn & scoot down to the EAF, park, go inside
> check the mail empty my bag a little

> lock up again & set off for the coffee shop
> where I'll read or write a poem or a
> review-or work on *Gwendolyn* ...
>
> (*Flash*, 3)

And later in that poem there is a more moody section, which this extraction, like most from Bolton's longer works, does not quite do justice to:

> Walking into town
>   to deliver an article to the
> *Advertiser*
>   feeling deliciously alone ...
>
>   winter light & clouds, the
> suggestion of rain
>   another article done, anonymous ...
>
> I see Tubby Justice across the street, waiting.
>   I wave.
> She waves, & disappears
>   hurries off, ahead. I smile
> & she reappears & we say hello. My friends
> are like ghosts in Adelaide
>   What is real here?
>
> (*Flash*, 6)

When *At The Flash and At The Baci* was published it was partly blurbed as follows:

> These poems were mostly conceived, written and worked on at the establishments which lend the collection its name, The Flash and The Baci, two coffee shops in Hindley Street, downtown Adelaide. (*Flash*, n.p.)

Since coming to live in Adelaide I have often wondered about these semi-legendary places and searched Hindley Street for them. And never found them. I even wondered if they'd been made up, or were composites. So I asked Ken, who told me via email:

> the Flash used to be where Short Black is now (near Tempo), but its last decade was across the road in what is now a discount clothes store, if it's open at all. It depressed most people in that new spot. The Baci was shorter lived—five or six years?—then became the would-be swishy *Tu Dish* which folded, despite its success, because someone wanted their lease. It's now a 'convenience' store, more or less across from the Cacas Chemist shop.
> There's no one place I go now. I needed a title—the places weren't really important, tho I suppose I was motivated to make all the thinking seen as somehow having 'a material base'. (Bolton, personal communication, 8 Feb 2012)

Some things that are always evident in Bolton's poems are the materials, as well as the sources, the references, the evidence of the moment. Names are named, speech is quoted and places are part of the poem's movement. This writing of place, or perhaps I should say in place—this imagining, this making in writing of a city that is both a source of thinking about other places yet also a place of busyness and business in its own particular form—relates to an idea of a provincialism (in the mostly positive sense of that word) that could be said to be Adelaidean. It is a place where life is negotiable yet busy enough, urban if not quite urbane enough for a super-abundance of ideas about art and poetry, but enough ideas anyway, in the way it is in certain, say European, provincial cities where a cultural life works without being so much in thrall to larger cultural movements or the more crass elements of capital, finance, deals, the weight of national and international politics.

In some of Bolton's poems, the movement is made through collage effects or working with fragments of texts written at different times. This way of working is not uncommon in contemporary poetry and could be said to be an effect of the poet living and writing the city, any city. Indeed, in 2012 Bolton re-released a small book of very early poems written while living in Sydney, *Four Poems*, which contains work constructed using a collage technique. As an aside, reading these earlier poems, and others of the time, it feels there is a difference in mood if not compositional style, from an exuberance to a calmness, which may be a function of age, inevitable changes in writing strategies, but possibly an effect of the place of writing, from Sydney's multitudinous curves to Adelaide's flatter, less frenetic ways. However, you would look hard to find in Bolton's Adelaide poems any reflection of Adelaide's more grid-like urban features. There is still the modernist drift or flâneurism in the poems, based on walking and contemplating, particularly the sky, possibly as a sign of looking elsewhere, and the weather, 'the breeze moving through the room' (*Bop*, 121).

Bolton also has a great interest in jazz, evidenced in so many of his poems throughout his career. To work with that analogy, you could also see many of his poems as improvisation, of movement and making as one goes along (again, this could be seen as a city effect), of selection of thought and movement. All of this is about decisions on the moment much as a musician might make decisions. In other words, it is not complete randomness but reflective of the way the mind makes choices in the making of work and ideas. It is about syncopation/syntax, about the page where the poem plays—something close to what poet and critic Peter Minter called 'kinetic' in Bolton's work (Minter).

Another way of putting it is in Frank O'Hara's words: 'You just go on your nerve' (Ford 247). Bolton references O'Hara in his work, and it is by way of explaining the title of this chapter, which in part refers to O'Hara's well-known poem, 'Having a Coke With You'. Bolton describes it this way:

> attending to the way thinking moves: inflected by, deflecting off and in deference to its surroundings—one's context—including other ideas and thoughts, memories, records playing, people going by on the street, the counter argument presented even by the appearance of other people in, say, a coffee shop—people who, sensibly, don't look like they hold the same ideas as you or hold them with larger or smaller pinches of salt. The shifts from idea to idea, the gaps and pausing, can provide poetically or aesthetically interesting shape or

form, that is, effectively, what a poem is: its motif if you like, in the
Cézanne sense. (Kinsella)

Bolton's poems contain a more flattened, democratic, sometimes sceptical or oblique, rather than any inflated 'poetic', diction; this is not poetry of the sublime, nor the 'high' lyric form. Nor is it pompous, though it can be serious in a teasing, inquiring and ironical way. Throughout his work, the flux and ephemera, the dailiness and detritus of life, feature and are worried over at times. And in thinking of that and looking, say, at the first section again of 'Home Town', I can't help wondering about the second-hand bookshops and record shops, the second-hand clothes shops, that flourish in Adelaide. In other words, there is nothing slick here; things, like words, have their uses. They aren't proud or inflated.

And, despite this, distance is also a factor in Bolton's writing, as it is a factor for Adelaide, and Australia, for that matter. Bolton's references to elsewhere, other than Australia, have always been primarily US American, whether written about from Sydney or Adelaide or on his travels—though he writes in a poem:

> Everything that's happened to me
> has happened in Australia.
> (*Untimely*, 52)

However, he went, not to America, but away from the biggest Australian city, Sydney, to one of the more provincial capitals, Adelaide. In one of his collaborative poems (with John Jenkins), 'The God of Trieste, Arezzo, Adelaide, Pisa, Leipzig and Other Smaller Cities Looks Down', mention is made of this god's observation about 'the hopeless crud/ that's going on in this town' (*Nutters*, 1). But the god also speaks of a fondness of such a place, a 'smaller city', of watching a figure by a river, say, the Torrens, which 'seems real enough' (2). Although it is a collaborative poem, it sounds as Boltonian as anything he would write solo.

Bolton's is an internationalism that can flourish quite well in Australia, in Adelaide:

> I worried about my own authenticity
> > in relation
> to the great art of elsewhere
>
> and the past. Ignoring or denying it
> seemed not the way to go—
>
> and anyway, I *liked* it: the fabulous clouds
> of Guardi and Tiepolo, the silky greys and whites and silvers
>
> of the skirts in a Gainsborough—like the winter skies
> of Adelaide; the beautiful surfaces in the poems
>
> of Frank O'Hara, Ted Berrigan, and later
> James Schuyler—and the work of
>
> some of my friends—which was great
> in *relation* to that.
> (*Untimely*, 58)

This is also how his poetry works, as relational, processural, writing aware of the conditions of its making.

Interestingly, in a 2005 interview Bolton says:

> I was all for internationalism when I began, but a very unexamined notion of it. Weirdly, now I see my stuff as strictly for the local market. I've absorbed and used a lot of influences—just to be grown up, fully qualified—but my poems are pretty much focused here, where they're not wanted. Maybe I'm not part of the culture. (Minter)

As already noted, Bolton has been part of the/an art scene in Adelaide for a long time and studied art in Sydney. He also has contributed drawings and artwork, pseudonymously, to some of his books. It is worth noting this when looking at, as opposed to reading, his work. Bolton uses the space of the page and the resources of punctuation and typography, though he has done this all along, in Sydney, in Adelaide. They are cities, places of movement, of walking, of thought.

But what of the specific Adelaide in the work? I won't provide an exhaustive list of every place, street, venue that is named in the poems. Some of the references are indirect anyway, and to places that undoubtedly disappeared from the 1980s onwards and to an outsider are, therefore, rather opaque.

The centerpiece is always Hindley Street, which can represent many things. To many Adelaideans, it's the place of tackiness, grunginess and late night violence, in a bad way, and to others it's a source of late night drinking, grunginess and possibly violence in not so bad a way. However, as well as pubs, bars and nightclubs, it's full of cafes, convenience stores, small businesses and cultural institutions, and Ken Bolton works nearby. It's his main daily place and there's not so much reference to its nightlife in his work but more its everyday plain ordinariness, Cacas Chemist, the now-defunct Flash and Baci, other shops, places to eat, places that sell T-shirts.

Other pubs and bars get a mention in the poems—the Exeter, the Austral over the other side of the CBD—as well as various gallery spaces, and also parts of suburbs. For instance, you can find traces of the inner southern suburbs in the poems published in the last decade or so. A hairdressing salon on Winston Ave features in one poem. An educated guess, therefore, might place the current Bolton residence in the inner southern suburbs. Indeed, home life, 'bounded comfort' (*Bop*, 88)—surely an Adelaide moment—the late night thinking and reading life, feature a lot in the poems. In a poem, Bolton will write about putting on a jazz or blues album, Joe Turner or John Coltrane, say, or maybe even Lou Reed, as if this is the occasion for a poem. It is also in these poems that one gets something of an Adelaide effect, of being one of only a few and therefore needing to contact friends in other cities and even imagine dialogues with writers and others the one admires. The poems are often conversations, or letters, directed to a particular friend, or in remembrance of a friend either dead, or living somewhere else and imagined. Thus, in the poem 'Halogen Pam':

> I picture
> Pam's halogen lamp sending
> a warm cone of light down
>
> onto her desk ...
> (*Flash*, 17)

The poem speaks of Pam Brown in the third person for most of its duration. Only on the last page is there a more direct address:

> Actually Pam, you *should move* down here: I go outside—
> & the air is exactly what I want from Sydney—so moist
> it is almost cool, & softly bright
>
> that is very Sydney—or Melbourne's idea of Sydney—the great
> doorway to the T-shirt shop, filled with the fake jaws of a shark—
> that you step through. ...
> (*Flash*, 24)

It is Bolton's determination to stick with dailiness and detail that prevents such poems becoming nostalgic, though a sense of melancholy, a great Adelaide emotion, may tinge them, via the vision of Pam's lamp, or a pencil dragging, or the memory of a kind of Sydneyness in the T-shirt shop on Hindley.

And now for something a bit more personal—some notes towards a poet's career, the poet in Adelaide. I don't propose Bolton as an exemplar of that; in a sense he is an anti-exemplar, and self-described as such (as noted above). Indeed, Bolton has noted publically in more than one place that he has never been a part of the Adelaide literary scene. Yet, paradoxically, he has done much of a literary nature here. This raises questions of whether there is ever one 'literary scene' in cities, let alone how various groupings, formal and informal, regard the activities of others beyond their circle, or intersecting with their circle.

From the mid-1980s to the mid-1990s Bolton produced *Otis Rush*, an influential literary journal out of Adelaide (it featured not only major Australian poets but overseas writers such as Gregory O'Brien, Jenny

Bornholdt, Harry Mathews, Tony Towle and Michele Leggott). He has run a small publishing press, admittedly mostly publishing his own work but certainly not exclusively. From time to time he has run a series of readings, the first being *New Writing Performed* organised with Brooke Watson in the late 1980s, the latest iteration being the Lee Marvin readings, which have run on-and-off again for some years in various venues. This does raise the issue of what precisely is 'the literary scene', particularly in Adelaide.

In an interview with John Kinsella, Bolton says:

> I started publishing *Otis* after I'd been in Adelaide a few years (in 1987). I did it for the same reason as before. There still weren't mags for me to appear in and I thought I'd like to publish somewhere. ... Adelaide's a long way from the publishing action and is not taken too seriously as an artistic centre by the east coast. And I was getting bored. So I started a new magazine. ... And there were a few Adelaide writers worth showing to the world who couldn't publish here and couldn't—from Adelaide—easily crack Melbourne or Sydney. (Kinsella)

In other words, he created a literary scene or milieu, although in interviews such as this he seems to suggest that the Adelaide scene (or scenes) is somewhere else. In an interview with Peter Minter he says:

> The Adelaide literary scene didn't find me very amusing—nor I it. ... It seemed to me that there was Friendly Street, a monthly open reading in a council-community centre ... There was *probably* a 'scene' around people like John Bray and Peter Goldsworthy and Noel Purdon and Peter Ward. I read at Friendly Street when I arrived. The 'Stooge' poem drew no laughs and no one spoke to me. They were trying to tell me something. I hope I didn't read it wrong. (Minter)

But he found a different community, via the visual art scene, that did nurture him, as he notes:

a kind of 'in' scene centered around the visual arts, music, alcohol, and more or less libertarian-leftist ideas and attitudes (and education, politics, design even). I wrote within that context—and to some degree to that context—in exile from the literary world I conceived of as Newtown, Fitzroy and maybe St Marks Place occasionally. (Minter)

He has stated in more than one place that the anonymity he experienced as a writer in Adelaide actually helped him. He expands on this in the Minter interview:

> But I'd had to adjust myself to the idea that I wasn't going to get much recognition and ask myself if the writing I was doing was any good or not. ... I think I began to take my work more seriously because no one else was. I wasn't looking for outside approval, since there was none. So it had to be good enough to make me happy ... (Minter)

As Bolton points out in the Minter interview, being isolated but also being involved with an organisation and an art scene which he was writing into, thinking into, provided energy and, as he puts it in relation to his work, 'more grist for the mill'. One may detect some disingenuousness in all this, or possibly an attempt to be positive rather than negative. This is the point, when talking about 'the poet' that it is tempting to overanalyse personal situations and biography, so I won't lean on this too much, albeit that I am quoting from material that is publically available.

It is also within a context where it could be argued that, while the current Adelaide literary scene is mainly imagined, and almost certainly by non-Adelaideans, through Adelaide Writers' Week, the SA Writers' Centre, perhaps Wakefield Press, and, for poets, the Friendly Street readings or some regular slam poetry events, and a few key figures, there is really not, even in as small a capital as Adelaide, a monolithic 'scene'. There are, expectedly, small nodes of activity that have some connections with some of the above as well as more informal, private gatherings and discussion plus, simply, individuals working pretty much alone or working via connections beyond Adelaide.

Bolton, despite being ignored by some of the more conservative Australian critics and anthologisers, is a key figure in Australian poetry. He may still see himself, sometimes, as 'Sydney' (Cook), and possibly be seen by some Adelaideans as 'Sydney', but he has lived in Adelaide for around 30 years in a way that is not just being anonymous or solitary, but through being an energetic focus for certain kinds of Australian writing, and art for that matter, beyond the east coast Sydney/Melbourne nexus.

It does not matter that certain Adelaide 'scenes' and Bolton do not coincide; the work is being done and a milieu, a casual but consistent one, has been created by him in Adelaide. And he has consistently featured an Adelaide in his work, a daily and nightly Adelaide life of a particular kind of worker and thinker and writer that lives in a small town but is not 'small town', not at all.

WORKS CITED

Bolton, Ken. *At The Flash & At The Baci*. Kent Town, SA: Wakefield Press, 2006.

___. *Four Poems*. Adelaide: Little Esther, 2012.

___ [with John Jenkins]. *Nutters Without Fetters*. Berry, NSW: PressPress, 2002.

___. *Sly Mongoose*. Glebe, NSW: Puncher & Wattmann, 2011.

___. *Untimely Meditations*. Kent Town, SA: Wakefield Press, 1997.

___. *A Whistled Bit of Bop*. Sydney: Vagabond Press, 2010.

Brown, Pam. 'Sly Mongoose by Ken Bolton: Pam Brown Reviews'. *Galatea Resurrects* 17 (December 2011). <http://galatearesurrection17.blogspot.com.au/2011/12/sly-mongoose-by-ken-bolton.html>. Accessed 8 February 2012.

Cook, R. 'Under the Counter: Interview Ken Bolton'. *Contemporary Visual Art-Culture Broadsheet* 39.1 (2010): 53-6.

Ford, Mark. Ed. *Frank O'Hara: Selected Poems*. New York: Alfred A. Knopf, 2008.

Kinsella, John. 'John Kinsella Interviews Ken Bolton', n.d. <http://www.johnkinsella.org/interviews/bolton.html>. Accessed 8 February 2012.

Minter, Peter. 'Ken Bolton in conversation with Peter Minter 12 October 2004 to 29 April 2005', *Jacket Magazine* 27 (April 2005). <http://jacketmagazine.com/27/bolton-mint.html>. Accessed 8 February 2012.

12 'A Dozy City': Adelaide in J.M. Coetzee's *Slow Man* and Amy T. Matthews's *End of the Night Girl*

Gillian Dooley

A blog post by Michael Duffy from May 2011, titled 'Is Adelaide Our Cruellest City?', begins:

> I was on a panel at the recent Sydney Writers Festival where novelists talked about the ideal cities in which to set crime fiction. Michael Connelly (Los Angeles), Gary Disher (Melbourne) and myself (Sydney) agreed the most important thing is for a city to be big enough to have experienced most types of evil, so that any horror will seem believable if set there in a novel.
>
> But Gary reminded us there is one city that fits this bill despite its relative smallness: Adelaide, the 'city of corpses'.
>
> Although Adelaide's murder rate is no higher than anywhere else in Australia, it has had more than its share of particularly gruesome and distressing murders. ... Salman Rushdie once nominated

Adelaide as 'the perfect setting for a Stephen King novel or horror film'.[1]

There are plenty of examples of books and films trading on this reputation, one of the most notable recent examples being the 2011 film *Snowtown*, which dramatises the gruesome series of murders committed in and around Adelaide in the 1990s by John Bunting and his associates. Susan Mitchell's book about these murders, *All Things Bright and Beautiful* (2005), emphasised the creepy quality she projected onto the northern suburbs where most of the so-called Snowtown murders took place and where Bunting lived. In local author Lisa L. Hannett's 2011 book of short stories, *Bluegrass Symphony*, which is set in an alternative version of somewhere like the southern states of the US, the author biography on the front flyleaf mentions the fact that she lives in Adelaide, 'city of churches, bizarre murders, and pie floaters'. Stephen Orr's award-winning novel *Time's Long Ruin* (2010) is a fictional version of the unexplained disappearance of the three Beaumont children in 1966, and in the following year he published a non-fiction book called *The Cruel City*, investigating the phenomenon of Adelaide's bizarre and murderous reputation.

Duffy's blog post quoted above continues 'In the past decade there has been nothing to equal the above horrors. Stephen Orr concludes his book [*The Cruel City*] with the hope that "in time Adelaide's reputation as evil, a city of corpses, will fade."' Orr, one might cheekily note, is not on the face of it particularly committed to dampening this reputation, given his preoccupation with exploring it in both fiction and non-fiction. I hasten to add that *Time's Long Ruin* is an excellent novel, and a deserving winner of the Adelaide Festival Unpublished Manuscript award and a 2012 National Year of Reading award.

However, Adelaide is not always seen in such an ominous light. Two other recent novels set in Adelaide use the city as a relatively benign, safe

---

[1] Although this post is signed only 'National Times', a check of the Sydney Writers Festival website reveals the poster to be Michael Duffy.

place, in contrast, implicitly or explicitly, with places where large-scale murderous and evil acts were perpetrated. In this chapter I explore this aspect of Adelaide as a setting for fiction in Amy T. Matthews's *End of the Night Girl* (2011) and J.M. Coetzee's *Slow Man* (2005).

End of the Night Girl is Matthews's first literary novel (though she has had a successful career as a commercial romance writer) and it won the Adelaide Festival unpublished manuscript award the year after *Time's Long Ruin*. It concerns an Adelaide waiter, Molly, who is haunted by the Holocaust. As a child, she saw a picture in a 1933 encyclopaedia of an unnamed Polish Jew, a teenage girl. Now, in her late twenties, she finds herself compulsively creating the story of this girl, whom she calls Gienia, taking her through the horrors of the camps to her death just as the Russians arrive to liberate them. Molly, like her creator Matthews, is not Jewish, and has no personal associations with Holocaust victims, but although this fact puzzles other characters in the novel, it is not unusual. Hana Wirth-Nesher points out that 'shocking images of the Holocaust appalled and shaped the collective memory of non-Jews as well as Jews born right after the war' (310), and it continues to exert a horrified fascination over subsequent generations—beyond the reach of personal memory—with a stream of memoirs, novels and films exploring many and varied aspects of the phenomenon.

The problems involved in writing about the Holocaust have been extensively discussed in the critical literature. Esther Marion notes that 'Writing on the Nazi genocide has been marked by the tension between rupture and continuity', and goes on to argue that 'positing the Holocaust as an ultimate rupture denies it a vital place in memory and history, leaving a space of erasure rather than inquiry' (1020). On the other hand, if Nazi atrocities are seen as continuous with some notion of human normality, this may open the door to a troubling moral relativism. Marion concludes that Auschwitz, and the Holocaust more generally, challenges writers 'to listen and forge responsive and responsible approaches', rather than allowing it to be set apart from the course of history (1022).

I argue that Matthews has taken up this challenge in a particularly thoughtful and responsible way. Early critical reaction to her novel has been positive on the whole, though some reviewers haven't quite got the point. Naomi Milthorpe, in the *Canberra Times*, understands that 'Matthews is a writer well aware of the limits of fiction, and of the brutalities inflicted upon readers and characters by a literary writer in search of meaning'. On the other hand, Christopher Bantick, in the *Australian*, writes, 'this is a bold novel, yet I can't help thinking Matthews should have written a stand-alone story about the Holocaust and not attempted to splice the contemporary with the historical. *Gienia's story matters; Molly's does not*' (added emphasis). This assessment seems to me extraordinary, with its morally dubious dismissal of the life of one young woman in favour of another. In any case, countless authors have mined the horrors of the Holocaust, whereas *End of the Night Girl*, as Matthews told me in an interview, 'is in essence ... a novel about the ethics of fictionalising the Holocaust'. She also spoke to me informally about the difficulties of getting this book published—about agents and publishers who suggested she remove the Holocaust sections of the book and turn it into more easily marketable 'chick lit'.[2] Without both elements, *End of the Night Girl* would be a competent novel, but would not have anything like the same searching power and impact, and the Adelaide setting is an integral part of its structure.

Molly is very much an Adelaide woman. She lives in the middle-class suburb of Parkside, and, after her shifts as a silver service waiter, parties at the Mars Bar nightclub or the Exeter Hotel. She used to go to the movies at the Piccadilly in North Adelaide with her unrequited love, Peter, who lived along the road in Childers Street. Peter has left for Sydney with his partner, another relationship has recently ended, and Molly is stuck in a dead-end waiting job, easy prey for the Chef whose marriage is on the rocks. Her stepsister, up to now always dauntingly

---

[2] Amy T. Matthews, personal communication 26 July 2011.

successful and unsympathetic, descends from interstate and turns out to be pregnant and in need of her help.

Meanwhile, Gienia's story is taking over Molly's life, and she doesn't understand why. One of the problems that this novel poses and does not entirely resolve is the troubling ethical question of the way Molly is using the story almost as therapy for her own difficulties. When she is treated cruelly and finds herself comparing her pain with Gienia's, she has to tell herself, 'There is no equivalence' (168). 'I build horrors, to make mine trivial, and send her into hell. This is something you're not supposed to do. It feels like digging up a corpse for its jewellery. Or worse, its organs' (172). But she keeps noticing links between the two worlds. She sits in her Parkside flat watching the television documentary *Shoah*, and the camera pans 'across the fields near Chelmno. It looks like Smithfield Plains. Like you could drive over the horizon and be on Main North Road, like you could drive to Elizabeth City Centre and order a cappuccino and a biscotti' (186).

But of course Adelaide in the early twenty-first century is not Poland during World War Two. Molly's pain is genuine but it is not inflicted by a powerful malevolent regime bent on destroying her and her whole community. 'You know what you've done,' she says to her character. 'You've taken away my right to be anything but happy' (193). At the same time, the propensity of human beings for casual cruelty is something she witnesses continually, and sometimes suffers, in her work. Matthews drew on her own experiences as a waiter when writing *End of the Night Girl*:

> You learn a lot about human nature when you're a waiter and a lot of it is depressing. People—both customers and workmates—can be awful to you over the most trivial things. I quit waiting forever one day when a man yelled at me about a side-salad. He was red-faced and furious and out to humiliate me because of a salad. ... That kind of behaviour in some ways made sense of the Holocaust for me. Because how many times have you heard someone ask in

> bewilderment 'How could they do something like that?' and yet I'd go to work and be cursed at and humiliated over a bowl of lettuce leaves. There is no equivalence, but those moments always struck me like a warning. Some people revel in having power over other people; or they're liable to forget that you're a human being at all. (Dooley)

Nevertheless, Molly's pain is something she can work through and conquer, with help from her family and friends and with her own growing maturity, in her own time, without interference, or indeed with help, if she needs it, from the government. She can quit her job if she is unhappy, and she won't starve or be sent to a camp. She can go back to university and finish one of the courses she has abandoned, or get another job. The only malevolent force in Adelaide is that inherent in human nature, and Molly comes to understand that she is not always faultless herself: she has her reasons, but she can be cruel to her nearest relatives. If there is a moral, or at least some kind of accommodation reached, in *End of the Night Girl*, it is that despite the fact that it is sheer luck which has granted Molly a life free of the unmerited and state-sanctioned persecution suffered by so many millions, she can and must overcome the guilt she feels which is holding her back and blighting her life.

J.M. Coetzee's Adelaide in *Slow Man*, similarly, is not a threatening place. In an essay about the Australian settings for Coetzee's late novels, Melinda Harvey has noted their difference from the novels set in South Africa where 'characters are locked into hierarchical power relations or ties of responsibility and obligation, be they loath to them or not, and the plots are, as if accordingly, wound as tightly as springs', while the sketchy settings and 'listless plots' of the Australian novels suggest 'that history and politics are hermetic discourses in Australia that have little to do with the private affairs of its citizens' (29). In *Slow Man* Paul Rayment's problems belong, like Molly's in *End of the Night Girl*, to the realm of the personal rather than the political. In this case, however, the contrast with the politically charged environment is not made explicit. When Coetzee spoke at Flinders University Library in 2004, he told a questioner that the theme of ageing was something he was exploring in his current work (Fridays). This theme is present in earlier novels like *Age of Iron* and *Disgrace*, but the political dimensions of those books rather overshadow it. As Harvey points out, 'for Coetzee in Australia rendering place becomes an option, not an obligation—something he had always dreamed of' (30). In his Australian books he is free to consider the personal divorced from the political, while in South Africa, like it or not, the political implications of writing are under constant scrutiny.

Adelaide, the city where Coetzee has lived since 2002, appears in *Slow Man* as a strange collocation of disconnected place names, often lacking in geographical logic. Why is Paul Rayment, who lives in North Adelaide, riding down Magill Road on a bicycle loaded with his grocery shopping? (41). Anybody who knows Adelaide would realise how implausible that is: there are no shopping destinations along Magill Road which are in any way superior to what is available much closer at hand, including the Adelaide Central Market. Magill Road is, however, an appropriate setting for a catastrophic accident involving a bicycle and a fast car. Similarly, Coniston Terrace, where Paul lives, does not exist, though most of the other places mentioned in the novel—the River Torrens, the suburb of Munno Para, Rundle Mall—do. There are, in fact, not many specific place names used in the novel, and even when they are there is no sense of the particularity of North Adelaide—nothing to match Matthews's Rundle Street East, or even her restaurant Green River, which is fictional and even geographically impossible but evoked with a strong sense of place, 'looking down over the sloping suburbs, the parklands, the winding river' (181). When Paul visits a shop in Rundle Mall, the main shopping area of the Adelaide CBD, his arrival there is not described at first. He relates it later, in interior monologue, and even then it is couched in the conditional, which has the effect of making the description rather abstract: 'If he battles the crowds on Rundle Mall, if he bargains and cajoles and pays for stuff he does not need, it is not, or not just, for the sake of a child he has never laid eyes on' (171).

I am not suggesting that this is a deficiency in Coetzee's writing. Susan Smit-Marais and Marita Wenzel, in an article about his novel *Disgrace*, observe that 'even though the events that are portrayed appear to be realistic, the verisimilitude of their representation is not the purpose of their portrayal' (209). Brian McAllister, further, claims that in postmodern narratives the accurate representation of space, and time as well, is not only irrelevant: 'a determinate chronotope becomes unattainable, unnecessary, and undesirable' (58), and 'the chronotopes of art and life are two different but interdependent levels of dialogue' (68). Postmodernism is, of course, a disputed term, and is often linked with an irresponsibility which is quite foreign to Coetzee's serious purpose,[3] but without entering into a debate about whether Coetzee is in all respects a postmodern writer, I think it is clear that many of his novels use techniques and modes which characterise what is generally accepted as postmodern. In Jean-François Lyotard's words,

> The postmodern would be that which, in the modern, puts forward the unpresentable in presentation itself; that which denies itself the solace of good forms, the consensus of a taste which would make it possible to share collectively the nostalgia for the unattainable; that which searches for new presentations, not in order to enjoy them but in order to present a stronger sense of the unpresentable. (xxiv)

From the beginning of his career, Coetzee's novels have 'search[ed] for new presentations ... in order to present a stronger sense of the unpresentable'. David Attwell, in a recent article on *The Master of Petersburg*, points out

---

[3] In *Doubling the Point*, Coetzee writes, 'There is a true sense in which writing is dialogic: a matter of awakening the countervoices in oneself and embarking upon speech with them. It is some measure of a writer's seriousness whether he does evoke/invoke those countervoices in himself, that is, step down from the position of what Lacan calls "the subject supposed to know"' (65).

that Coetzee inserts a nineteenth-century shot tower into St Petersburg for the purpose of his narrative:

> There is no shot tower in St Petersburg. Nor has there been one. ... Shot towers are conical structures of up to seventy meters tall, designed for the manufacture of ammunition. ... J.M. Coetzee puts a shot tower in St Petersburg, on Stolyarny Quay, to be precise, in his novel. ... It is a brilliant insertion, appropriate to the period if not to the place, and it looms organically out of the world of the novel, which is full of perverted fantasy, obscure motives and dark threats. (25)

Dostoevsky scholars complain that 'he makes only a very perfunctory stab at filling in the St Petersburg background' (Attwell 27). But what he has done is create a St Petersburg to suit his literary purpose, and similarly in *Slow Man* he creates an Adelaide to suit his purpose. In *Elizabeth Costello*, the first chapter, or 'Lesson', is titled 'Realism', and throughout it there are deliberate references to the constructed nature of the illusion of reality created in fiction, the 'signs of a moderate realism' with which the author carefully studs the narrative (4). Zoe Wicomb sees the a-topic aspect of *Slow Man* similarly as a function of its metafictional nature; perhaps a further 'lesson' on the nature of realism, as demonstrated by Elizabeth Costello (the character in *Slow Man*) when she and Paul visit the Jokićs' house in Munno Para:

> When Costello repeatedly comments on the Jokićs' house with its Japanese garden, – 'So real! ... So authentic! ... Who would have thought it!'(242) – Paul, who exists on a different level of reality, assumes that she is being ironic. For the reader, however, it is surely a reference to the protean nature of representations, the propensity of fiction to slip beyond the author's control, and to beget further fictions. The Jokićs as characters ... have, unlike Paul, taken off, and represent a level of reality at which even the author must marvel. The fiction, turned in upon itself, cannot be cut adrift from referentiality; even the illusionary must refer to the world of things,

> so that the simulacral nature of a Japanese garden in an Australian suburb does not detract from its reality. (Wicomb 225)

It is often difficult to know, in this prosaic novel, despite its sceptical and unimaginative narrator, what is 'really' happening. Paul wonders at one stage whether he has entered a bizarre life beyond death, and Elizabeth Costello, also, refers to Magill Road as 'the very portal to the abode of the dead' (*Slow Man*, 83).

Nevertheless, although evoking Adelaide as a concrete location might be beside the point for Coetzee's purposes, the city, and Australia in general, do have certain important qualities in *Slow Man*. Paul is the victim of an accident caused by careless driving, which could happen in the best-regulated city. He is not abandoned by society: rather, it offers more help than he is willing to accept: 'Why should he not,' he asks himself, 'settle for a modestly circumscribed life in a city that is not inhospitable to the frail aged?' (26). Authority is not threatening: lost in thought in Rundle Mall, he finds himself addressed by someone: 'He is staring into the eyes, the entirely kindly eyes, of a young woman in blue uniform. A police officer' (172). Sue Kossew is of the opinion that Adelaide's 'famously sedate pace may ... account for the "slow" in the title' (63). Elizabeth Costello, who is a Melbourne resident, adds weight to this argument: Adelaide is, for her, a place where you can still get Friar's Balsam (226), 'just the place for a bath chair' (262) and 'too much like a graveyard' (231): 'a dozy city that does not provide outlets for all the restlessness' in the bones of 'lively young chaps' like Drago Jokić (219). Indeed, the 'liveliness' of the young male seems to be the principle threat in the Adelaide of *Slow Man*, whether embodied in the reckless Wayne Blight, behind the wheel of the car which hits Paul on Magill Road, or in Drago, who, with his mate Shaun, 'a pimply red-head ... to whom he has taken a dislike at first sight' (181), replaces Paul's precious antique photos with his photo-shopped versions. Marijana worries that her teenage son is running with 'wild friends, wild boys' (74), and that 'Adelaide no good, just pull him down' (90), but it is hardly a reflection on Adelaide's safety per se. Paul replies,

> This is not an easy country for a boy to grow up in. ... A climate of manliness prevails. A lot of pressure on a boy to excel in manly deeds, manly sports. Be a daredevil. Take risks. It is probably different back where you came from. (75)

He immediately rethinks: 'What does he know about the forms that manliness takes in south-eastern Europe?' (75). Indeed, he speculates that the Jokićs have come to Australia because 'if a better, more peaceable life is not to be found in Australia, where is it to be found?' (40). The question of migration and national identity is another significant theme in *Slow Man*. Kossew points out that 'a number of the characters in *Slow Man* ... do not identify themselves as "Australian"' (68), having been born overseas. Marijana's observation that, according to European perceptions, Australia has no history to speak of 'because in Australia everybody is new' (49) seems to resonate throughout the novel: even Paul's photograph collection seems a disembodied, abstract form of history, easily altered to include 'new Australians'. Paul himself is 'a foreigner by nature' (231) as well as an immigrant. According to Kossew, 'Being an outsider ... is both a physical and spiritual state of being for Paul. It is also the way he is able to mark out his own sense of individuality or difference' (68). In Adelaide such individuality is tolerated, if not welcomed. The pressures to conform are not absent but are relatively easy to resist.

In the Adelaide of *Slow Man* and *End of the Night Girl* there are no sinister forces at work. Elizabeth Costello tells Paul that 'this tranquil-seeming world we inhabit contains horrors' (97), but in Adelaide such horrors are caused by illness, injury and old age, not malign ideologies or dictatorships, and unhappiness is a matter of personal relationships going wrong and individuals treating each other badly. In each of these novels Adelaide is the ideal setting to explore a difficult phase of life. For Molly in *End of the Night Girl* it is the transition from the irresponsibility of young adulthood to a more mature acceptance of the needs of those who have claims on her, in stark contrast to the same period in the life of Gienia, who is brutally denied the chance to attain that maturity. Even while she survives, her life becomes gradually reduced to a frenzied, selfish competition for food, clothing and shelter with others equally victimised; altruism and care for the weak becomes an unaffordable luxury. In *Slow Man*, Paul is brought face to face with old age. At one stage he wonders whether Elizabeth has 'descended on him ... not to write him into a book but to induct him into the company of the aged' (191). Harvey points out that Coetzee's 'late novels ... attempt "to face directly the one question that truly engage[s] his soul: how to live," and this project is *en train* thanks to the escape from place that Australia has made possible' (32).[4] What I am about to conclude is a little like Ava Gardner's famous but apocryphal comment that Melbourne is 'the perfect place to make a film about the end of the world'. Instead of a cruel or murderous city, I contend that for Coetzee Adelaide is the perfect setting for a novel not just about how to live, but about how to grow old and die.

Works Cited

Attwell, David. 'The Shot Tower: History, *Autre*-biography and Madness in *The Master of Petersburg*'. *Ex-centric Writing: Essays on Madness in Postcolonial Fiction*. Ed. Susanna Zinato and Annalisa Pes. Newcastle upon Tyne: Cambridge Scholars Press, 2013. 25-42.

Bantick, Christopher. 'On Alienation and Murder, Accidental and Otherwise'. *Australian*. 27 August 2011. 22.

Coetzee, J.M. *Diary of a Bad Year*. London: Harvill Secker, 2007.

___. *Doubling the Point: Essays and Interviews*. Ed. David Attwell. Cambridge, Mass.: Harvard University Press, 1992.

___. *Elizabeth Costello*. New York: Viking Press, 2003.

---

[4] Harvey's quotation here is from Coetzee's *Diary of a Bad Year* 192-3.

___. 'Fridays at the Library'. Flinders University Library, 6 August 2004.

___. *Slow Man*. Sydney: Knopf, 2005.

Dooley, Gillian. 'Walking on Graves: An Interview with Amy T. Matthews'. *Transnational Literature* 4:1 (2011). <http://fhrc.flinders.edu.au/transnational/home.html>. Accessed 18 March 2012.

Duffy, Michael. 'Is Adelaide Our Cruellest City?' [Post by 'National Times']. *The Age Blog*. <http://www.theage.com.au/opinion/society-and-culture/blogs/crime-and-punishment/is-adelaide-our-cruellest-city-20110530-1fbhq.html>. Accessed 18 March 2012.

Hannett, Lisa L. *Bluegrass Symphony*. Greenwood, WA: Ticonderoga, 2011.

Harvey, Melinda. '"In Australia You Start Zero": The Escape from Place in J.M. Coetzee's Late Novels.' *Strong Opinions: J.M. Coetzee and the Authority of Contemporary Fiction*. Ed. Chris Danta, Sue Kossew and Julian Murphet. London: Continuum, 2011. 19-34.

Kossew, Sue. 'Border Crossings: Self and Text'. *J.M. Coetzee in Context and Theory*. Ed. Elleke Boehmer, Katy Iddiols and Robert Eaglestone. London: Continuum, 2010. 60-70.

Lyotard, Jean-François. *The Postmodern Condition: A Report on Knowledge*. Ed. Wlad Godzich and Jochen Schulte-Sasse. Trans. Geoff Gennington and Brian Massumi. Minneapolis: University of Minnesota Press, 1984.

Marion, Esther. 'The Nazi Genocide and the Writing of the Holocaust Aporia: Ethics and *Remnants of Auschwitz*'. MLN 121.4 (2006): 1009-22.

Matthews, Amy T. *End of the Night Girl*. Kent Town, SA: Wakefield Press, 2011.

McAllister, Brian. 'I Am Becoming and Island Dweller: Postmodern Space-Time in J.M. Coetzee's *Foe*.' *On and Off the Page: Mapping*

Place in Text and Culture. Ed. M.B. Hackler. Newcastle: Cambridge Scholars, 2009. 55-76.

Milthorpe, Naomi. 'Where the Wild Fears Are'. *Canberra Times*. 6 August 2011. 22.

Smit-Marais, Susan and Marita Wenzel. 'Subverting the Pastoral: The Transcendence of Space and Place in J.M. Coetzee's *Disgrace*'. *Beyond the Threshold: Explorations of Liminality in Literature*. Ed. Hein Viljoen and Chris N. van der Merwe. New York: Peter Lang, 2007. 209-21.

Sydney Writers Festival 2011. Online Program, 'Cities of the Dead'. <http://www.swf.org.au/component/option,com_2011/Itemid,310/agid,2570/task,view_detail/>. Accessed 18 March 2012.

Wicomb, Zoe. '*Slow Man* and the Real: A Lesson in Reading and Writing'. *J. M. Coetzee's Austerities*. Ed. Graham Bradshaw and Michael Neill. Farnham: Ashgate, 2010. 7-24.

Wirth-Nesher, Hana. 'This Sand, These Beaches'. *Novel* 40.3 (2007): 309-11.

This book is available as a free fully-searchable PDF from
www.adelaide.edu.au/press

www.ingramcontent.com/pod-product-compliance
Lightning Source LLC
Chambersburg PA
CBHW081131080526
44587CB00021B/3832